Janet Martin Soskice is a Tutor at Ripon College, Cuddesdon, Oxford member of the Faculty of Theology University of Oxford.

VISIONS
OF
APOCALYPSE

VISIONS OF APOCALYPSE

End or Rebirth?

Saul Friedländer,
Gerald Holton,
Leo Marx,
Eugene Skolnikoff
editors

HM
HOLMES & MEIER
NEW YORK   LONDON

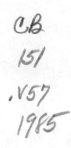

First published in the United States of America 1985 by
Holmes & Meier Publishers, Inc.
30 Irving Place
New York, N.Y. 10003

Great Britain:
Holmes & Meier Publishers, Ltd.
Unit 5 Greenwich Industrial Estate
345 Woolwich Road
Charlton, London SE7 9TX

Book design by Stephanie Greco

Library of Congress Cataloging in Publication Data
Main entry under title:

Visions of Apocalypse. End or rebirth?

  Bibliography: p.
  1. Regression (Civilization)—Addresses, essays,
lectures. 2. Civilization, Occidental—Addresses, essays,
lectures. 3. End of the world—Addresses, essays,
lectures. I. Friedländer, Saul, 1932–   . II. Title:
Visions of apocalypse.
CB151.E54   1985   909′.09821   84-19246
ISBN 0-8419-0673-4
ISBN 0-8419-0755-2 (pbk.)

Manufactured in the United States of America

CONTENTS

1

INTRODUCTION

Saul Friedländer

FOR THE FIRST TIME IN HISTORY, THE HUMAN SPECIES now has the capacity for its own immediate, total obliteration. In retrospect, however, this fearful circumstance would seem to have been prefigured by the many thinkers who, in almost every epoch, have set forth distinctive visions of "the end." Western culture is a storehouse of apocalyptic prophecy, and during the last century, a strikingly large number of artists and thinkers have called into question the validity—and durability—of the concept of "Man" itself. In one way or another they have announced the eclipse of the ancient belief that humanity is blessed with a unique endowment of soul, or some other distinctive core of spiritual or psychic autonomy or moral integrity. When contemplated from the perspective of humanity's obsessive interest in versions of its own ultimate demise, either as a physical entity or as a species capable of sustaining its self-reflexive character, today's nuclear predicament acquires a different, somewhat less novel, if no less frightening, aspect.

This volume attempts, among other things, to place these ancient themes in their widest historical context: What are the roots of Western thinking about the End? How has the apocalyptic imagination expressed itself over the centuries? To what extent is the contemporary perception of imminent danger influenced by the legacy of hopes and fears about the future of humanity, whether their origin be mythological, historical, religious, psychological, literary, or scientific?*

I am deeply grateful to my friends Leo Marx and David Stern for their help in vastly improving the original version of this Introduction. Most of all, I would like to express my thanks, in my own name and in the name of the editors of and contributors to this volume, to Jessie Janjigian for her constant help in the coordination of the project and in editing the texts at their various stages. Her help was of major importance for the preparation of this volume.

*The impetus for this endeavor came from a faculty seminar held under the auspices of the Center for International Studies at the Massachusetts Institute of Technology in 1978.

The first group of essays (Harald Reiche, Amos Funkenstein, Saul Friedländer, and Frank Kermode) deals with apocalyptic beliefs, beliefs in End and Renewal, including beliefs in a total End; the next group (Harvey Brooks, Robert Morison, Robert Jay Lifton) assesses specific contemporary threats of catastrophe; the third (Matei Calinescu, André Reszler, Richard Poirier) analyzes modern thinking and writing about the end of "Man." The concluding essay, by Philip Morrison, considers the fate of our species from the vantage of a distant star.

Each section considers a different way of envisaging the End, yet the striking fact is that today all such visions seem to be converging. The dark prospect we now foresee derives its credibility not only from the existence of our new science-based military technology. As the essays that follow demonstrate, it also derives from two other contemporary developments. One is the latent persistence, not to say (in some parts of the world) the resurgence, of apocalyptic beliefs that might well provide a fanatic believer with the justification for using that awesome technology. The other is a recession of that ancient faith in "Man" as a uniquely endowed being, a faith that has been a countervailing force to humanity's self-destructive propensities.

There is an astonishing continuity in apocalyptic beliefs. Each period has its prophets of doom, its annunciators of new beginnings, its heralds of the unthinkable. Hopes of total change and fears of catastrophe: the fears linking the Great Year to planetary and terrestrial catastrophe in ancient times, the earliest Jewish and Christian apocalyptic visions, the fears surrounding the Year 1000, those behind the cultural and intellectual changes of the Renaissance and the Reformation, those donning a new garb during the nineteenth century when, suddenly, God seemed to have foreknown the calculations of the astronomers and the marvels of electricity, and when He threatened to effect an early and terrible End by means of a comet or of general electrocution.[1] Then, too, the year 2000 is approaching. For many people, almost any kind of apocalyptic accounting is an irresistible temptation, and the unveiling of divine schemes of the End, through the reading of omens or the interpretation of numbers, elicits as much passionate attention today as it did in what we like to think of as the benighted past.

But are we, in fact, entitled to use the terms "apocalyptic imagination" or "apocalyptic beliefs" or "apocalyptic tradition" in referring to the modern scene? One contributor would impose radical restrictions on the use of the term. "Apocalypticism in the full sense of the word," writes Amos Funkenstein,

> a balance of myth, method, and way of life, existed for only about 200 years, and formed a unique mentality. . . . I do not mean to deny the

enormous impact and influence of the apocalypticism of Judaism and Christianity. On the contrary: because apocalypticism was so captivating, it has remained a constant theme. Yet, the history of its reception has been the history of its constant dilution. Apocalypticians were the first who were believed to possess a unique key for unlocking "the secrets of the times." Other keys have since been found and discarded, but we need not identify all of them with apocalypticism just because they retained general similarities, or simply because apocalypticism came first, or even because they assume some demands from the apocalyptic tradition.

But other contributors would allow a less strict and literal approach to the history of apocalypticism. Frank Kermode believes that "it is natural that people should look from the evils of the present, brought to them by a deplorable past and now reaching what may seem an intolerable pitch, to a better future; that they should conceive of theirs as a between-time, with decadence before it and renovation to follow." For Kermode, "the history of apocalyptic thought is the history of the interaction of these three elements": an apocalyptic "set" (a "sociological predisposition to the acceptance of apocalyptic structures and figures"); "canonical apocalypse" (that is, "Daniel, Revelation, and the other apocalyptic passages of the New Testament"); and "interpretative apocalypse" (that is, secondary accretions or "material other than the strictly canonical which became attached to it in the course of its transmission").

The three elements adduced by Kermode may be found in various guises in modern apocalyptic beliefs and imagery. While canonical apocalyptic tradition may not be widely invoked, it often makes its presence felt by a similar structure of imagery and beliefs. With regard to such indirect evidence, Kermode notes, "the accretion of secondary elements is endless, and the subject of endless studies. For our purposes it is sufficient to mention a few of the most important and enduring additions. They come from Sibylline writings about Rome's destiny, from the legends of the medieval Alexander, and from many other sources. Among the apocalyptic legends which have had powerful historical consequences are those of the Last World Emperor, the ultimate conversion of the Jews, and the Everlasting Gospel."

But, then, if we turn to the apocalyptic "set," to those kinds of experience which are likely to foster apocalyptic beliefs—oppression, despair, uncertainty, disaster, overall chaos, loss of collective identity—we are led to speculate about the particular forms that this set takes nowadays, at a time when thoughts about the End again have come to weigh heavily upon many minds.

As an undercurrent of Western imagination, apocalypticism is always with us. Consider its part in such sudden surges of intellectual and artistic life in our century as modernism, and, in particular, expressionism; com-

munism and fascism, the most powerful apocalyptic political currents of
our time; the unwelcome beginnings of the nuclear era and the cold war;
then the countercultural explosion of the 1960s with its fear of technology,
its yearning to recover the natural, and its millenarian dreams of a new
Heaven and a new Earth. The sixties and its dreams are gone, but the
general uneasiness has remained with us, perhaps more than ever,
through the seventies and into the eighties: a deep uneasiness sometimes
verging on panic about the onward rush of technology; about increasing
centralization and social control; about ecological, demographic, and nuclear threats; about the new extremes of poverty and affluence; uneasiness, in short, about humanity's inability to shape the fate of societies
and our own ability to control our individual lives. If violent protest has
subsided, it is partly because even protest seems pointless; instead, there
is subdued restlessness, a sense of aimless drifting as recognizable in
Stockholm as in San Francisco, in Toronto as in Paris, in New York as in
Berlin.

This mood is enough, in itself, to evoke a widespread "sense of an
ending," as Frank Kermode so aptly puts it. No wonder that we are seeing
the resurgence of apocalyptic beliefs, simultaneous visions of total up-
heavals and new beginnings, sometimes imagined in their traditional
religious forms, but often as yet inchoate.

This volatile mood surely is exacerbated by the imminent possibility of
technologically effected catastrophe—so vividly assessed in the second
section of this book—and the concurrent latency of alternative outlets for
the expression of apocalyptic impulses.

The crisis of modernism, for instance, is so widely acknowledged by now
that many speak of the dawn of a postmodern age. In his essay Frank
Kermode forcefully demonstrates that apocalypse as revelation belongs to
the very essence of modernity: "What we think of as truly Modern or
Modernist," writes Kermode, "is always relatively apocalyptic. Cézanne
plotting against his world mountain, Kandinsky deserting appearances in
favor of his abstract proclamations, the novelists with their unique plots
against time and reality, all are apocalypticists and in their measure
Joachimite. They honor the *transitus,* announce new orders, restructure
the world, utter their once-only but Everlasting Gospels. In their own
estrangement they are one-man sects, their books the modern equivalent
of the scrolls at Qumran or of the 'fiery flying roll' of the Ranters, annunciations of a new order superseding the old law and the old book: every
artist his own gospel." Still, at the end of his essay, Kermode announces
the demise of Apocalypse in its Modernist form: the hope does recur, the
possibility of new gospels cannot disappear.

If, for the intellectual elite, intellectual and aesthetic modernism provided an apocalyptic outlet to the few, yesterday's extremist political

ideologies offered apocalypse at a much broader mass level. These ideologies were apocalyptic dreams at their most dangerous: visions of a world about to die, of the final crisis and the ultimate salvation, be it the classless society or the Thousand-Year Reich.

In fact, the similarity between modern and traditional apocalyptic beliefs and imagery in the case of Nazi ideology was noticed many years ago, initially by Eric Voegelin in *Die politischen Religionen* published before the Second World War, then by Norman Cohn in *The Pursuit of the Millennium*, more recently by James Rhodes in *The Hitler Movement*.[2] Rhodes stresses the similarity by pointing out that Nazi ideological imagery, like that of the traditional apocalypticists, approximated the following sequence: disaster, revelation of the way to salvation, discovery of the fundamental forces of Evil and of the imminence of a final attack by those forces, discovery of one's own election to fight the ultimate battle against the evil forces—all leading to a vision of the subsequent millennium (the Thousand-Year Reich). Rhodes's structural comparison would have been even more convincing had he added two crucial elements: among the elect, there is one who is outstanding, a messianic figure, a savior, the leader of the ultimate battle; and the revelation is laid down in a Gospel-like text, its fundamental tenets being the keys to unlock "the secrets of the times."

Thus, when Karl Liebknecht, in his last article in *Die Rote Fahne*, heralds the Day of Wrath, when Ernst von Salomon's "Outlaws" march through the burning towns of the Baltikum, portent of a world going up in flames, when the Cadets of the Alcázar of Toledo decide to sacrifice their lives to the very last, or when the International Brigades storm the enemy lines at Guadalajara, on each side of the barricades there is a belief that the hour of the ultimate sacrifice, the hour of the final battle for the ultimate change, has come. *Today, these ideologies remain like smoldering embers and apocalyptic politics is just a latent but always present possibility.*

Although apocalyptic dreams of modernity as revelation are fading, the theme that accompanied modernity from the start—the idea of the eradication of Man or self—haunts the contemporary imagination. Matei Calinescu, André Reszler, Richard Poirier, and Saul Friedländer reach back to the nineteenth century to trace how the notion of the disappearance of humanity arose and was given expression. Then, when modernity had exhausted itself, the thinker and writer, as if standing at the outer fringe, was able to become the cool observer of "arrangements of knowledge" reaching their end; it was these arrangements that had led to the emergence of Man as a concept, and the disappearance of which would entail the erasure of the traditional self-conception of Man as if he had been "a face drawn in sand at the edge of the sea."[3]

Here again, we find the pervasiveness of that diffuse feeling of unease, that portentous mood mentioned at the outset. In the 1950s the Beckettian vision of the end of Man seemed to be inseparable from the then prevalent notion of the Absurd. Then the "humanistic" trend of thought which had veered close to orthodox Marxism—Sartrian existentialism—disappeared, in part, with the recoil from Stalinism. In France, where thinking and writing about the total freedom of man has had a special hold, structuralism came as a reaction both to existentialism and to orthodox Marxism (Louis Althusser's synthesis of Marxism and structuralism did not succeed in changing the general trend). In that context, Claude Lévi-Strauss's polemic against Jean-Paul Sartre's *Critique de la Raison dialectique* marked a turning point, as did Michel Foucault's *The Order of Things* (1966), where he announced the probable disappearance of Man, in the sense of being the central actor and object of History.

In recent decades commonplaces about the destructiveness of industrial society have been echoed in the utter pessimism of Lévi-Strauss's finale—the closing pages of the last volume of *Mythologiques*. The disruption of the natural order, the desecration of primitive societies that still embody some of the innocence we associate with the myth of the Golden Age and the Christian Eden call for punishment. Destructive modern Man will destroy himself. With Foucault, we remain at the level of concept, with Lévi-Strauss, we dangerously approach the notion of literal retribution. These gloomy forecasts lend specificity to the vague forebodings of an epoch.

We thus return to our primary concern about the human prospect. *This volume, in its general structure and its varied angles of approach, suggests the possibly ominous convergence of apocalyptic beliefs whose future form cannot be foreseen, of technological means of total destruction, and of more or less diffuse theories about the End of Man. Such a convergence may well be the real "set," however dimly perceived by most, for contemporary forebodings of doom.*

The idea of the End, be it technological catastrophe or the death of civilization, may evoke the hope of renewal or the fear of destruction; it may, as well, awaken excitement at the disintegration of that ephemeral concept, Man, or despair, profound despair at the possibility of ultimate destruction; or it may call forth detachment in the face of individual death, or of the cyclical inevitability of disaster, or of the many possible vagaries of our known prospect.

"The death of an individual," writes biologist Robert Morison, "is a matter of no great moment. Certainly it is no mystery. It is the inevitable corollary of a system dedicated to change." This way of considering individual death helps to neutralize some of the fear aroused by forecasts of the extinction of the species; for the same logic is applicable to the span of collective life on earth and the more so, Morison states, because we have no proof that evolution represents an evolution toward higher and better stages of life: "Some commentators," notes Morison, "may have been a little too ready to assume that evolutionary change is always for the better. . . . Your orthodox, value-free scientist, if he still survives, prefers not to say whether this complexity is better or worse than the simplicity that preceded it. Such judgments must be left to the humanities, whose business it is said to be."

Robert Morison's essay expresses in modern language what the mainstream of Greek and Roman philosophy considered to be the only dignified attitude in the face of the necessarily recurring catastrophes in the cycle of being: "Ancient philosophers like Heraclitus, Plato, Aristotle, and the Stoics," writes Harald Reiche, "were expected to resist the impulse. Stoics went out of their way to demonstrate that what might terrify others—imminent cosmic catastrophe—did not terrify the true philosopher. Although, or rather because, he acknowledges the doctrine of catastrophes, he does not dignify it with apprehensiveness. Quite the contrary. The implication is that if and when catastrophe, even the ultimate catastrophe, does strike, it will come as a challenge. It will then afford him a not unwelcome occasion for proving, in the dual sense of testing and demonstrating, imperviousness to all manner of adversity."

The modern scientist's detachment about the fate of the species is reminiscent of classical Stoicism. Whatever the fearsomeness of the prospect, a scientific gaze allows us to weigh all of the possible consequences and still keep them at a serene distance. "Nuclear weapons, the most present of all dangers," Philip Morrison writes,

> do not seem likely literally to end our species. Should the worst happen, I would expect a severalfold decimation of the two or three big warring nations. They would sink, their cultural properties as well. All that would remain in the United States, say, would be a few portions of certain less-populated regions, amidst vast unvisitable wastelands. Barren, dying fields and forests might be found worldwide, amidst general hunger. But it still seems to me that some of our far-flung species would survive, its population, wealth, and hope sadly dwindled, but not finally ended. The Southern Hemisphere is actuarially the better off—airborne radioactivity and the dark clouds cross the equator only slowly—though it would not remain unthreatened. The best guesses are still that a factor of ten, though not much more, stands against the death of the whole species by nuclear war. Certainly the average danger does not strike every individual; and distances and environmental differences are great. Once again, diversity is the key to survival. The false winter or two have come and gone; the ozone layer is at risk; epidemics of tumors and birth defects persist for centuries; the best

croplands are unusable for a long time. The very air holds chemical toxins. The tale is genuinely tragic. Yet there will be people left, plenty of them miserably surviving here and there by their wits on the unused storehouses and the residual life.

But there are times when the idea of judgment is divested of all hope. Robert Jay Lifton quotes the reaction of a Protestant minister after the explosion of the atomic bomb on Hiroshima:

> The feeling I had was that everyone was dead. The whole city was destroyed. . . . I thought all of my family must be dead—it doesn't matter if I die. . . . I thought this was the end of Hiroshima—of Japan—of humankind. . . . This was God's judgment on man.

At other times, the very people who announce the imminent end assume that they, the announcers, will not be swept away by the catastrophe, because they are the elect, hence they are immune from general destruction. Amos Funkenstein demonstrates the presence of that attitude among the apocalypticists:

> While the prophetic visions of ultimate doom and delivery were addressed to the whole of Israel, [writes Funkenstein,] including the lost tribes, the Qumran sect seems to have written off most of Israel. They alone are "the remnant," the avant-garde of the new eon in the midst of the old, doomed one. They alone are the true Israel. . . . Their eschatological hopes were confined to their own group, while the rest of Israel would have to share, so it seems, the lot of the other nations.

When we turn to modern metaphors of the End of Man, we find a similar complacency, and a similar jubilation at the end of those others who do not belong among the Chosen: "We have been listening to voices," writes Richard Poirier, "that invite us to join in the drama of apocalypse," a receptivity to doom that accords with the fact, as Frank Kermode has shown,[4] that human beings seem always to have found in the End a thrilling opportunity for advancement. But what is the basis for that thrill? Why is it that with Nietzsche and Foucault we get as excited by the drama of self-obliteration as we might with any popular writer? Some curious motives are at work here, perhaps including a kind of cultural and social snobbery. Surely some measure of our excitement comes from the fact that the speaker's voice seems to assume that we who listen, like those who speak, are somehow *more* than human. We are being offered some exclusive, transcendent or exonerating privilege, an inducement to a kind of pride that, on the other side of extermination, would in earlier times have made us ineligible for sainthood. Though the words we hear condemn mankind, the sound of them, the mode of address, clearly exempts the speaker and his auditors. These are not the voices of ordinary mortals speaking to other ordinary mortals.

One cannot help but remember the hallucinations of Daniel Paul Schreber, reported in Robert Jay Lifton's essay:

> During the latter part of my stay in Flechsig's Asylum [Prof. Flechsig was the director], I thought this period had already expired and *therefore I was the last real human being left,* and that the few human shapes I saw apart from myself—Professor Flechsig, some attendants, occasional more or less strange-looking patients, were only "fleeting-improvised men" created by miracle.[5]

This feeling of immunity that attaches to the annunciator of the end may explain in part, but in part only, the most crucial of the attitudes mentioned here: not only detachment or fear, or fear *and* hope, in the face of destruction, but the desire for destruction, the appeal of destruction. As Robert Jay Lifton puts it, "the impulse to 'press the button' and 'get the thing over with,' even the orgiastic excitement of the wild forces let loose—destroying everything in order to feel alive." According to Lifton, this very impulse also creates its own antidote, a topic to which we shall come back later.

This attitude usually is linked to a desire for renewal, but the bare fact remains, as Lifton shows, that in a devious and complex way people tend to worship the agents of their own destruction, which they also consider to be agents of a potential renewal: ". . . a pseudoreligion I call 'nuclearism,' involving the deification and worship of the very agents of our potential destruction, seeing in them a deity that cannot only destroy but also protect and create, even depending on them to keep us and the world going."

In fact, Robert Lifton could have gone one step further, for there is a desire for utter destruction which knows of no renewal, which awaits no purification, no aftermath, nothing at all. Saul Friedländer brings forth some of this attitude in describing the *fin de siècle* atmosphere, as reflected in the following passage from Mario Praz's *The Romantic Agony:*

> The oft-repeated lament over the downfall of Latin civilization, the 'Ohé!!! Ohé!!! les races latines!' of Péladan, the conviction of d'Aurevilly that the race had arrived 'à sa dernière heure,' Verlaine's 'Je suis l'Empire à la fin de la décadence'—such things show not so much the terror, as the attraction, of disaster: the very ideas of Decadence, of imminent Divine punishment like the fire of Sodom, of the 'cupio dissolvi,' are perhaps no more than the extreme sadistic refinements of a *milieu* which was saturated to excess with complications of perversion.[6]

The attraction of disaster felt by so many authors of the late nineteenth century may appear to have been a fleeting fad of tired aestheticists. But, a longing for catastrophe, death, and apocalyptic destruction, a cult of death and destruction, was also at the core of Nazism and of fascist movements in the twentieth century. "Viva la Muerte!" This sinister motive no doubt is bound up with a more universal urge toward the void, which explains some of its appeal to so many during the thirties and the forties. Similar motives also may account for some of the "aesthetic" fascination it still holds for many today.

In *The Myth of the Eternal Return*, Mircea Eliade stresses the fear that all primitive societies had and have of "history," the passing of time.[7] The cyclical conceptions of history with their recurrent catastrophic endings were actually expressions of hope: time was periodically renewed and man could again and again partake of the beginning. This, in a sense, is the millennial pattern of resistance to history, to change. But with the growth of modern skepticism, the idea of a cyclical return faded away, just when history, the pace of change, accelerated to a point almost unbearable for many. The craving then arose: stop this mad course by all means, stop this insane rushing forward and let us rest—even if it be in the sleep of an eternal night, when no world remains. A rest for weary men, a rest for the cosmos itself—from the sickness of technological change produced by man—a craving magnificently expressed by Italo Svevo:

> A man, made like all other men of flesh and blood, will in the quiet of his room invent an explosive of such potency that all the explosives in existence will seem like harmless toys beside it. And another man, made in his image and in the image of all the rest, but a little weaker than them, will steal that explosive and crawl to the center of the earth with it, and place it just where he calculates it would have the maximum effect. There will be a tremendous explosion, but no one will hear it and the earth will return to its nebulous state and go wandering through the sky, free at last. . . .[8]

But what, in fact, is the prospect—the destruction or survival of humanity? The implications of the essays that follow seem contradictory. Philip Morrison foresees "that some of our far-flung species would survive, its population, wealth, and hope sadly dwindled, but not finally ended." But Harvey Brooks's assessment has a far more pessimistic ring (and, on that same scale, Jonathan Schell would be even more extreme[9]). "The overwhelming threat from modern technology that dwarfs all others," writes Brooks, "is the threat of large-scale thermonuclear conflict. While it is doubtful whether even the largest nuclear exchange possible with current weapons stockpiles would wipe out all human life on earth, or completely destroy the world ecosystem, the face of the earth would be so altered that it is improbable that any form of civilized society would survive." One can hardly get much consolation from Brooks's belief in the ability of humanity to survive a nuclear war if, as he puts it, "it is improbable that any form of civilized society would survive." This pessimism returns in the conclusion of his essay:

Finally, of course, the huge stockpiles of nuclear weapons, and the dedication of enormous managerial and technical skill, as well as capital investment, to the building of an ever-escalating destructive capacity continue to be the principal threat of doom, and perhaps the only one that seems to this commentator, at least, to be fully credible and real.

But another aspect of the problem of survival, less often mentioned, but no less crucial, is the political cost of averting disaster. Brooks expresses it forcefully:

> If the human prospect proves to be as dim as the prophets of doom would have it, the cause will not lie in the direct consequences of technology, but in the complex interplay between technological development and the evolution of the individual and social character. There are almost certainly workable technical solutions to all the problems and dilemmas of the next hundred years. The question is whether humanity can summon the collective wisdom and consensus necessary to implement these solutions without compromising other social and moral values that we also hold dear. *Or will the implementation of solutions require so much social coercion that they are not really solutions in the larger human sense?*[10]

Here Brooks poses what may well be the real alternatives: destruction or, possibly, the rise of a coercive society that will in effect put an end to the kind of human life worth living. Some years ago, in *An Inquiry into the Human Prospect*, Robert Heilbroner had already touched upon the same dilemma; and he had appealed for a voluntary restriction of freedom as the necessary price to pay for survival:

> This general admonition applies in particular to the intellectual elements of Western nations whose privileged role as sentries for society takes on a special importance in the face of things as we now see them. It is their task not only to prepare their fellow citizens for the sacrifices that will be required of them but to take the lead in seeking to redefine the legitimate boundaries of power and the permissible sanctuaries of freedom, for a future in which the exercise of power must inevitably increase and many present areas of freedom, especially in economic life, be curtailed.[11]

The alternatives described by Brooks and Heilbroner point to the grim prospect held forth by André Reszler: the survival of tiny islands of freedom within a predominantly totalitarian world. Heilbroner also assumes that such islands of freedom can survive; Brooks does not say so, and indeed he poses the question in a rather pessimistic way. Reszler also leaves the question open: "The fact that the last man has the unlimited power of the state and of public opinion against him," he writes, "might make him lose faith in his ideals. How can he affirm his right to exclusiveness—difference—his nostalgia for the forbidden realm of the past, from a position of total isolation?" But, on the other hand, "in [Zamiatin's]

We, when D-503 is told that a soul has formed within him, he also learns that individual soul formation has spread like an epidemic. Around the figure of the last man, whole islands of individual resistance are constituted. And on these islands, conspiracy prevails."

For most Western readers of the counterutopias mentioned by Reszler the choice is likely to be clear: they will be on the side of the last man, which is to say, on the side of individual freedom against the undifferentiated "harmony" and "peace" imposed by totalitarian society. But, what if totalitarian peace and harmony turn out to be the only alternative to physical destruction—the only guarantee of the species' continued existence? After all, is not the survival of life the ultimate goal, whatever the conditions?

The question takes us to some of the issues raised by Philip Morrison:

> Are we alone as self-conscious appraisers of our future? Or among the suns are there many like us in insight, however different in biology? It seems probable that we will know that within a modest time, perhaps by catching radio signals from Others far away. Perhaps we are The People, solitary on our planet-island, someday soon to be surprised by other beings from far away, with radio beams if not white sails, easily our masters in many domains of life. It has happened before: it may happen again. We do not know, but perhaps we will find out by an active if vicarious radio or laser search. To be sure, those Others will not be of our species, but they will by hypothesis share the niche we hold; conscious beings, surviving and spreading by a new form of evolution, changing more by hand and eye than by the gamble of inheritance.
>
> We have never seen anything like that before: a new species which shares our functions though not at all our image, our descent, even our biochemistry. If our culture and our history pass into the keeping of a wider society than earth's, the issue of species survival becomes somewhat moot. Here we touch questions of philosophy, of the very definition of the end. What does it mean? Would we be held to survive if our new partnership with natural selection led to a filiation into something rich and strange? The older speculators, say George Bernard Shaw, saw the deep future as the rise of an etiolated but powerful race of philosophers, perhaps even of pure thought; the more silicon-bound speculators of our day foresee the inheritance of our culture by subtle machines which we set on a path of machine evolution.

Again and again the question recurs: is the only choice between survival under any form (and at any price) or possible extinction? "Our exploration of end-of-the-world imagery suggests, in itself, a countering force," Robert Jay Lifton writes:

> It is a precarious one, because it hovers on the anxious edge of ultimate destruction. Consider the two dimensions of the Dr. Strangelove image.

There is, on the one hand, the impulse to "press the button" and "get the thing over with," even the orgiastic excitement of the wild forces let loose— destroying everything in order to feel alive. But the other side of the Strangelove image, what I take to be its wisdom, is the insistence that we confront the radical absurdity or "madness" of the world destruction we are contemplating. It is similar to what Teilhard de Chardin had in mind, as an evolutionary theorist and mystic, in writing about the expansion of the "noosphere" or area of knowledge as the other side of our capacity to destroy ourselves. And it is what Erik Erikson means when he speaks about the relationship between our destructive capacity and our first glimpses of a form of human identity so inclusive that it embraces the entire species.

We must imagine something close to nuclear extinction in order to prevent it. We must extend our psychological and moral imaginations in order to hold off precisely what we begin to imagine.

Robert Lifton believes that notwithstanding the evergrowing danger of humanity's total self-annihilation—because of that very possibility, in fact—we may witness the rise of a new consciousness; it might take the form of a psychological mutation of humanity, in effect, a new stage in the development of the human species. Harvey Brooks rests his hopes upon the existence of some "collective wisdom" which could ward off the imminent dangers of catastrophe. For Philip Morrison the realistic view is this:

One day, the sun dead, the universe itself perhaps collapsing to a fiery rebirth, it will all be over, long before matter itself decays away as likely it will do. But we are a long-lived, widespread, and marvelous species, all the same, marked by a symbiosis unique on earth, living intimately with a creature of wonderful talent and sinister cunning, our Monkey of the Mind.

André Reszler speculates that the "last man" of the totalitarian nightmare might become the first of a new beginning. "We know that classical utopia has been the forerunner of the collectivist intellectual tradition of the nineteenth and twentieth centuries. Negative utopias may well be the harbingers of a new age of individualist humanism, thus announcing the renaissance of pluralism and anarchist-conservative pragmatism." Frank Kermode takes the view that the demythologizing, deconstructing tendency which is spreading through our culture probably will not provide the last word:

For the time being, the apocalyptic, certainly in Western literature, is out of fashion, and the Gospel is not being written. . . . Popular fundamentalist apocalypticism thrives, but the educated, the heirs of Joachim of Fiore and his heirs, have given it up. Deconstructors write no gospels. But it is hard to believe there will never be another.

In recent philosophical literature Matei Calinescu discerns a "resurrection" of man, although a very tentative one: "All we can say is that it would
be as wrong to gainsay the significance of man's recent and as yet incomplete resurrection, as it would be to blow it up. On a more modest plane,
though, it seems in order to look at the banalization of the language of the
end of man with a philosophical smile." And Richard Poirier reasserts,
beyond all theory, beyond all the intellectual stances, all the glittering
rhetoric of those who aim at "writing off the self," an incoercible belief in
life, in being—as such. "It is fitting," writes Poirier,

> that as [William] James came to the end of his life one of his last essays, "A
> Pluralistic Mystic," was a tribute to his friend Blood, at the conclusion of
> which he writes: "Let *my* last word, then, speaking in the name of intellec-
> tual philosophy, be *his* word:—'There is no conclusion. What has con-
> cluded, that we might conclude in regard to it? There are no fortunes to be
> told, and there is no advice to be given.—Farewell!' If this is an echo of
> Emerson in 'The Poet' or 'Nature' or 'Experience,' it is an echo that reaches
> toward the last poem of Wallace Stevens, a poem called 'Of Mere Being,'
> where he celebrates 'The poem at the end of the mind, / Beyond the last
> thought.'"

Each essay in this volume, in its own way, charts a possible descent
toward the abyss, and each in its own way leads toward an act of faith—
faith in man, in life, in mere being beyond the last thought.

Robert Jay Lifton contends that it is necessary to think about the End
in order to prevent it; Richard Poirier argues that writing about nonexistence always carries the tacit rhetorical affirmation of the writer's existence. Both suggest that a consideration of the end of life involves and, in
fact, virtually requires a commitment to its continuity. This is true, it
seems to us, of an authentic thinking and writing about the End, and
therefore it is the fundamental justification for this book. Our investigation, with its manifold approaches, and with the strong personal feelings
that come through so many passages, is not a mere exercise in theoretical
speculation, nor an expression of a morbid attraction to vistas of destruction; it evinces our conviction that the human mind still offers the best
possible means of finding a way out—of reasserting our commitment to
life.

NOTES

1. Perry Miller, "The End of the World," Chapter 10 in his *Errand into the
Wilderness*, (Cambridge, Mass.: Harvard University Press, 1956), pp. 229 et seq.
2. Eric Voegelin, *Die politischen Religionen* (Stockholm: Bermann-Fischer,
1939); Norman Cohn, *The Pursuit of the Millennium* (London: Secker & Warburg,

1957); and James M. Rhodes, *The Hitler Movement: A Modern Millenarian Revolution* (Stanford, Calif.: Hoover Institution Press, 1980).

3. Michel Foucault, *The Order of Things* (New York: Pantheon Books, 1971), p. 387. (Originally published as *Les Mots et les choses* [Paris: Éditions Gallimard, 1966].)

4. Frank Kermode, *The Sense of an Ending* (New York: Oxford University Press, 1967).

5. Emphasis added.

6. Mario Praz, *The Romantic Agony*, trans. Angus Davidson (Oxford: Oxford University Press, 1933), p. 381.

7. Mircea Eliade, *Cosmos and History: The Myth of the Eternal Return*, trans. Willard R. Trask (New York: Harper & Row, 1959).

8. Italo Svevo, *Confessions of Zeno*, trans. Beryl de Zoete (New York: Vintage Books, 1958), p. 398. (Originally published as *La Coscienza di Zeno* [Bologna: L. Cappelli, 1923].)

9. Jonathan Schell, *The Fate of the Earth* (New York: Alfred A. Knopf, 1982). Also Jonathan Schell, *The Abolition* (New York: Alfred A. Knopf, 1984).

10. Emphasis added.

11. Robert Heilbroner, *An Inquiry into The Human Prospect* (New York: W. W. Norton & Company, 1974), pp. 137–38.

PART I

2

THE ARCHAIC HERITAGE: MYTHS OF DECLINE AND END IN ANTIQUITY

Harald A. T. Reiche

THE SENSE OF DECLINE AND END, IMMINENT, PERHAPS catastrophic, yet not necessarily terminal, the variety of phenomena responsible, its various formulations, and its human consequences—these form the thematic focus of the essays assembled in this book. The present chapter concentrates on the ancient, largely Greco-Roman evidence for this sense of decline and imminent end. Pessimistic in content and expressed in traditional mythic form, this sense notoriously antedates, coexists with, and survives the flowering of optimism and rationalism associated with Athenian democracy. The paradox has attracted scholarly attention ever since the nineteenth century, when the Basel historian Jacob Burckhardt redrew Greek politics, and the German philosopher Friedrich Nietzche (then also at Basel) redrew pre-Socratic philosophy, in new, more somber tones. Our focus here, therefore, can afford to be more limited. Concentrating on the actual myths of decline and end, we shall successively examine the linguistic form and corollary conservatism with which they were transmitted within a predominantly oral culture; the cosmological, terrestrial, human, and politicoeconomic data that gave rise to these myths in the first instance and continued to lend them support; and the different emotions—resignation, anxiety, panic, studied indifference, or grim satisfaction—which such myths inspired, whether in experts or laymen, in those at the apex or at the base of the social pyramid, and whether in terms of cognitive-technological progress or moral regression or of cosmic or purely personal salvation.

That such a preliminary reassessment may be worth attempting at this time is suggested by recent advances along several formerly unrelated but increasingly convergent lines of inquiry. One of these has to do with the formulation, transmission, and special hold of knowledge in oral, that is, memory-based, cultures. Another concerns the unsuspected sophistication of even Stone Age sky watchers as evinced by the relatively recent discipline of archaeoastronomy. A third concerns the evidence, amassed by comparative ethnologists, that there existed, and in some parts of the world still exists, a configurational, above and beyond a purely positional, astronomy that requires us to assume unsuspectedly long attention spans on the part of naked-eye observers; and that certain recurrent mythological motifs in these cultures seem, with a probability verging on certainty, to have furnished sky watchers of considerable sophistication with, among other things, the requisite technical language in which to express, transmit, and theorize about the meaning of their observations.

MYTH AS LANGUAGE

Like other myths, those dealing with decline and catastrophic end demonstrably originate in a world as yet devoid of literacy and numeracy.[1] In such a world, personification and narrative are the primary linguistic vehicles for formulating, interpreting, recalling, and communicating information, knowledge, and meaning. Myths of decline and catastrophic end deal with knowledge at once technical and sacred whose mastery, recital, and even reenactment, because linking past, present, and future, are deemed vital to the survival of community and cosmos alike.

Evidence abounds that in oral cultures poetic skills are as indispensable to science as to leadership. Until quite recently, Polynesian navigators managed—without benefit of maps, compasses, or clocks—to effect pinpoint landfalls on islands hundreds of miles away. Their secret: navigational directions in the form of catalogues of successive star risings (at a fixed azimuth) linked by "mythic" plots that helmsmen had memorized for recital to themselves while at sea. Even Agamemnon, it has plausibly been suggested, would have had to issue his sailing orders to the captains of the Greek expeditionary force to Troy in versified, that is, memorizable, form.[2] The Polynesian material suggests what sort of content these verses might have had.

Massive evidence assembled by archaeoastronomy, moreover, shows that Stone Age people, notwithstanding their primitive technology, were capable of prodigious feats of observational astronomy and of the megalithic engineering required to embody them in stone alignments. Yet how are we to suppose these people to have described their findings without benefit not only of letters and numbers but also of our very notions of coordinates and multivariate systems? Again, the only answer consistent with the evidence is that they did so in story, that is, in "mythic" form. Thus, they might conventionally have described what to us is the midwinter full moon's 18.6-year cycle (from minimum to maximum back to minimum elongation from the point of midsummer sunrise, marked, at Stonehenge, by the so-called Heelstone) as the up-and-down pacing of a caged animal that cannot or dares not go beyond certain limits.[3] Just so, the Greek philosopher Heraclitus speaks of the sun as confining his annual journey to within the solstices, lest—so his readers would supply—like Aegisthus (at once Clytemnestra's paramour and accomplice in the murder of her husband Agamemnon) he become liable to blood vengeance for harming others in the process of overstepping his allotted measures.

Even the literate and numerate sequel of Western history has never wholly forgotten that myth is mankind's mother tongue. Aristotle all but says so outright in the *Metaphysics;* and Plato, for profound epistemological reasons of his own, actually emulates it in his *Timaeus* (and elsewhere). By and large, the Stoic downgrading of myth to the level of mere allegory remained ineffective. So did the Epicurean rejection of everything except atomic doctrine as mythology. And so, apparently, is the early modern refusal to accord cognitive import to any languages other than those of philosophical logic and mathematical physics (and Newtonian at that). The refusal at issue is implicit in the work of Immanuel Kant. Because of this refusal, Kant left unconsummated the insights of, among moderns, the seventeenth- and eighteenth-century philosophers Giovanni Battista Vico, Johann Georg Hamann, and Johann Gottfried von Herder, leaving it to our contemporaries to realize the full implications of his own central insight that understanding is, quite broadly speaking, symbolic transformation. Even today the effects of Kant's arbitrary restriction linger on in the specious alternative of myth either as mere social cement devoid of cognitive import or as possessed of such import only in the trivial, derivative sense of allegory.

CONVENTION AND INNOVATION

The fact, then, is that in cultures without our numeracy, literacy, operational symbols, and coordinate systems a properly crafted oral statement *(mythos)* involving personification and narrative was virtually the only way in which knowledge could be described and transmitted.[4] Indeed, personification and narrative offered the sole linguistic matrix within which experience could not only be recollected and communicated but also be obtained in the first instance. So much would be clear, even if comparative ethnology had not independently confirmed it, from what Gestalt psychology and phenomenology have shown to be the role of intention and expectation in ordinary experience. There remains still another, major characteristic of the way in which oral cultures "schematize" experience. It is that their very perceptions seem to take place in a time frame and, by that token, within an attention span very much longer—and thus capable of registering far slower phenomena— than what we routinely take for granted. Specifically, expert sky watchers in such cultures are demonstrably capable of transcending positional in favor of configurational astronomy. By extraordinary feats of mnemonic synopsis they seem capable of linking together into quasi-continuous geometric figures (usually inscribed within the zodiac) what to our naked eye appear as so many discrete luminous dots.[5]

Like everything else, configurational astronomy finds verbal expression in dramatic form. To express and save from oblivion discoveries imperfectly accessible to laymen, experts had no choice but to avail themselves of the language of laymen, indeed to enlist the communal memory in the task of preservation. Only if embodied in a rattling good yarn appealing to, even if not fully understood by, a constituency much larger than the one represented by expert minorities, could technical knowledge be handed on. Inevitably, so close a dependence upon appeal to the broad base of the social pyramid within a given oral culture exacted its price. The same matrix that preserves stories from casual changes proves inhospitable, too, to deliberate updating no matter how justified by changes in the objective (say, astronomical) situation. Witness the sheer unbelievable conservatism (profusely documented by Willy Hartner and Hertha von Dechend) with which astronomical and astrological iconography and mythic formulas are accurately retained long after they have ceased accurately to reflect reality.[6] From a purely scientific point of view, there would be a point of diminishing returns beyond which, as in the case, say, of navigational or observational directives, the very cost of oral conservation, rigidity, would begin to diminish the immediate usefulness of the knowledge so conserved. But then, as already noted, science concurrently discharged the ritual function of helping to maintain the predictability of that which it described. In that context, exact replication of proven if obsolescent formulas, as compared to innovations however factually justified, may well have seemed the lesser of two risks.

Certain aspects of the way in which even such critical minds as Thucydides and Aristotle portray, respectively, historical causation and political governance betray their continuing indebtedness to the older, oral culture. At issue here are not so much their particular, overt conclusions as their tacit presuppositions. Thus Thucydides's perception of the behavioral constant which he thinks responsible for the likelihood of historical repetition is decisively colored by the dramatic matrix of the same oral culture that produced Attic tragedy. The point is not that, as E. R. Dodds put it, "history repeats, but only ritual repeats exactly." It is that our historian's conclusion reflects an antecedent conditioning of his mind by mythic conventions that, despite everything, have remained the very idiom of a still predominantly oral culture. Francis Cornford termed such involuntary assimilation of history to myth "infiguration."[7] Mutatis mutandis, the same will account for Aristotle's capping his eulogy to the "nonepisodic" order of the universe (*Metaphysics* XII) with a citation of Homer's line in praise of monarchy: "The rule of many is not good; let one be ruler." Notwithstanding his own *Politics*, Aristotle is here reassimilating causal and geometric analysis to the older mythical language that he knew by heart (and had codified for Alexander the Great in the form of a new edition of Homer). Ever since Cleisthenes (who extended Solon's constitutional reforms and who had even commissioned a special recension of Homer), radical democracy was bound to think of Homer and Hesiod as a somewhat ambivalent legacy. For a whole spectrum of alternative forms of governance—for the informal leadership of men like Pericles and Alcibiades to formal monarchy of the Spartan or Macedonian type and Plato's philosopher-king—could and did, tacitly or overtly, derive from it their psychological legitimacy. Such, then, were the values that continued to be latently associated with the Homeric epics and with Hesiod's myth of declining world ages where each age is governed by a celestial monarch and Zeus in particular is invoked as guarantor of justice.

Plato, of course, had no illusions as to the enormous power of suggestion implicit in the traditional oral culture. He held its poetry responsible for keeping the majority of men in that condition of mindless bondage which in the Cave allegory of the *Republic* he diagnoses and castigates. By reinforcing people's native emotionalism and literal-mindedness, such poetry, he held, unfits them for objective, analytic, that is, properly rational, thought. His remedy: replace traditional mythology by philosophical myths of the sort he himself was to compose in *Politicus* and *Timaeus*.

THE ASTRONOMICAL DATA BASE

Passing reference has already been made to configurational, as against purely positional, astronomy, in which attention focuses not, or not primarily, on the length of specific planetary periods per se but on the geometric figures which planets inscribe in the zodiac in the course of their synodical or sidereal periods (or of submultiples or multiples thereof).[8] Thus, the moon's four major phases appear to mark off the corners of a square in the course of one month; Mercury as evening and as morning star, a hexagram per year, which rotates once every twenty years; Venus as either evening or morning star, a pentagram every eight years; the conjunctions of Jupiter and Saturn, a trigon every sixty years, and so on. Reference, too, has been made to the massive archaeological evidence showing that Stone Agers all along the coasts of Northwestern Europe knew and kept trace of the lunar declination cycle, presumably for the twin purposes of eclipse and tidal prediction.[9]

Observation was by means of backsight-foresight combinations aligned to a level horizon, the stone arrangements themselves being equivalent to systems of numeration. Quite extraordinary precision would have been attainable with simple but widely spaced foresight-backsight combinations.[10] In due course, these same alignments would have been bound to reveal to the same expert observers yet a third class of phenomena, namely, the slow eastward drift of the constellations marking the four year-points at any given time. Actually, according to Professor Philip Morrison, physicist and cosmologist at the Massachusetts Institute of Technology, all that would have been needed to pick up this drift was an old tree and faith in one's grandfather. Observation by means of the more elaborate backsight-foresight method would then have served merely to confirm such family tradition. Let it be noted once and for all that to think Stone Agers capable of this observation is not in any way to detract from the originality of the Greek astronomer Hipparchus's hypothetical explanation (ca. 150 B.C.) that this apparent eastward drift of the year-point constellations is in reality the westward, circular motion, or "precession," of the equinoxes, those invisible intersections of our two invisible coordinates, equator and ecliptic. The distinction is as crucial as it is all too often ignored. In order to keep it before the reader's mind, the naked-eye phenomena at issue, i.e., the eastward drift of year-point constellations, will from here on be referred to as "quasi-precessional" only.

The case for Stone Age familiarity with these quasi-precessional phenomena, then, has three distinct aspects. There is, first, the claim that observation of the phenomena at issue falls well within the range of the accuracy embodied in dozens of preserved megalithic alignments; i.e., that, on principle, it was possible. There is, second, the claim that, with a probability verging on certainty, this observational possibility was actually realized. The first claim can appeal to cognate evidence assembled by archaeoastronomy; the second to the convergent testimony of myths and mythic motifs collected by the Frankfurt ethnologist and historian of science, Professor Hertha von Dechend; in particular to the myths of decline and catastrophe under discussion. As configurational astronomy freezes long stretches of time into geometric figures, so myths of decline and catastrophe froze such stretches into narrative plots. Once detected, the periodic obsolescence of any given set of year-point constellations had people looking for evidence of a beginning and of an end; the latter to be followed (everywhere except in orthodox Zoroastrianism and Judaeo-Christianity) by a new beginning in the form either of linear reversal or else of fully circular renewal. There is, finally, the question of why, if realized, quasi-precessional phenomena were never expressed in other than mythic terms, even after the rise of Ionian science; and why, even after Hipparchus had succeeded in astronomically expressing the phenomena at issue, his restatement remained in virtual limbo for centuries. The answer to be suggested in what follows is that expression in the anthropomorphic terms of myth piously acknowledged the linkage of man's moral destiny to that of the cosmos—and the risks, to the cosmos as well as to man, of hubristically replacing it by geometrico-mathematical expression.

TYPICAL MYTHS OF DECLINE AND END

To anyone looking for visual evidence of a beginning, the Milky Way was bound to appear crucial. Its role in many myths confirms this assumption. For its lingering golden-white glow seemed to proclaim that once, long ago, it had served as the path of the equinoctial sun, a path long since abandoned, in consequence of some sort of catastrophe variously specified. Backward extrapolation, then, equated the astronomical beginning with the time when two galactic constellations in particular, Gemini and Sagittarius, marked the sun's horizon position on the two equinoctial days of the year, spring and fall.[11] The galaxy, too, seemed visibly to justify the universal belief that the evident ills afflicting our mortal condition deepened and multiplied in proportion as the sun progressively departed from his ancient equinoctial path. So long as the galaxy had in fact been that path, men, gods, and the dead were thought still capable of communing by way of this luminous bridge. Both astronomically and morally, that arrangement exhibited perfect parsimony. To a perpetual equinoctial day corresponded a human life which despite or because of its extreme simplicity was virtuous and as yet unblemished by all the familiar woes of aging, hunger, drought, sex, war, and death. Thereafter, in consequence of some wrenching catastrophe, galaxy and equinoctial sun came unstuck. The galaxy ceased to link gods and men, and their erstwhile communion now became something only intermittently realizable by ritual and calendric means. As Hesiod expressed it in the language of Greek mythology, the Golden Age opened when Cronus, Uranus's youngest son, forcibly separated the sky from the earth, by mutilating his father. The Golden Age closed when Phaëthon, the sun god Helios's son, lost control of the solar chariot and, even while searing the earth's surface, swerved onto a more westerly track, which left the galaxy forever marking the sun's now abandoned path. The Silver Age followed when Cronus was overthrown by his own son, Zeus; and it was terminated, in its turn, by Zeus kicking over the table in disgust at a cannibalistic dish offered him by Lycaon, an Arcadian king who was then transformed into a wolf for presuming to test the divinity of Zeus.

Thus, the virtue and simplicity of the Golden Age disappeared. In its place came the Silver Age, an age less blissful because it purchased such progress as it made in civilization at the price of moral decline. Next came the Copper Age, a period worse still because it put a budding metal technology to the nasty uses that have since become so familiar. Next, the Age of Heroes, selflessly conquering as at Troy even while beholden to grand and fatal passions. Finally, the present or Iron Age, most wretched of all because it unites the apex of civilized sophistication with viciousness, unending conflict, and great suffering. In sum, man's simultaneous advance in civilization and decline in moral sanity was precipitous. After quasi-precessional drift had run through no more than a bare handful of year-point constellations, the Iron Age and its inevitable sequel, end, and reversal, were already at hand. How was a predominantly oral culture to anchor in its collective memory this awesome sequence? Clearly, by casting it all in a narrative form peculiarly suited, then as now, to recollection, i.e., in the form of plots replete with blood, lust, and physical violence.

So far, then, two observations were involved. People observed the equinoctial sun's ever-widening remove from the Milky Way. They also observed, or at least thought they observed, that human decency declined in proportion as civilization progressed. They observed, finally, yet a third thing. After a given set of year-point constellations has thus slipped through one quadrant of the zodiac, it necessarily repeats if in scrambled sequence. To the first century B.C. the point was of more than purely academic interest. For the year-point constellations then about to return, if in scrambled sequence, were precisely those of the erstwhile Golden Age. Well might educated Romans, sickened by the climactic savagery of revolutions and civil wars, yet remembering Plato's doctrine (in the *Politicus*) of a reciprocating cosmic cycle, take this as evidence that the cosmic and moral decline had reached its nadir and was about to reverse direction.

That is what Vergil's *Fourth Eclogue* tells us. "Already [he writes] Virgo [the mark of summer solstice in the Golden Age] is returning [to mark autumnal equinox]; the reign of Saturn [the Golden Age itself, therefore] is [eventually] returning [too]." Allegorically equating the imminent new era with the imminent birth of a child, he projects the return of a Heroic Age comparable to (though not, of course, identical with) the one once associated with the Trojan War and the Argonauts' Voyage, and the return, eventually, of another Golden Age. Astronomical, biological, and moral phenomena are here treated as parallel—as befits a cosmology for which mathematics, astronomy, biology, etc., are essential but merely auxiliary disciplines. Vergil does not allude to catastrophes coincident with the end of the old and the start of the new cycle. He does not mention, that is, the panplanetary conjunctions in one of the solstitial signs which (according to Aristotle) trigger terrestrial fires or floods; or the eventual desiccation of the very cosmos which (according to the Stoics) follows upon its exhaustion of humid nutriment. Evidently, he thinks the return of the Golden Age's year-point constellations and man's present depravity are quite sufficient to justify the expectation of an imminent reversal. He seems content with the reciprocating model implicit in Hesiod and explicit in Plato.

Nothing, moreover, suggests that he thinks of the moral trend as reversing but of the trend of the year-point constellations as continuing forward. His construal of quasi-precessional drift as reversing, despite Hipparchus's long-standing thesis that precession is circular, is instructive. After all, by the time of Vergil's poem (41 B.C.) Hipparchus's theory of precession (like some of his other work, familiar even to Cicero forty years earlier) had been in the public domain for a full century. That should have been long enough for it to displace the older, reciprocating model— if Hipparchus's conclusion that precession is circular had in fact been promoted to the same rank of "normal science" (in T. S. Kuhn's phrase[12]), as the measurements whereby he had established the reality and rate of precession in the first instance. On the evidence of Vergil's *Fourth Eclogue*, however, this promotion never occurred. In educated perception, the fact of precession, though now properly defined and quantified, remained separate from Hipparchus's extrapolation to its circular direction.

What explains this selective reception of one of the great scientific contributions? The reason is plainly unrelated to, say, an empiricist's objection to extrapolation as such. Nor does there seem to be any other, obvious, explanation.

Now, more than a century ago, Thomas-Henri Martin devoted a whole monograph to the question of whether there is any evidence for ancient awareness of precession prior to Hipparchus.[13] Ignoring the iconographic and mythic evidence presently to be cited, he concluded in the negative. In the process, he cited ancients who rejected Hipparchus's theory on the pseudoempirical grounds that his very data are unsupported by what they mistook for Egyptian and Babylonian observations of prehistoric antiquity. To those of us, however, prepared to view myths of declining world ages as a technical language appropriate to the oral stage of early cultures, the Babylonian Gilgamesh epic (like Hesiod's later myth of world ages) contains one of "the clearest statement[s] ever uttered by men or gods concerning the [sc.quasi-]precession[al phenomena]."[14] And the iconography of Babylonian seals and Iranian vases (from 4000 B.C. till the seventh century of our era) is demonstrably unintelligible except in terms of precisely the quasi-precessional phenomena at issue.[15] Throughout four and a half millennia, that iconography persisted in depicting a celestial situation that, empirically speaking, had long since ceased to exist.

Thus, to the extent that ancient critics of Hipparchus may be presumed to have been familiar with the iconographic and mythic evidence cited, their true reasons for resisting Hipparchan theory were not, or at least not primarily, empirical as alleged. Instead, their objections were aimed not at the quasi-precessional phenomena per se, but at the language (mathematico-astronomical rather than mythic) in which Hipparchus expressed them and at the kinematic model (circular rather than reciprocating) from which he extrapolated them.

But why should Hipparchus's choice of language and of model have aroused such resistance? Nothing is explained by tautological appeal to "religious conservatism." An explanation must be sought, instead, in three specific beliefs as widespread as they were deep-seated. There was, first, the association of changing year-point constellations with the decline at once of the astronomical cosmos and of the world of man. There was, second, the belief that human language in the broadest sense, i.e., as including but not reducible to the language of mathematical astronomy, not only describes but potentially affects, "spellbinds" its referents. And there was, third, the belief that the cosmos is alive and divine and, as such, accessible to magical coercion and the objective pollution potentially effected by verbal blasphemy.

Thus, unless prudently tempered by apotropaic euphemisms or outright silence, the mere description of cosmic decline might turn out to reinforce and accelerate to catastrophic proportions what it thus described. Greco-Roman examples are legion (and the same may be supposed for Egypt and Babylon, thus explaining the lack of nonmythic references to quasi-precessional phenomena). Witness the popular reaction to Anaxagoras's cosmology; Aristotle's attack, in a popular work, on those who take Plato's creation account literally; and Lucretius's attempt to dispel the fear, widespread even among the educated, lest a denial of the divinity of the cosmos threaten the survival of the cosmos and invite divine retribution.[16] Under the circumstances, Hipparchus's model of precession, just because it was purely astronomical, could hardly escape becoming the object of popular apprehensions of the sort associated with Anaxagoras, with the literalists attacked by Aristotle, and with the heliocentric hypothesis of Aristarchus (d. 250 B.C.) as challenged by the Stoics. In the religious view, then, the only safe way to describe quasi-precessional phenomena would be one that would temper the description of cosmic decline by something the language of mathematical astronomy was ill equipped to provide, viz., ritualized expressions that all would turn out well in the end, and another Golden Age be already under way.[17] Conversely, the language that could provide this ritualized optimism was precisely the language of myth. Witness, for example, the Athenian practice of having a special college of priests assess the religious significance of· eclipses long after their "mechanism" had been understood. The importance which Aristotle accords to myth—at the first and fourth stages of the cycle of human culture myth occurs as the prefigurement or allegorizing enshrinement of perennial truth—could not but reinforce this view.[18] But the real strength of the optimistic coda that myth alone could supply derived from two, ostensibly empirical, pieces of evidence: the return (albeit in scrambled order) of the Golden Age year-point constellations after quasi-precessional drift had run through no more than one quadrant of the zodiac and, concurrently with it, the conviction that man's moral corruption (which, after all, mirrors the drift at issue) had already reached its nadir. Instant moral reversal and instant quasi-precessional reversal (not Hipparchan progression), therefore, had to be at hand.

By Vergil's time, man's moral decline had literally achieved historic proportions. For ever since Rome had achieved mastery of the known world, i.e., ever since about 146 B.C. (which, ironically, was also the *floruit* of Hipparchus), Rome's record, plain for all to see, had been one of ever widening, deepening, and accelerating moral crisis.[19] But now, in the unspeakable savagery of the second civil war, bottom had been reached, and reversal had to be at hand, if only because man could sink no lower. "Where all is bad, it must be good to have known the worst" (as a survivor of World War II's horrors has put it in our time).

Such are the reasons that induced Vergil to ignore Hipparchus's purely theoretical contribution (even though Hipparchus himself is reported to have believed in man's kinship with the cosmos).[20]

As late as the middle of the first century B.C., then, the older, reciprocating model, with the prestigious endorsement of Platonic cosmology, prevailed over mere technical astronomy. In *Timaeus* 39D, Plato had spoken of a generic "perfect year" which was equivalent, presumably, to the least common multiple of all planetary periods and evidently in step with the reciprocating motion of quasi-precessional drift.[21] But he had prudently omitted to specify both its overall length and how he took it to relate to the fiery and watery catastrophes which Babylonian theory (alluded to in *Timaeus* 22C) associated with periodic panplanetary conjunctions in the signs of summer and of winter solstice respectively. Notwithstanding these calculated imprecisions, Plato's point is clear: the cosmos itself is subject to a quasi-biological life cycle which, consistently with the conservation of energy, has its own versions of gestation, birth, maturing, aging, death, and rebirth.

This is not the proper place for a comprehensive typology and history of ancient schemes of macroperiodization involving celestial, or celestial and terrestrial, or purely terrestrial catastrophes of fire *(ekpyrōsis, conflagratio)* and deluge *(kataklysmos, diluvium)*.[22] Suffice it here to discuss the earliest extant Greek text (so far imperfectly understood) which combines the notion of world ages, opening and closing with celestial catastrophes, with the notion of terrestrial catastrophes simultaneously triggered by panplanetary conjunctions at the solstices. That text is Plato's well-known report, at the beginning of his *Timaeus* (composed around 365 B.C.), of the Athenian lawgiver Solon's encounter with an Egyptian priest, almost exactly 200 years earlier. To draw out the priest on Egyptian traditions, Solon cites the Greek myth of a flood visited by Zeus upon wicked humanity, with only two people, Deucalion and his wife Pyrrha, being allowed to survive so as to start the human race anew. Solon's tactic succeeds. After exclaiming, "You Greeks are ever children!" the Egyptian priest proceeds to offer the "true," that is, as he makes clear, astronomical, explanation of the terrestrial fires reportedly started by Phaëthon's loss of control over the solar chariot. Note that the fire which the priest chose to comment upon was the one which both temporally and causally had preceded the Deucalian flood. Zeus reportedly sent the flood in order to extinguish the fires started by Phaëthon's mishap. Thus, when *Timaeus* has "the gods" periodically "purge the earth with waters," this purging is not, or at least not primarily, moral but physical: the ashes left by the preceding fire must be washed away. The priest hints at the astronomical explanation of the fire. "In reality" there occurred, as there does "at vast [presumably periodic] intervals," "a *parallaxis* of [unspecified] celestial bodies orbiting the earth." One and the same term, *parallaxis* (or what Berossus, the third-century B.C. Babylonian priest-historian, describes as the planets being "so positioned under the same sign that a straight line could pass through all of their disks") is here used to explain two distinct conflagrations, one celestial, the other terrestrial, both mythically traced to Phaëthon's accident with the solar chariot.

The celestial catastrophe is clearly that associated with the opening of an ever-widening gap between the sun, with its current set of equinoctial constellations, and the galaxy. However, once the sun has started to leave that path which long-past usage has forever burned into the sky, the language of "burning" ceases to be applied to the current solar track. Instead, it seems to have been reserved for the fate of obsolescent year-point constellations. Drawing ever nearer the rising sun, these are typically spoken of as "burned" into invisibility before "drowning" beneath the eastern horizon.

According to the Phaëthon myth, however, Phaëthon's accident is responsible for a terrestrial as well as a celestial conflagration. The solar chariot, that is, is said to have swerved not only laterally but also earthward. It is this latter component of its swerve which, in the myth, is credited with causing the fiery destruction of much of the earth's surface and population. Comparable, though unspecified, "dislocations" presumably underlie parallel myths of terrestrial deluges. Because Egypt, so the priest claims, is immune to both kinds of destruction, it alone has preserved intact ancient traditions that everywhere else are fragmented or lost. This claim obviously implies that at least the terrestrial fires and floods, however caused "in reality," were real, not metaphorical, and that it was the actual, historical Egypt, not its homonymous counterpart in Egyptian astronomy, which was spared.

In a sort of conceptual shorthand, then, the interpretation of the Phaëthon myth by the Egyptian priest imputes to the sun of yore the following two distinct catastrophes: first, one of the celestial "conflagrations" which preliterate astronomy associated with the drifting year-point constellations; and second, one of the terrestrial conflagrations which Babylonian astronomy, in particular, traced to panplanetary conjunctions in the sign of summer solstice. In his explanation, of course, the priest makes no overt reference to planets at all. This has left commentators unable to tell us how an unspecified "deviation" *(parallaxis)* in the orbits of an unspecified plurality of earth-circling bodies can possibly account (as the priest clearly claims it does) for what in the Phaëthon myth is the earthward plunge of the (singular) solar chariot.

All would become clear if the "deviation" *(parallaxis)* at issue could designate a panplanetary conjunction as well as the lateral displacement of year-point constellations. A medical meaning of the term, so far neglected in this context, seems capable, I submit, of doing just that. For it signifies overlap, as of broken bones. And "overlap" would accurately describe the placement of the planets when "so positioned under the same sign that a straight line could pass through all of their disks,"[23] that is, when in conjunction. In sum, if we are to make sense of the priest's alleged explanation—and of Solon's ready comprehension—we must suppose the priest to have used the technical term at issue in two distinct senses: in the sense of deviation with reference to the sun's departure from the galaxy, and of overlap with reference to the attendant panplanetary conjunction (presumably in the then constellation of summer solstice, Leo).

COSMIC ANXIETY

Catastrophes, cosmic or terrestrial, mythological or historical, did not always inspire anxiety. Take the expectation, just discussed, that panplanetary conjunctions in one of the two solstices produced fires or deluges. This doctrine could account, as it does in Plato and Aristotle, for what appeared to be the periodic loss and reachievement of high culture throughout human history. But these periods were too large to seem humanly relevant. And when they did seem so relevant, as when one such catastrophe was thought imminent, at least the conflagration (ekpyrōsis) was thought to occur not all of a sudden but only at the end of a long, prior process of gradual desiccation. Whatever ended here, ended, in T. S. Eliot's phrase, "not with a bang but a whimper."

Yet there was the belief—firm, ancient, and widespread—in the active interdependence, above and beyond mere parallelism, of the astronomical universe and man's biological, scientific, and ritual activities. The cosmos depended as much upon human support as man depended upon the cosmos. Periods as short as a year or a few decades could, therefore, inspire truly cosmic anxiety. Witness the Babylonian New Year ritual of reciting the cosmogony, the so-called Enuma Elish. This clearly implies that every year, prior to the vernal equinox, apprehension was widespread—or at least simulated. The same may be inferred, if at fifty-two–year intervals, for the Aztecs: all fires, we are told, had to be, and to stay, extinguished until the Pleiades had safely rearisen in their constellation, Taurus. As for the early Christians, their expectation of an imminent Second Coming, heralded and accompanied by a whole panoply of apocalyptic events in the sky, notoriously accounts for their omission to undertake a conventional biography of Christ, for their fear of exclusion from the company of the Elect, and for their certainty that those presently contemptuous of their apocalyptic astronomy would find themselves tormented in their turn.

On the whole, however, even major, unexpected, and prolonged adversities (such as plagues, crop failures, floods, and invasions) were not invested with cosmic anxiety until and unless they coincided with ostensibly significant astronomical, or astrological, indicators. And even then these indicators were thought of as contingent rather than absolute in their cogency. Much depended upon the presuppositions of the observers, their relative expertise and social status, and the kind and magnitude of evidence being considered. Different observers might differ in their assessments of the same evidence; one and the same observer might, as already noted, perceive, say, its cognitive strand as progressive, yet its moral component as marking decline. An incipient convert to Christianity like the Roman Emperor Constantine could profess to derive confidence before battle from signs like a flaming cross in the sky, signs that others found unconvincing. And the Jutlanders of A.D. 412 and 413 (about whom we shall hear more presently) appear to have panicked at major astronomical conjunctions which, topping an unusual series of eclipses, seemed to confirm the Norse Sibyl's apocalyptic predictions of the end *(ragnarók)*, and may have been preceded by a series of disastrous spring tides like the ones that 500 years earlier had driven the Cimbri and Teutons from their homesteads.

Like an active volcano, then, cosmic anxiety smoldered even when not actually erupting. It fed, as we saw, on the ever-widening gap between sun and galaxy on the one hand, and between present and original moral conditions on the other. Whenever that decline seemed to accelerate, to approach its nadir, and/or to be accompanied by events like eclipses and unusual conjunctions (which continued to be viewed as ill omens long after they had become predictable), cosmic anxiety habitually erupted. But it remained latently active even during periods of steady, if undramatic, moral decline—even when that was concealed, as it often was, by intellectual and material progress.

Now the ancient paradigm of decline was locked into, and hallowed by, its ancient oral matrix. As fared the matrix, so therefore fared the paradigm. Along with the former, the latter demonstrated the greatest staying power both at the broad, nonliterate base and at the literate but latently anti-intellectual apex of the social pyramid. These social extremes were bound to reinforce one another, given the tendency of Athens's democratic culture to "level up" and assimilate the aristocratic values, and given the landed gentry's natural partnership with the peasantry. Thus, only a relatively small segment of society succeeded, and only for a relatively brief span of time, in detaching the pessimistic paradigm from its oral matrix and fusing it with rationalism. The result: tragedy and pre-Socratic as well as Platonic philosophy. All around them, however, the pessimistic paradigm continued to survive in its oral, Homeric-Hesiodic matrix and to shape, decisively and mostly silently, the very terms of popular perception, feeling, and thinking. Only the pressure of prolonged adversity could be relied on to bring it out into the open. Such then is the steady organ bass which accompanies and tacitly qualifies the sense of euphoria at democracy achieved, Persia repulsed, empire established, Athens beautified, and destiny mastered. Here, as in the later case of the Christian Gnostics, the accidents of documentation, articulateness, and relative stridency must not be allowed to distort the historical realities.[24] Seen in proper perspective, that progressivist euphoria is but an episode within a longer cycle. By 411 B.C. democracy had voted itself out of power. The Greek philosopher Protagoras, for whom man was "the measure of all things," may or may not have found cause to revise his belief in progress.[25] For once, the majority was not blind. Even the sovereign people finally realized that King Demos wore no clothes. Such disenchantment, of course, was not born overnight—nor did it remain unique. It is implicit throughout the Fifty Years in Sophocles' darkling hints in his tragedies at the ambivalence and hence precariousness of reason and all its works. It is implicit in Aristophanes' lampooning of the Athenian statesman Cleon as a demagogue and in Thucydides' unblinking diagnosis of democracy's pathology. It becomes explicit in Plato's alternative polity of the philosopher-king—and in his clear suggestion that even it is subject to the decline of the cosmos as a whole as portrayed in the *Politicus* myth.

DIFFERENTIAL RESPONSES

Different people, we noted, were capable of differently perceiving one and the same situation. The reasons so far examined were the "subjective" ones of social position and membership in the corresponding cultural matrix. To identify them, the historian will obviously want to discover who, at what level of the social pyramid, perceived a given set of phenomena as decline, as progress, or as an epicycle of progress, temporally and qualitatively limited, and astride a larger, secular cycle in whose declining phase our present happens to be contained.

There is another set of reasons, however. It is "objective" in the sense of being internal to the logic of any cyclical paradigm. Thus, on the assumption of declining world ages, the last of which is our present one, and of the progressive character of knowledge and material civilization, the following combinations typically result.

Once the midpoint in a steadily degenerative cycle is reached, qualitative moral degeneration begins to be offset by diminution of the quantitative, temporal distance remaining to be covered before the Golden Age returns. Hence, if one focuses on the coming birth of a new era, one will share Vergil's and the early Christians' sense of confidence increasing in proportion to deepening darkness. For is it not always darkest just before dawn? Conversely, if one focuses on the coming end of an era, one will, as did Hesiod, feel deepening gloom. If, finally, one oscillates between both foci, one will oscillate, too, between both emotions, since not infrequently both phenomena are being contemplated simultaneously in a sort of visual counterpoint. Depending upon which part of the cycle one looks at, an infant will seem happy or pitiable; a conqueror, enviable or, like Shelley's Ozymandias, doomed; a defeated country, doomed or destined, Phoenix-like, to rise victorious from the ashes of defeat. This explains the twin paradox: that Rome's sense of decline was born precisely when Rome was victorious, and grew along with its Empire; and that, conversely, as the Roman theologian Tertullian observed, the blood of the Christian martyrs proved the seed of an era to come.

Nor does pessimism with respect to the present cosmic era preclude optimism with respect to some limited aspect thereof. Indeed, a necessary connection between the two is sometimes thought to obtain. The worse the universe at large, the more intense an individual's efforts either to escape by frenzied labors in an ivory tower or to save at least his soul, as in Pythagoreanism and Platonism, by single-minded devotion to the so-called *mathēmata*—arithmetic, geometry, harmonic theory, and mathematical astronomy. These exacting disciplines are credited with the power of purifying and unifying the essential self, the *psychē*, even during its mortal, incarnate sojourn. Such efforts were normally confined to small groups of like-minded individuals, though sometimes intended vicariously to save or at least reform the community at large. In no case would one expect to halt or reverse the trend of the universe, but would be content to follow Dr. Samuel Johnson's maxim of retarding what one cannot halt, mitigating what one cannot cure. Xenophanes, sixth-century B.C. Greek philosopher, is the earliest clear case in point. That he combined belief in the dissolution of the cosmos with belief in the progress of human knowledge has been observed.[26] What appears to have gone strangely unnoticed is that he coupled this progressivist persuasion with the attempt, futile in the event, to wean his fellow Colophonians from preoccupation with luxury goods and athletic victors lest that unfit them for defense of their liberty.[27] The attempted intervention, equally futile, by Pythagoreans and Platonists alike in contemporary Italian politics was clearly inspired by the same spirit of political apocalypticism. The ancient doctrine of the mixed constitution, finally, so important for the authors of *The Federalist Papers*, explaining and urging adoption of the American Constitution in 1788, belongs in this context. According to that doctrine, the tendency of constitutions to follow the macrocosmic pattern—to decline, to grow corrupt, and to engender their opposites—can be arrested, albeit not forever, by institutionalizing a judicious mixture of monarchy, aristocracy, and democracy.

Yet general pessimism must not invariably turn into cosmic anxiety. Ancient philosophers like Heraclitus, Plato, Aristotle, and the Stoics were expected to resist the impulse. Stoics went out of their way to demonstrate that what might terrify others—imminent cosmic catastrophe—did not terrify the true philosopher. Although, or rather because, he acknowledges the doctrine of catastrophes, he does not dignify it with apprehensiveness. Quite the contrary. The implication is that if and when catastrophe, even the ultimate catastrophe, does strike, it will come as a challenge. It will then afford him a not unwelcome occasion for proving, in the dual sense of testing and demonstrating, imperviousness to all manner of adversity. Nothing less, after all, is consistent with the heroic ethic in philosophic guise. Thus Plato's Atlantis myth presents the victorious Athenians, perishing alongside the defeated enemy, as the heroic executors of a larger, divinely sanctioned law. Post-Socratics like Cynics and Stoics notoriously go farther still. Their *fiat justitia, pereat mundus* ("let justice be done, [even if] the [very] universe perish [thereby]") proudly proclaims an ethic of intrinsic value. Disdainful of any calculus of consequences to their physical selves, to society, or (hypothetically) even to the cosmos, they justify the Latin poet Horace's prediction that if the universe were to collapse, its ruins would strike the man of integrity still standing upright.[28] Such moral rigorism is compatible with preemptive suicide, if the sage feels the immovable object that is his integrity seriously threatened by an irresistible force of historic, or even cosmic, origin. "The very gods favored Caesar's cause by granting him victory; yet Cato by committing suicide continued to favor the cause now lost." So the Latin poet Lucan's *victrix causa diis placuit sed victa Catoni* pithily and untranslatably puts it. The true mark of success, then, is indifference to it in its vulgar form.

To the twelfth-century Christian mystic, Joachim of Fiore, his proto-Spenglerian parallel between the decline and fall of Rome's Empire and the life cycle of an individual was a source of profound regret. To a true Stoic it would merely be another challenge. He would press the argument that an Academic Skeptic, Carneades, had merely presented as an option: if the Roman Empire were found to be unjust, decline and liquidation were deserved; if just, it would remain so regardless of its outer fate—and afford the philosopher a test of his moral fiber in the bargain.

In yet another combination, all segments of a society, rulers and ruled alike, spectators and participants, can experience not confidence but anguish as the future prospects of the cosmos darken. There has been one occasion for which, quite recently and unexpectedly, such a sense of truly cosmic panic has been documented. The time is late antiquity (A.D. 413, to be precise); the place, southern Jutland, well east of the Roman *limes;* the evidence, two golden horns (now lost) covered with astronomical, calendric, astrological, and eschatological iconography of demonstrably syncretic character—Teutonic, Hellenistic, Babylonian. One of these Gallehus horns has been shown to refer to the lunar eclipse of November 4, 412; the other, to the subsequent solar eclipse of April 16, 413. The latter also contains a crypto-runic inscription, "May I, the potion of this horn, bring help to the community." The point of this inscription is intimately related to that of at least eleven iconographic and other references to eclipse periods and the Great Year.[29] It is that of bolstering the sun's will and ability to resist being permanently eclipsed. The parallel logic of the Babylonian New Year recital of the cosmogonic epic, earlier referred to, leaps to mind. In the case at hand, the bolstering in question is achieved by means of repetition, that hallmark of all magical incantation, mnemotechnic fixation, and aretalogical invocation. What is being repeated are the eclipse periods by virtue of which the sun has in the past triumphed over the threat of permanent extinction. The threat is here presented in its Teutonic form, as the *ragnarók,* the conception of the end of heaven, earth, and hell as described by the Norse Sibyl in the Elder Edda's *Voluspá* ("The Witch's Prophecy").

True, this evidence of cosmic anxiety, associated with deluge or conflagration since Babylonian days, is late and from outside the Roman Empire. Yet it permits two arguments by analogy. First, it is probable that an anxiety so overt in late antiquity and so syncretic in character was not unknown among the populace and astrologers of polyethnic Rome itself. Among the evidence favoring this belief is the "much demanded Oracle of Cronus, the so-called Little Mill" from a fourth-century Paris Magical Papyrus. Here is the ancient tale of Cronus/Saturn's quasi-precessional mill, sunken to the bottom of "the sea" at the end of the Golden Age, yet still alive in late antiquity. Pompeian graffiti similarly afford us wholly unexpected glimpses of a linguistic subculture, an underground link, as it were, between archaic and vulgar Latinity, between both ends of the chronological spectrum.

Second, an anxiety so pronounced in largely preliterate northern Europe at so late a date is unlikely to be of recent origin. On the contrary, barring decisive evidence to the contrary, it may safely be assumed to reflect a state of mind reaching back into the Stone Age—certainly into the period among whose few surviving witnesses are the mute alignments which archaeoastronomy has evinced for hundreds of megalithic structures. Of course, the unavailability to our Stone Age ancestors of literacy and at least our sort of numeracy defines the limits within which archaeoastronomy and allied disciplines must operate. Still, the tie-in between eclipse prediction by means of the oscillation of the midwinter full moon, on the one hand, and prediction bearing on the end of a world era, on the other, is too clear to be ignored. If *ragnarók* were, on general grounds, thought to be imminent, then, given the link between lunar declination and the probability of subsequent eclipses, the actual date of *ragnarók* would be thought predictable by reference to the lunar declination cycle. In the case at hand, as I have argued elsewhere, *ragnarók* might have been expected to occur at the new moon nearest the summer solstice after the midwinter full moon cited—but for one embarrassing fact. By A.D. 406 the actual incidence of eclipses had far outpaced the predictive capability of the lunar declination cycle. Thus the link between it and the imminent termination of the Great Year would have been statistical, not sharp. Instead of pinpointing *ragnarók* itself, the lunar declination cycle would have defined the time frame within which a period of *ragnarók* danger, comparable to the familiar periods of eclipse danger, had to be expected. That the unnatural crowding of eclipses preceding the dates mentioned made *ragnarók* seem at hand is beyond all reasonable doubt.

So is the fact, already noted, that 1,100 years after Hesiod, a wave of truly cosmic anxiety swept over these Jutlanders. Indeed, unlike Hesiod, they seem to have felt it so keenly that not even the routine desparation of their day-to-day lives could numb them to it. Nevertheless, though thus succumbing, they did not therefore react—or overreact—by welcoming, let alone embracing, the threatening catastrophe. To do that, at once grimly and joyfully, to welcome a truly universal destruction as the price of their own defeat, was, as we shall presently see, left to other, more recent claimants to the heroic ethos.

The mythical notions of decline and end, based on pagan notions of declining world ages and imminent catastrophe, underwent successive modifications and attenuations. Some, as in ancient Iran and Palestine, might retain the empty shell of the story, out of priestly conservatism or for missionary effect. But—and this is the point—it was always infused with new significance. The new beginning following upon the apocalyptic phase would be neither cyclic nor reciprocating, but millennial in format. The earliest attentuation came at the hands of biblicists intent—on grounds neither empirical nor rational but purely revelational—on exculpating the Deity. Man himself, not cosmic agencies, had henceforth to be held responsible for man's troubles. Whence that shift of emphasis which is still discernible as on a palimpsest held up to light in the Biblical creation accounts as they stand. Whence also Tertullian's claim that by their prayers the Christians have effectively interceded with God to stave off the end of the world—and of the Roman Empire along with it. There is, finally, the Romantic yearning, apparent in certain nineteenth-century German works of historical fiction—as well as in marching songs of both world wars—to identify with the Norse vision of catastrophe (ragnarók), as somberly intoned in the brooding minor chords of Richard Wagner's Die Götterdämmerung. The effect is that of conferring cosmic significance and grandeur upon the heroic death struggles of Goths, Nibelungs, and latter-day claimants to their ethos. "If we go under, so will—so must—the very universe." For long, the weaponry of war had, mercifully, proved unable to consummate this somber, self-fulfilling vision. The advent of the nuclear age has, alas, moved its consummation from the realm of mythological language and historical rhetoric into that of technological feasibility. But that is another, sadder, story.

NOTES

1. In his pioneering statement of the problem of literacy, Sterling Dow, "Minoan Writing," *American Journal of Archaeology* 58 (1954), esp. 109–112, distinguished within each historical situation a quantitative and a qualitative vec-

tor, the one ranging from zero through "selective" to "habitual," the other from zero through "stunted" to "fluent." Thus, Linear A, like the Mayan syllabary, instantiates selective, yet stunted literacy; Linear B and the Cypriote syllabary, selective yet fluent, or "special" literacy. Opinions divide as to the state of literacy in classical, that is, fifth-century, Athens. Dow seemed to date it to the start of the century, and Eric A. Havelock, *Preface to Plato* (Cambridge, Mass.: Harvard University Press, 1963), pp. 53, 294, to the end.

2. Havelock, *Preface to Plato*, p. 94.

3. David Lewis, *We, the Navigators* (Honolulu: University of Hawaii Press, 1972), and *Voyaging Stars* (New York: W. W. Norton & Company, 1978); Alexander Thom, *Megalithic Sites in Britain* (Oxford: Clarendon Press, 1967), and *Megalithic Lunar Observatories* (Oxford: Clarendon Press, 1971); Gerald S. Hawkins, *Stonehenge Decoded* (New York: Dell, 1965) and *Beyond Stonehenge* (New York: Harper & Row, 1973). See also their papers in "The Place of Astronomy in the Ancient World" (symposium), *Philosophical Transactions of the Royal Society of London* 276 (1974), 1–276.

4. See Karl Reinhardt, "Personifikation und Allegorie," *Vermächtnis der Antike* (Göttingen, 1960), pp. 7–9; and Geoffrey Stephen Kirk, *Myth: Its Meaning and Function in Ancient and Other Cultures* (Cambridge: Cambridge University Press, 1970), p. 240. See also my chapter "The Language of Archaic Astronomy: A Clue to the Atlantis Myth?" in *Astronomy of the Ancients,* ed. Kenneth Brecher and Michael Feirtag (Cambridge, Mass.: MIT Press, 1979), pp. 153–89, and the bibliography there given.

5. Marcel Hinze, "Studien zum Verständnis der archaischen Astronomie," *Symbolon, Jahrbuch für Symbolforschung* 5 (1966), 162–219.

6. Willy Hartner, *Oriens-Occidens* (Hildesheim, 1968); Hartner, *Die Goldhörner von Gallehus* (Wiesbaden: Steiner, 1969); and Hertha von Dechend and Giorgio de Santillana, *Hamlet's Mill* (Boston: Gambit, 1969).

7. Francis M. Cornford, *Thucydides Mythistoricus* (1907; Philadelphia: University of Pennsylvania Press, 1971), pp. 131–32. John Finley, "The Origins of Thucydides' Style," *Harvard Studies in Classical Philology* 50 (1939), 35–48, demonstrated the extent to which this infiguration of thought was matched by the stylistic infiguration of Thucydides's prose, through antithesis chiefly into the elevated, poetic mold. Though subsequently justified in a variety of ways, both infigurations betray a primal, involuntary aspect: the pull of oral, poetic, "musical" tradition. For as the accompaniment of poetry music is part of that tradition. What horizon alignments are to numeracy in astronomy, and antithesis to subordination in Greek style, the "commensurational" is to the computational expression of intervals in Greek music.

8. Hinze, "Studien zum Verständnis der archaischen Astronomie."

9. Thom, *Megalithic Sites in Britain* and *Megalithic Lunar Observatories;* Hawkins, *Stonehenge Decoded* and *Beyond Stonehenge;* Otto Sigfrid Reuter, *Germanische Himmelskunde: Untersuchungen zur Geschichte des Geistes* (Munich, 1934); and Rolf Müller, *Der Himmel über dem Menschen der Steinzeit* (Berlin, 1970).

10. Thom, *Megalithic Lunar Observatories,* p. 11.

11. See von Dechend and de Santillana, *Hamlet's Mill,* pp. 242–62.

12. Thomas S. Kuhn, *The Structure of Scientific Revolutions,* 2nd ed., en-

larged (*International Encyclopedia of Unified Science,* 2:2) (Chicago: University of Chicago Press, 1970).

13. Thomas-Henri Martin, *Mémoire sur cette question: La Précession des Équinoxes a-t-elle été connue des Égyptiens ou de quelque autre peuple avant Hipparque?* (Paris: Imprimerie Impériale, 1869), pp. 47–51, 74, 83, argued that under the twin influence of undue respect for the data of Babylonian and Egyptian astronomy and of the requirements of astrology, most Greco-Roman writers on astronomy, including Ptolemy, either ignore Hipparchus's discovery or else treat it as poorly substantiated and as, in any case, of narrowly astronomical import.

14. See von Dechend and de Santillana, p. 325, for statement and reference.

15. See Hartner, *Die Goldhörner von Gallehus,* pp. 54 ff., on the Babylonian asterisms portrayed as heliacally rising at two of the four year-points, viz., Pleiades before Alpha Tauri at vernal equinox; Ibex (i.e., part of our Aquarius) and Stag (i.e., our Cassiopeia) at winter solstice; Leo marking summer solstice.

16. For all the details and bibliography see my "Myth and Magic in Cosmological Polemics: Plato, Aristotle, Lucretius," *Rheinisches Museum für Philologie* 114 (1971), esp. 304–12.

17. Cf. the "Say woe, woe, but may the good prevail" of the first chorus in Aeschylus's *Agamemnon;* Hesiod, *Erga* 174–75; line 60 of the Edda's *Voluspá;* and the corresponding motifs on the Gallehus horns in Hartner, *Die Goldhörner von Gallehus,* pp. 99, 103–5; and Harald A. T. Reiche, "Gallehus Horns, Lunar Declination Cycle, and *Ragnarók,*" in *Prismata: Naturwissenschaftsgeschichtliche Studien. Festschrift für Willy Hartner,* eds. Y. Maeyama and W. G. Saltzer (Wiesbaden, 1977), pp. 321–24.

18. See Reiche, "Myth and Magic in Cosmological Polemics: Plato, Aristotle, Lucretius," pp. 318–19.

19. That judgment, of course, is not original with Vergil. Its fullest and most influential statement is (or rather, was) to be found in the Stoic philosopher Posidonius's 52-book ecumenical history from Rome's triumph (145–144 B.C.) through Sulla's dictatorship (79 B.C.). See K. Reinhardt, *Real-Encyclopädie* s.v. "Poseidonios" coll. 627–35.

20. By contrast, Cicero's failure to make use of Hipparchus's rather than Eudoxus's less accurate, planetary periods for the computation of his Great Year of 12,954 years in the *Hortensius* is due to purely literary reasons. He himself evinces familiarity with Hipparchus's critique of Aratus (a follower of Eudoxus) and Eratosthenes. (Cf. M. Ruch, "Météorologie, Astronomie et Astrologie chez Ciceron," *Revue des Etudes Latines* 42 (1964), p. 204. For purely literary reasons Cicero preferred to follow Aristotle's *Protrepticus* and the use there made of Eudoxus's (obsolete) periods. After all, even Posidonius managed to combine his reception of Hipparchus's better planetary periods with continuing admiration for the organismic cosmology of Plato's *Timaeus.* See my forthcoming study of Cicero's Great Year in the *Hortensius.*

21. See B. van der Waerden, "Das Grosse Jahr und die ewige Wiederkehr," *Hermes* 80 (1952), 129–55; on Vergil's connection with it, see A. D. Nock, *Conversion* (Oxford: Oxford University Press, 1933), pp. 244–45; and E. R. Dodds, *The Greeks and the Irrational* (Berkeley: University of California Press, 1951), p. 21.

22. Good introductions to the problem are the series of articles on "Ages of the

World" in *Encyclopedia of Religion and Ethics*, ed. James Hastings, with John A. Selbie and others (New York: Charles Scribner's Sons, 1928), vol. 1, pp. 183–210; Arthur O. Lovejoy and George Boas, *Primitivism and Related Ideas in Antiquity* (Baltimore: Johns Hopkins University Press, 1935); Bodo Gatz, *Weltalter, Goldene Zeit und sinnverwandte Vorstellungen* (Hildesheim, 1967); and H. A. T. Reiche, "Aristotle's Great Year of 12,954ᵃ Explained," *Bulletin of the American Astronomical Society* (Historical Astronomy Division) 14 (1982), 896–97.

23. Berossus, fg. 37 Schnabel, with P. Schnabel, *Berossus und die babylonisch-hellenistische Literatur* (Leipzig: Teubner, 1923), pp. 98 ff.

24. For all their other merits, the three standard works most often cited in reference to the topic virtually neglect this aspect of the question. See John B. Bury, *The Idea of Progress* (1932; New York: Dover, 1955); Lovejoy and Boas, *Primitivism and Related Ideas in Antiquity;* and Ludwig Edelstein, *The Idea of Progress in Classical Antiquity* (Baltimore: Johns Hopkins University Press, 1967).

25. See Dodds, *The Greeks and the Irrational*, p. 184; Edelstein, *The Idea of Progress in Classical Antiquity*, p. 56n., (who disagreed, on the ground that progressivism suffered only a "temporary crisis"); and E. R. Dodds, *The Ancient Concept of Progress* (New York: Oxford University Press, 1973), p. 13.

26. Edelstein, *The Idea of Progress in Classical Antiquity*, p. 29.

27. H. A. T. Reiche, "Empirical Aspects of Xenophanes' Theology," in *Essays in Ancient Greek Philosophy*, ed. John P. Anton with George L. Kustas (Albany: State University of New York, 1971), pp. 98, 109n.

28. See also Lord Mansfield's famous ruling in the Wilkes case: "We must not regard political consequences; how formidable soever they might be, if rebellion was the certain consequence, we are bound to say *Fiat institia, ruat coelum*." In Mozart's *Don Giovanni*, Act 1, Scene 21 (end), Don Giovanni blasphemously dares the world to fall into ruins: not even that would deter him from philandering.

29. Harald A. T. Reiche, "Gallehus Horns," pp. 317–28.

3

A SCHEDULE FOR THE END OF THE WORLD: THE ORIGINS AND PERSISTENCE OF THE APOCALYPTIC MENTALITY

Amos Funkenstein

Q*UONIAM FESTINANS FESTINAT SAECULUM PERTRANSIRE:* "Our world," says the Ezra apocalypse, "hurries toward its end." Written about a generation after the catastrophic end of the first Jewish revolt against Rome (A.D. 71), the vision restates the motifs common to all apocalyptic visions: the end of the world is very near; only a few will survive it to see the outbreak of a new, magnificent eon. The old world is full of "sorrow and pain"; it will crumble under the weight of its own wickedness. The new world will be new in all respects: a new society, a new cosmic order; "all periods and years will then be destroyed, and thereafter will exist neither month nor day, nor hours."[1] The new order of things, albeit anticipated and prophesied, will come "like a thief in the night," sudden and terrible.[2] Very little can be done by anyone, including those who know, to precipitate the end or to prevent it. Its exact time is known to God only: it has been set in a divine plan, written "in heavenly tablets" preceding history and predestining its course.[3] This blueprint for the course of history is immutable, and so is the end of history. It will come soon, but "not by the hands of man" (Daniel 2:45).[4] A passive, predestinarian posture allowed the apocalyptic visionary to withdraw from this world and to cast all hope on the other world. And though passivity does not always characterize the apocalyptician—the Dead Sea Scrolls, for example, anticipate a final battle between the "children of light" and the "children of darkness"—he is, whether active or passive, filled with a profound sense of alienation within this world. His political resignation, caused by internal persecution and external loss of political autarky since the end of the Hasmonean (Maccabean) dynasty, was complete: nothing in this world seemed to him worth amending or ameliorating.

Apocalypticism was a new and well-defined phenomenon in the history of the Jewish religion since the second century B.C. It was also the main source for future Jewish and Christian eschatological images, images concerning the "last things." Both the novelty and the uniqueness of apocalypticism are far from being self-evident. After all, visions of cosmic doom and delivery are not confined to the Jewish and Christian traditions. They appear in just about all cultures and societies in times of want as well as in times of affluence. Every culture seems to harbor thanatic fears of an ultimate catastrophe and hopes of rebirth of a new world. It is hard to overlook the ties between the myth (and cult) of the yearly regeneration of the earth out of darkness and barrenness and the myths of a future, final recreation of the world out of immense chaos and pain. "Millenarian" movements in different and disparate cultural horizons employ similar myths of rebirth.[5] Even if this is all these were to say of apocalypticism—which is not the case—apocalypticism would be a watershed in the history of the Jewish religion. On a very basic level, its novelty consists in the renewal of the almost severed umbilical cord of the Jewish religion to the domain of creative mythology. The mythopoetical imagination of the apocalyptician remythologized, in a sense, both cosmos and history. His language, his symbols are mythical through and through: unlike the prophets he not only employs current residues of myth, but rather creates a new mythical imagery to express the cosmic battle between good and evil, order and chaos, God and primordial beasts.

Yet if we attend only to the mythopoetical aspect of apocalypticism, important as it is, we shall hardly appreciate its uniqueness. For the sake of clarity, I wish to introduce the (ideal) distinction between apocalyptic imagery and apocalyptic knowledge: the significance of apocalypticism lies not only in the fact that the apocalyptician envisions the end of the world in very vivid images; no less important is the manner in which he proves the veracity of his visions, convinces himself and his community that the end is inevitable and inevitably close. Only with the aid of this distinction can the paradox of apocalypticism be understood—that it enhanced at one and the same time a sense of myth and a sense of history as a distinct unity.

Apocalyptic visions of a final universal trial took the place of the older prophetic visions of an ultimate "day of Jahweh." The later prophets did not invent hopes of a sudden, miraculous delivery. Such hopes were part of popular beliefs during the last one and a half centuries of both monarchies, Israel and Judea, when internal disintegration and political impotence generated hopes for a miraculous relief, prefigured by the exodus from Egypt.[6] The prophets rather tried to cut such hopes down to size. Vis-à-vis the professional optimists of their times, the "false prophets," they did not deny the coming of the "day of Jahweh" but insisted that it would be a time of "darkness, and not light" (Amos 5:20) which would precede the future redemption.[7] The catastrophe could not be avoided; only a radical devastation would atone for internal corruption. Their message also demanded a new theodicy. Then as now, it was difficult to maintain allegiance to a God who seemed incapable of protecting his chosen people; cults are covenants which bind two sides. Could it be that Israel's God was powerless against the gods of mighty Egypt and Assyria? The prophets introduced a revolutionary, dialectical theodicy, an inversion of the popular belief that the measures of power of a deity are the success and prosperity of the community obliged to that deity by the bonds of *religio*. They insisted, to the contrary, that God's immense, universal powers were manifested by the very plight of the chosen people: only God could employ the mightiest empires as a "rod of wrath" to purge Israel, while these empires were unaware of their role in the divine plan, of their objective role in history (Isaiah 10:5–7).[8] The "remnant of Israel" (Zephaniah 3:13) that survived the day of judgment imposed on all nations would also witness a new and just order of things.

Many of the leading prophetic images reappear in the apocalyptic literature—exaggerated almost to the point of an involuntary caricature, and without the strong realistic sense which permeated the writings of the prophet. At times—though by no means always—the apocalyptic vision of history is rooted within a sectarian counterideology.[9] The Qumran sect, for example, regarded only itself as the "holy community." The establishment, particularly "the wicked priest and his community," constituted the "city of vanity"; other Jews were either part of the adversary or, at best, "fools."[10] And while the prophetic visions of ultimate doom and delivery were addressed to the whole of Israel, including the lost tribes, the Qumran sect seems to have written off most of Israel. They alone are "the remnant," the avant-garde of the new eon in the midst of the old, doomed one. They alone are the true Israel, preparing for, and knowing about, the imminent final war between light and darkness. Their eschatological hopes were confined to their own group, while the rest of Israel would have to share, so it seems, the lot of the other nations.

The period between the last Hasmoneans in the first century B.C. and the revolt against the Romans (A.D. 66–71) was more sectarian than any other period of Jewish history. All over the Hellenistic-Roman world (*oikumene*), old religious, social, and political institutions were disintegrating. The classical political ethics of the Greeks gave way to the individual ethics of the Hellenistic period: the individual, not the city, strove now to attain autarky.[11] Traditional, national, or local cults were replaced by consciously syncretistic cults which centered around newly formed groups striving for individual salvation through true knowledge *(gnosis)*.[12] Even normative Judaism was affected by the spirit of individualization, as the Pharisaic commitment to an individual eschatology shows; Judaism, in a time which lacked a firm central religious-legal authority, was all the more affected. A century later, this lack of consensus at the eve of the revolt was blamed as the chief cause of the catastrophe, so much so that, according to a learned legend, even a small, insignificant incident could lead to the destruction which neither the Roman Emperor nor the Jews wanted: "The Temple was destroyed because divisions multiplied in Israel."[13]

APOCALYPTIC MODES OF PROOF

Before they became widespread and watered down, some apocalyptic visions were a part of sectarian or quasi-sectarian interpretations of history. A peculiar unity of form and content is likewise the distinctive mark of authentic apocalyptic writings, and both are subservient to the actual social role of apocalypses. The apocalyptic visionary employed three modes of proof for his contentions: first, "uncovered" prophecies (apocalypses in the strict sense); second, a new method by which to "decode" old, well-known prophecies *(pesher);* and third, a technique of "interpreting" the course of history itself "typologically." All of these modes have in common the indication of secret knowledge.

The invention of "rediscovered" or "uncovered" prophecies reveals an unspoken assumption which the apocalyptician shared with normative Judaism of his time, namely, that the age of authentic new prophecies had ended sometime in the very beginning of the second Temple period in the sixth century B.C. Then and there prophecy ceased to be an active social, public institution and was relegated to "the deaf, the dumb and the minor" only.[14] For the same reason, normative Judaism refused to add any recent books, no matter how valuable, to the canon of sacred Scripture: ancientness was the prime principle of canonization. At the same time, the legal portion of the Talmud (Halakah) insists on its legitimate disregard of inspiration. The apocalyptician, on the other hand, ascribed his prophetic writings to famous biblical figures. The biblical book of Daniel, perhaps generated in the circle of "the first pious man" in the beginning of the Hasmonean era, came first and became the paradigm for a host of similar prophecies-after-the-event. Daniel supposedly lived during the Babylonian exile and experienced four apocalyptic visions. Later visions were ascribed to even earlier figures, back to Adam and Adam's grandson

Enoch, in part in order to enhance veneration toward the apocalypse, in part to convey the growing sense within the apocalyptic tradition that all of history, from the first entanglement in sin down to the ultimate end of this world, is predestined and follows an immutable course. Sealed and concealed by their illustrious authors, these prophecies were destined to be rediscovered by the right persons at the end of days. The circumstance that most of the events prophesied in an apocalypse, in symbols transparent to contemporaries, were already fulfilled vouched for its authenticity even more. The very fact that an apocalypse was rediscovered proved that the end was close indeed, and that those who found it were what they claimed to be—the small avant-garde of the new world within the old, whose function now was to spread the knowledge about the end:

> And I heard, but I understood not; then said I: "O my lord, what shall be the latter end of these things?" And he said: "Go thy way, Daniel; for the words are shut up and sealed till the time of the end. Many shall purify themselves, and make themselves white, and be refined; but the wicked shall do wickedly; and none of the wicked shall understand; but they that are wise shall understand. . . . But go thy way till the end be; and thou shalt rest, and shalt stand up to thy lot, at the end of the days." (Daniel 12:8–13)

Should we call apocalypses forgeries? Could it be that the authors of pseudepigraphic materials believed that they were merely recreating, by inspiration, an ancient ideal codex? Such questions may be addressed to the books of Daniel or Enoch no less than to the Book of Mormon, the most recent genuinely apocalyptic text.

More subtle than apocalypses proper, was the apocalyptic decoding of already well known canonical prophecies. The technical term employed for their exegetical acrobatics—*pesher*—was once used to indicate the technique of decoding dreams (Genesis 41: 12; Daniel 2: 26) by identifying their symbolic contents. The apocalyptician is convinced that all prophecies of old are latter-day prophecies. The prophet himself may not have understood what he was prophesying; he may have (subjectively) believed he was prophesying the approximate events of his time, whereas in reality he was predicting the events of our days, events close to the end of history. Again, as in the case of apocalypses, the proof of the method is a vicious circle, a proof by self-reference. The fact that the apocalyptician was given a key to unlock the hidden meaning of ancients texts, the fact that God "announced" to the "teacher of righteousness"—the founding father of the sect—"all the secrets of his servants the prophets"[15] proves the proximity of the end and the chosenness of the sect. For only close to the end will "wisdom," that is, knowledge about the end, multiply (Daniel 12: 8–13). The apocalyptical exegesis develops great ingenuity in identifying even the smallest details of present history in ancient prophecies: the

book of Habakkuk, for example, referred to the Roman consuls and sen-
ate. Formally, the actualizing exegesis of apocalypticians may not differ
much from the Midrash of normative Judaism in its methods: but the
latter exposition is conscious of violating the grammatical meaning of the
Scriptures and does so with a grain of salt, at times even with self-
mockery.[16] No trace of humor or relativization will be found in the apocalyptician when he exploits the Scriptures. He is as dead earnest as his
subject.

His subject, his obsession, was the end of the world. He was called by
later adversaries "a calculator of the end." Self-produced prophecies and a
new key to decode old prophecies helped him to ascertain how close the
end was. His understanding of the structure of history, his method of
reading it, his technique of interpreting history typologically served the
same purpose. Nowhere before was historical time, the course of history
as a whole, so strongly perceived as a unity structured by very precise
periods.

The periods, albeit distinct, follow the same pattern; they are the eon
in miniature. The book of Enoch distinguishes clearly three periods of
cosmic weeks: the first two from the creation to the "first end," the
deluge, five others to the present, and three additional weeks to prepare
for the "grand eternal judgment." The Ezra apocalypse has five periods
which repeat the same new beginning followed by the triumph of evil:
from Adam to Noah, Noah to Abraham, Abraham to Moses, Moses to
David, and David to the first destruction. The Baruch apocalypse sees its
twelve periods in an antithetical order: a "bright" stream is always followed by a "dark" one; only the time before the end will witness the
boundless reign of evil.[17] Guided by the analogy between the number of
days of creation of periods of the world, and armed with a realization of
the biblical metaphor "for a thousand years in your eyes are like one day,"
apocalyptic calculations find a scriptural rationale for ancient Iranian-
Babylonian traditions of a "grand year": "six thousand years the world
endures, and is devastated for one thousand"; "six thousand years the
world endures, of which two thousand are chaos, two thousand law, and
two thousand the messianic days." The treatise Sanhedrin of the Babylonian Talmud, which mentions the last two traditions, also lists many
more—probably in order to discard them. The list concludes with the
dictum, "Let the spirit of those who calculate the end expire."[18]

The fascination with historical time and its structure was the most
important contribution of the apocalyptic mentality to the Western sense
of history. The apocalyptician grasped all of history as a structured, well-
articulated, meaningful unity. His detailed account of the future drama of
the end, down to days, hours, and precise actors, was drawn from the

background of his perception of the whole of history as a dramatic struggle between the forces of good and evil.

With these methods, the apocalyptic visionary "proved" his contentions. Visions of an end, as was said above, have also occurred in other cultures at different times. In classical antiquity, however, I know of only two variants which required a proof: the Greek anticipation of the periodic devastation of the world *(apokastasis, ekpyrosis)* and the apocalyptic expectation of the transition of eons. The difference between these two is not that the one views history as cyclical while the other, as has been sometimes contended, endorses a linear view of history—this distinction is a recent scholarly invention. It is very clear that the apocalyptic tradition does not exclude eternal return, at times even alludes to it under the influence, perhaps, of Iranian tradition. Nor indeed does the Bible exclude eternal return—it simply is outside the horizon of biblical imageries. The *uniqueness* of history, or at least of its central event, became thematic only in the Christian horizon. Against Origen's theory of world succession, Saint Augustine (A.D. 354–435) insisted that Christ came only *once* for all times. The difference is rather that while the apocalyptic writer takes his proof from Scripture and history, the Greek philosopher relies on astronomical-cosmological speculations.[19] And, of course, for the Greek scientist as well as for the modern, the cosmic end is not so pressing, so urgent an issue as it was to the apocalyptician, who lived in the tense, daily expectation of the end to come. The life of the apocalyptic community revolved around this expectation.

THE JEWISH TRADITION

"Let the spirit of those who ponder upon the end expire." The rabbinical establishment had good reasons to suspect apocalyptic fantasies even when they ceased to be sectarian. Jewish apocalypticism proper died out somewhere during the second century A.D. A strong religious-legal leadership, formed after the first revolt against Rome (A.D. 66–71) and consolidated after the second (A.D. 132–135), systematically eradicated sectarian subcultures. It placed national unity above all other concerns—even the integrity of the priesthood.[20] It also feared messianic-apocalyptic eruptions. The suspicion was well grounded. Christianity grew out of a messianic-apocalyptic heresy into a formidable adversary. The second, or Bar Kochba, revolt against the Roman Empire was a catastrophe greater than the first revolt: it left Judea depopulated and the Jews barred from Jerusalem.[21] Beyond the danger of promoting uncontrollable messianic eruption, apocalypticism was suspicious on another count. It smacked of mythology, of a mythopoetic mentality. And even though apocalyptic images, traditions, and motifs, taken out of their original context, survived and continued to be embellished, the invention of authentic new apocalypses ceased almost entirely.

Normative Judaism, however, could not rid itself of apocalyptic motifs altogether, because it was, and remained, committed to a utopian ideal, no matter how "realistic" its interpretation. A utopian mentality[22] is an integral component of the Jewish religion: a belief in the ultimate redemption of the nation by a Messiah, the restoration of sovereignty for the rest of the historical time, the return of all Jews from exile, the rebuilding of the Temple at its place, the establishment of peace and justice throughout the world. In view of the ever-present danger of a messianic eruption out of unrestrained apocalyptic fantasies and expectations, the normative attitude toward messianism was a continuous balancing act between affirmation and caution. As a result, no normative interpretation was formulated at all. The rabbinical establishment may have felt instinctively that the best messianic doctrine was no doctrine at all; otherwise, if definite characteristics of the Messiah and his age were given, no matter how restrictive, a generation pregnant with acute messianic hopes would find it all the easier to identify such criteria with the present age and with some present contender. The vaguer the criteria, the less room there was for an actualizing interpretation—such as Christianity, to develop out of the apocalyptic tradition.

Against apocalyptic fantasizing, normative Judaism consolidated the distinction between "the messianic days" and "the world to come" and warned against exaggerated, premature hopes for the former. From the triple repetition of the formula "I beseech you, the daughters of Jerusalem, in the name of the gazelles of the fields, not to hasten nor to precipitate love until it desires," the sages inferred that an oath was laid upon Israel not to precipitate the end nor to rebel against "the nations of the world"; while another oath was laid upon the kingdoms of the world "not to subjugate Israel too much."[23] The "messianic days" entail only the restitution of sovereignty, according to a famous dictum of Mar Shmuel; even poverty will not be abolished, for it is said that "the poor shall never cease out of the land" (Deuteronomy 15:11).[24] Rather than a binding doctrine concerning the last things, the rabbinical sayings amount to the warning not to expect too much and not to expect it too soon. Within the whole Talmud, only one genuine, new apocalypse is mentioned, and even the discovery of this one is ascribed to a Persian soldier.[25]

"When you see empires in conflict, expect the footsteps of the Messiah."[26] The conquest of the land of Palestine by the Persians in A.D. 614, its brief reconquest by Byzantium, and its final conquest by the Muslim Arabs in A.D. 637 incited the renewed production of apocalyptic visions, all the more so since, for a very short while, it seemed as if the Persians were allowing a Jewish administration of Palestine. Some of the disappointment and the expectations are attended to in the book of Zerubbabel, an intermediary between ancient and medieval apocalypticism. To the gallery of dreadful events at the end of days, the book of Zerubbabel adds, both under Christian influence and in an anti-Christian vein, a Jewish version of the Antichrist, the last Roman emperor!

> And as I heard his words I fell on my face and said: reveal me the truth about the leader of the sacred people. And he held on to me and brought me to a church and showed me a statue in the image of a woman whose appearance was very, very beautiful. . . . and he said to me: upon this stone Satan [Beliya'al] will come and lie with [her] and she will bear Armillus. He will rise and reign in terror, the dominion of Satan his father. These are his signs, his hair is green as gold, his hands reach his heels, his face a finger in breadth, his eyes irregular, and he has two skulls; everyone will flee him [but] all the nations of the world will follow him to heresy, except for Israel which will not believe in him. And he will attack the saints in Jerusalem with mighty force.[27]

During the First Crusades (1095–1099), there was a resurgence of apocalypses, at times mixed with astrological-astronomical speculations.[28] On the whole, however, it is astonishing how few genuine apocalypses were produced throughout the Middle Ages, all the more so in view of the fact that apocalyptic images and motifs persisted as an integral part of messianic folklore. In other words, medieval apocalypticism, unlike ancient apocalypticism, ceased by and large to be a science, the systematic secret knowledge it once was. "Calculations of the end" are here and there carried forth—by scholars, at times even with astronomical-astrological reasoning—but it is not in the strict sense apocalyptical. Apocalyptic images, on the other hand, permeate the popular fantasy; they are always ready to nourish acute messianic hopes, but they are not part of a secret system of knowledge.

How much this is so we learn from the latest and widest messianic eruption, the Sabbatai Zvi movement in 1665–66. The famous letter in which Nathan of Gaza, the prophet and the moving force behind the Sabbatean propaganda, first argues for the messiahship of the Jewish mystic, Sabbatai Zvi, has two, almost disconnected, parts.[29] In the first part, the whole battery of Lurianic cabalism is adduced to prove why belief in Sabbatai Zvi and in the fact that the new eon has already begun is the litmus test of Judaism today. The language and symbols are Lurianic, not apocalyptic. In the second part of the letter, a timetable is set for the further deeds of the messiah in the coming years. There is nothing Lurianic here, rather a repetition of apocalyptic images—all of which are expected and need no proof, and none of which is tied to cabalistic symbols.

THE CHRISTIAN TRADITION

The recent realization that the Christian community may have begun as an apocalyptic Jewish sect has thrown Protestant theology into a severe crisis. All reform movements wished a return to the *ecclesia primitiva*, to the original Christian community; this is the leading connotation of *reformatio* even prior to the Reformation in the sixteenth century. But the early Christian community was neither committed to humanistic-ethical ideals as such nor did it wish to make the whole world a better place to live in. It seems to have been a world-withdrawn Jewish sect which expected the end of this world any day. Its earliest written documents attest the possession of certified knowledge about the stages of the end-of-the-world drama and the establishment of the Kingdom of Heaven in the new world to come. Christ's first presence on earth initiated the new eon, the Kingdom of God; his imminent Second Coming would bring its triumph. In the meantime, the community may have lived in urgent expectation, and all that could be done while this world still prevailed was to spread the good message of Christ's life, sacrifice, and Second Coming.[30]

From previous and contemporary Jewish apocalyptic sects, the earliest Christian writings inherited most of its leading motifs, albeit with shifts of emphasis. In contrast to the Dead Sea sect, for instance, Christianity deemphasized priesthood and was from the outset an open community. Their apocalyptic knowledge of the latter-day drama was likewise grounded on a predestinarian, dualistic vision of history as a battleground between good and evil. The Christian community also inherited, perhaps even in a mitigated form, the hatred of some apocalyptic sects toward the "city of vanity," the establishment of priests, scribes, and Pharisees.[31] In Jewish apocalypticism, the Qumran sect regarded the belief in the "teacher of righteousness" as a condition for salvation, for belonging to the community of the elect. Christianity demanded belief in the Messiahship of Christ in spite of his overt failure and ignoble end, a paradoxical belief—"*et ressurexit die tertio, certum est, quia impossible est,*" according to Tertullian. With other apocalyptic sects, early Christianity expected daily the outbreak of the heavenly kingdom.

Christian literature also inherited some of the apocalyptic modes of expression such as "decoding" old prophecies and the periodization of world history; but it did not hurry to produce apocalypses of its own. On the whole, early Christianity was much less fascinated with the written word than other apocalyptic movements. Instead of a written revelation, it possessed a living one: the life of Christ, his acts and teachings. In them, Christianity recognized the "fulfillment" of the open and secret message of the prophets. The events of Christ's life and the events of the community were prefigured by all the cardinal events and figures in Jewish history. He was Moses, David, and a new Adam in one. He came to establish a new priesthood "after the order of Melchizedek."[32] The community awaited daily for the descent of the "heavenly Jerusalem" to replace the corrupt one.

But Christ failed to come again, and a community cannot live for much more than one or two generations in the tense climate of urgent expectation. Sooner or later it had to adjust to life in the interim, to lose some of its apocalyptic sense of utter alienation in this world, even without abandoning the belief in the close end altogether. At the same time it needed a rationale to explain why the end of this world, the Second Coming of Christ, had been postponed. With its spread and mission, Christianity became more world oriented. Indeed, since the end is not in sight, it must have been postponed, because there still is a mission to be fulfilled on earth. The good message has to reach everywhere; everyone must be given the chance to be among the Saved. With the mission and spread of Christianity, with its growing Hellenization, came also the shift away from collective toward individual eschatology and the watering down of apocalyptic motifs. Instead of the revolutionary expectation of a sudden, radical end to this world came the evolutionary conception of a gradual ennoblement, even deification, of human beings; of a gradual advance of humanity within history toward an ultimate (or pristine) perfection. The new version of the sacred history of humankind pertained not only to Jews: Jews and Greeks alike "prepared" the coming of Christ, as did also the political unification of the *oikumene* under one empire.

The Apocalypse of John, the first genuine Christian apocalypse, was written close to the end of the first century A.D., probably to fortify and comfort the community under the persecutions of the Roman Emperor Domitian. To the martyrs and martyrs-to-be, the book of Revelation promises, before the final end of the world, a millennium of "the new Jerusalem" here on earth—a distinction similar to the recent Jewish distinction between "the messianic days" and "the world to come." But it is different from the older apocalyptic tradition in that its author does not hide his identity or his knowledge; nor, which is more important, does he speculate on the date of the end. He only describes its essential phases with as rich and colorful symbols as the apocalyptic tradition he draws from, and he projects the fears and hopes of his generation upon the end: even the millennium will conclude with a general lapse, a temporary triumph of Satan. It may be an exaggeration to call it a nonapocalyptic apocalypse: it has nourished Christian apocalyptic fantasies until today, but it lacks a most essential ingredient of apocalypses—an exact timetable for the end-of-the-world drama.

Normative Judaism, we have seen, neutralized the apocalyptic tradition by refusing to formulate a methodology to discern the signs of the end and of the Messiahs; it relegated the apocalyptic motifs to the level of folklore. Christianity went the opposite way, with similar intents and similar results. It absorbed both the content and the methods of apocalypticism by giving them new meanings. In part it formulated a precise doctrine of the last things and forbade other expectations; in part it allegorized apocalyptic images, as when Origen (A.D. 185?–254?) rails against those who identify the descent of the "heavenly Jerusalem" with the millennium too literally.

To those, however, for whom too much philosophical allegorization seemed just as pernicious for Christian doctrine as apocalypticism itself, Saint Augustine showed how to utilize every single apocalyptic motif or method as building blocks for a deapocalypticized philosophy of history. *The City of God (De civitate Dei)* employs an apocalyptic image in its title: the confrontation of "the earthly city" and the city of God throughout history is the theme of Augustine's *magnum et arduum opus*. The tale of the two cities is a tale of contrast in spite of similarities. The subjects of both cities may adore one and the same God: the earthly so as to use Him, the heavenly so as to be of use to Him. Both of them strive for peace—the one for an earthly peace which is imitable because it can be achieved by power, the other for eternal peace. Membership in the one or the other is in part a matter of will,[33] in part a matter of predestination known to God only. But the inhabitants of God's city while on earth are, in a legal as well as metaphysical sense, resident aliens *(peregrini)* in the earthly state: they neither obstruct it nor do they contribute to it.

Augustine denies categorically the attempts to tie the history of Christianity to the prosperity of the Roman (or any earthly) Empire. The bankruptcy of such "imperial theologies" became evident with the very real chance of an end to the Roman Empire, and Augustine wrote his essay in part so as to make it very clear that the end of the Roman Empire was not, as many Christians thought, the end of the world. The end of the world is unpredictable; the city of God counts its progress "not by years, but by steps."

An old apocalyptic tradition fixed the duration of the world at six thousand years, analogous to the six days of Creation together with the realization of the psalmist's metaphor, "For a thousand years in Thy sight / Are but as yesterday when it is past / And as a watch in the night" (Psalms 90:4).[34] This calculation of the end found its way into both Jewish Midrash and Christian literature. How deliberately Augustine tried to deapocalypticize apocalyptic images can be seen from the way he tampered with this tradition. On the one hand, he elaborates the analogy between the days of Creation and the periods of history far beyond the inherited images: he shows in great detail how the contents of each day of Creation prefigure the events in the corresponding period of history. On the other hand, the very elaboration of the analogy enables him to shift emphasis from the duration of the world (which nobody can calculate) to the structure of history. Under his hand, the analogy became a commonplace for every future Christian philosophy of history.

Analogies such as this one (between the days of Creation and the period of the world) belong to the domain of figurative-symbolic reasoning. Since antiquity, Christian theologians have exposed the structure and meaning of sacred history with the aid of immanent historical symbols called "types" or "figures": events, persons, and institutions of the Old and New Testament are matched to each other; one is seen as the "prefiguration" of the other. Cain and Abel, Leah and Rachel are "prefigurations" of the synagogue and the Church. The Twelve Tribes prefigure the Twelve Apostles; Melchizedek and David prefigure Christ as priest and king. A figure is not merely an image or metaphor; it constitutes a symbolic unity between two separate events or persons within the various periods of history.

The typological mode of reading history was part of apocalyptic knowledge (as distinguished from apocalyptic imagery) since antiquity. The detachment of "apocalyptic science" from "apocalyptic myth" (or imagery) culminated in Augustine's philosophy of history. While apocalyptic images were suppressed, the typological exegesis became a central mode of cognition. In the twelfth century, a new sense of the importance of the immediate presence within God's plan of salvation incited new interest in historical speculations. The men of this century of the War of Investiture, the Second and Third Crusades, and the rediscovery of classical science believed that there is more to present history than merely "the aging of the world" between the First and Second Coming of Christ. Present events seemed to them as pregnant with meaning, worthy of detailed exegesis as biblical history. The new speculative moment culminated in the vision of Joachim of Fiore (c. 1132–1202): to each person of the Trinity he attached one period of history. The period of the Old Testament was the period of the Father, that of the New Testament was the period of the Son, and he predicted the outbreak soon of a new period of "eternal testament" and a nonhierarchical church—the period of the Holy Ghost.[35] This expectation was based not on divination, but on a meticulous study of analogous persons, institutions, events, and sequences of events within each period of history. The structure of the imminent millennium could thus be deduced from the course of history. Some radical Franciscan spirituals after Joachim saw in him and his writing the very eternal Testament which he anticipated: his influence on millennial movements in the later Middle Ages was profound.

The authority of Augustine, the official stand which the Church took against apocalypticism, was not strong enough to suppress altogether the creation of new apocalypses. But these remained scattered and unimaginative, a mere rearrangement of inherited motifs.[36] Yet, while apocalyptic imagery declined, apocalyptic science, employed by the Church itself, became an ever more imaginative tool, and eventually came to serve in its new garb the very same utopian mentality from which it originally embarked. In the speculations of Joachim and the Joachimites I see the only creative, genuine apocalypticism in the Middle Ages—in spite of the fact that no single "apocalypse" emerged from their circles. Apocalyptic hopes and motifs continued after them; apocalypses continued to be written; the Apocalypse of John and other apocalypses continued to be applied to present events. But never again, not even during the Reformation, did the apocalyptic mentality rise to become a creative force, either socially or intellectually. The utopian mind found other forms of expression, bound to new cultural configurations.

A full history of Jewish and Christian end-of-the-world visions is outside the scope of this chapter. Yet we can argue one main point, that even if apocalyptic motifs, images, methods, and texts persisted, their career in Judaism and Christianity was that of elements taken out of an original context. Apocalypticism in the full sense of the word, a balance of myth, method, and way of life existed only for about 200 years, and formed a unique mentality. The reader ought to be warned that this is not a commonly accepted view; the terms *apocalypse* and *apocalyptic* are loyally and lavishly employed in current studies. It has been argued that secular utopian movements, even Marxism, are legitimate heirs of apocalypticism. I disagree, although lack of familiarity with Muslim apocalypticism and Iranian sources, as well as lack of space, prevents me from giving a detailed proof of my thesis. I do not mean to deny the enormous impact and influence of the apocalypticism of Judaism and Christianity. On the contrary: because apocalypticism was so captivating, it has remained a constant theme. Yet the history of its reception has been the history of its constant dilution. Apocalypticians were the first who were believed to possess a unique key for unlocking "the secrets of the times." Other keys have since been found and discarded, but we need not identify all of them with apocalypticism just because they retained general similarities, or simply because apocalypticism came first, or even because they assume some demands from the apocalyptic tradition. Our fears and dreams of the end of the world are different in color, method, and, alas, in their chance for realization, from those of other times. To quote the German poet Rainer Maria Rilke:

> O Herr, gib jedem seinen eigenen Tod.
> Das Sterben, das aus jenem Leben geht,
> darin er Liebe hatte, Sinn und Nott.
>
> (Lord, to everyone his own death grant,
> The act of dying, which departs that life
> Wherein he once had meaning, love and hardship.)

NOTES

1. 4 Ezra 4:26, 27, in B. Violet, ed., *Die Esra-Apokalypse,* vol. 1, *Die Überlieferung* (Leipzig, 1910), p. 36; vol. 2, *Die kritische Ausgabe* (Leipzig, 1927), p. 17. For references hereinafter to 4 Ezra or the Ezra Apocalypse, see Violet, *Die Esra-Apokalypse;* or G. H. Box, "4 Ezra," in R. H. Charles, ed., *The Apocrypha and Pseudepigrapha of the Old Testament,* 2 vols. (1913; Oxford: Oxford University Press, 1963), vol. 2, pp. 542–624. On apocalyptic "pessimism," see Rudolf Bultmann, *Das Urchrislentum im Rahmen der antiken Religionen,* 2nd ed. (Zurich, 1954), p. 79; and W. Bousset, *Die Religion des Judentums im späthellenistischer Zeitalter,* ed. H. Gressmann, 3rd ed. rev. (Tübingen, 1926), p. 243 ff.

2. Matthew 24:3–51; 2 Peter 3:10; 4 Ezra 4:34 ff.; see Amos Funkenstein, *Heilsplan und natürliche Entwicklung* (Munich, 1965), pp. 11–15.

3. Ethiopian Enoch 81:2, 93:2, Jubilees 1:29; Funkenstein, *Heilsplan und natürliche Entwicklung,* p. 173n. For references hereinafter to the Ethiopian Enoch or the Ethiopic version of the Book of Enoch, see Charles, *The Apocrypha and Pseudepigrapha of the Old Testament,* vol. 2, p. 163 ff.; for the Book of Jubilees or the Ethiopic version of the Hebrew Book of Jubilees, see Charles, *The Apocrypha and Pseudepigrapha of the Old Testament,* vol. 1, pp. 1–82.

4. See Aage Bentzen, *Handbuch zum Alten Testament,* ed. Otto Eissfeldt, 2nd ed. (Tübingen, 1952), p. 33. For exceptions to this passive ideology, see Funkenstein, *Heilsplan und natürliche Entwicklung,* p. 124n.; and, on the Hasmoneans, J. Efron, *Studies of the Hasmonean Period* (Tel Aviv, 1960), pp. 30–34, 41–125.

5. Mircea Eliade, "Cosmic and Eschatological Renewal," in his *The Two and the One,* trans. J. M. Cohen (Chicago: University of Chicago Press, 1962), pp. 125–59, and *Cosmos and History: The Myth of the Eternal Return* (New York: Harper & Row, 1959).

6. Isaiah 11:15–16. See S. A. Loewenstamm, *Masoret yetsiat mitsrayim behishtalsheluta,* 2nd ed. (Jerusalem, 1952), pp. 16, 103. On other typologies of reenactment in the Bible, see Amos Funkenstein, "Nachmanides's Typological Reading of History," *Zion* 45:1 (1980), 37.

7. See Gerhard von Rad, *The Message of the Prophets*, trans. D. M. Stalker (New York: Harper & Row, 1972), pp. 95–99.

8. See Amos Funkenstein, "Maimonides: Political Theory and Realistic Messianism," *Miscellanea Medievalia* 11 (1977), 90–93; 93n.

9. Peter L. Berger and Thomas Luckmann, *The Social Construction of Reality* (Garden City, N.Y.: Doubleday & Co., 1966), pp. 116–17.

10. See J. Light, "Mata'at olam ve'eam pedut el," *Mechkarim bemagilot hagnuzot, Sefer Zikaron le A. L. Sukenik* (Jerusalem, 1951), pp. 49–75; and David Flusser, *Judaism and the Origins of Christianity* (Tel Aviv, 1979), pp. 324–32, 335–37.

11. W. W. Tarn, *Hellenistic Civilisation* (1930; New York: New American Library, 1961), 327 ff.

12. Gilbert Murray, *Five Stages of Greek Religion* (1925; Garden City, N.Y.: Doubleday & Co., 1955), pp. 119 ff, esp. 154 ff.; Hans Jonas, *Gnostic Religion*, 2nd ed. (Boston: Beacon Press, 1963).

13. Babylonian Talmud, Gittin. 55b–56a.

14. See A. A. Urbach, "When Did Prophecy Cease?," *Tarbits* 17 (1947), 1–11, and *The Sages*, 2nd ed. (Jerusalem, 1978), pp. 502–13.

15. See Matthew 13:35 (as in Proverbs 2:6–8).

16. Babylonian Talmud, Sanhedrin: "*hincha shochev im avotecha vekam.*" Vedilma: "*vekam ha'am haze vezana?*"

17. Ethiopian Enoch 93:3–10, 91:12–17; Bousset, *Die Religion des Judentums*, p. 281; D. Rössler, *Geseh und Geschichte* (Neukirchen, 1960), p. 57. Also see 4 Ezra 3:45; and Funkenstein, *Heilsplan und natürliche Entwicklung*, p. 128n. See as well *Syriac Baruch* 69 (cf. 4 Ezra 14:11). The underlying image may be that of the Zodiac. For references hereinafter to Syriac Baruch, see "2 Baruch or the Syriac Apocalypse of Baruch," in Charles, *The Apocrypha and Pseudepigrapha of the Old Testament*, vol. 2, pp. 470–526.

18. Babylonian Talmud, Sanhedrin 97a, Avoda Zara 9a. On similar Christian traditions *(ante legem, sub lege, sub gratia)*, see Funkenstein, *Heilsplan und natürliche Entwicklung*, p. 129nn. See also my "Changing Patterns in Christian-Jewish Polemics in the 12th Century," *Zion* 33 (1968), 170.

19. See, for example, Eliade, *Cosmos and History*, pp. 112–37; also M. Pohlenz, *Die Stoa*, 2 vols. (Göttingen, 1959), vol. 1, p. 79 ff., and vol. 2, p. 47 ff.

20. Mishna, Yadayim 4:3.

21. M. Avi Jona, *Biyme Roma u'Bizantion* (Jerusalem, 1946), pp. 1–4.

22. Karl Mannheim, *Ideology and Utopia*, trans. Louis Wirth and Edward Shils (1929; New York: Harcourt Brace, 1955).

23. Babylonian Talmud, Ketubot 3a; cant. Rabba 2.

24. Babylonian Talmud, Berakhot 34.

25. Babylonian Talmud, Sanhedrin 97a.

26. Genesis Rabba 42.

27. Jehuda Eben-Shmuel, *Midreshe Geula* (Jerusalem, 1952), p. 79. On the Christian attributes of this Jewish Antichrist, combined with attributes of Christ himself as some Jewish traditions saw him, e.g., "The Book of History of Jesus" in

"*Das leben Jesu nach judischen Quellen*," ed. S. Krauss (Vienna, 1902). It seems likely that the Apocalypse was written in Byzantium; Byzantium was also the place where rabbinical authofity was weakest.

28. J. Baer, "Ein Judische Messias-Apocalypse aus dem Jahre 1186," *Monatshefte zur Geschichte und Wissenschaft des Judentums (MGWJ)* 70 (1926), 113 ff.

29. Jacob Sassportas, *Sefer Tsitsat Novel Tsvi*, ed. J. Tishbi (Jerusalem, 1956); included in Gershom Scholem, *Sabbatai Sevi*, trans. R. Zwi Werblowski (Princeton, N.J.: Princeton University Press, 1973). pp. 270–75

30. On the balance between apocalyptic expectations and life in the present with its obligation, and on the danger of overexaggerating the one against the other moment, see Flusser, *Judaism and the Origins of Christianity.*

31. Amos Funkenstein, "Anti Jewish Propaganda: Ancient, Medieval and Modern," *Jerusalem Quarterly* 19 (1981), 60–61.

32. Funkenstein, "Nachmanides's Typological Reading of History," pp. 35–39.

33. Funkenstein, *Heilsplan und natürliche Entwicklung*, pp. 45–46.

34. Ibid., p. 27.

35. See Herbert Grundmann, *Studien über Joachim von Floris* (Leipzig, 1927).

36. On various apocalypses, see Norman Cohn, *The Pursuit of the Millennium* (London: Secker & Warburg, 1957).

4

THEMES OF DECLINE AND END IN NINETEENTH-CENTURY WESTERN IMAGINATION

Saul Friedländer

translated from the French by
Susan Rubin Suleiman

IT WAS IN THE NINETEENTH CENTURY, IN THE WEST, THAT
the vision of the total end of man appeared for the first time in a
systematic and repeated fashion. A note of growing pessimism accompanies the theme of progress from the very beginning of the century; it
becomes louder as the century draws to its close. In that context, the
notion of a complete disappearance of humanity takes form.

The pages that follow, after dwelling very briefly on the general background of pessimism, will approach the theme of total end on two different levels: that of explicit theories or literary constructs and that of symbols and myths of destruction. The whole chapter will attempt to answer
the question: Is there a fundamental theme that seems to underlie, to
characterize, and perhaps to explain the visions of total destruction which
appear during that period?

As the nineteenth century begins, we already hear a strong note of gloom:
it is the voice of the ideological enemies of the Revolution proclaiming
their visions of catastrophe; it is the disenchanted voice of the Romantics,
seduced and then disappointed by the Revolution; it is the fearful voice of
all those who felt themselves threatened by the new spirit which spread
throughout Europe during the first decades of the century. Already then,
civilization itself was seen in deadly peril: thus, a Bavarian scientist,

62   SAUL FRIEDLÄNDER

A. H. F. Schlichtegroll, proposed using Iceland as a sanctuary for all the achievements of a civilization that was about to disappear (a kind of Shangri-la before its time), and F. G. Wetzel, a friend of the German poet E. T. A. Hoffmann, wrote in his *Magischer Spiel* as early as 1806: "The light will be taken from Europe, when Europe will be full of demolished sites, when goblins will meet each other on her deserts, and the paradise will have vanished in the great flood and the rage of fire."[1]

As the historian of Romanticism, H. G. Schenk, has noted,

> It is true that prophets of doom have existed at all times, and especially during the closing stages of the Middle Ages. Yet it would seem that the spirit of foreboding had never been so widespread. Surely it is remarkable that the feeling of an approaching deluge was shared by Romantic thinkers rooted in such diverse backgrounds as the Germans F. Schlegel and Lasaulx, the Frenchmen Chateaubriand, Lamennais and Baudelaire, the half-Scot Byron, the Irishman Mangan, the Pole Krasiński, the Italian Leopardi, the Spaniard Larra, the Portuguese Garret and the Swiss Bachofen.[2]

In Germany, the cosmic pessimism of a Schopenhauer belonged to the early part of the century, but it was with the foundation of the new Reich that "cultural pessimism," to use Fritz Stern's term,[3] became more and more widespread. For some, Bismarck's Reich was none other than the expression of the most sordid materialism, the triumph of the bourgeois philistine, the death of traditional Germany, the end of the dream of an ideal Reich, a monstrous reality. If Nietzsche's thought can be mentioned only incidentally on this level, that is not the case with the biblical scholar and polemicist Paul de Lagarde or his disciple Julius Langbehn, who fully express this state of mind, as do the Romantic historians Carl W. Volgraff and Ernst von Lasaulx with their apocalyptic tones. But it was Jacob Burckhardt, the historian from Basel, who more than any other expressed the profound sense of despair provoked by the rise of what appeared to be an era of abjection; according to Burckhardt, European culture was about to go under, was about to enter a long night, the reign of Satan the Barbarian.[4]

The Austro-Hungarian Empire at the end of the century became, as one hardly need point out, the very symbol of disintegration and decadence. Soon, the "Cacania" so pitilessly analyzed by Robert Musil would go under forever; it was there that, during World War I, Karl Kraus would write *The Last Days of Mankind;* it was there that, in the first years of our century, Alfred Kubin, author of *The Other Side*, would evoke the gradual decline and then the monstrous fall of an imaginary country that could be none other than the child of our nightmares and the symbol of our society; it was there that, in 1905, Hugo von Hoffmannsthal wrote: "We must take leave of a world before it collapses. . . . Many know it already, and an undefinable [*unnenbares*] feeling makes poets out of many."[5]

In France, where the defeat in the Franco-Prussian War added national humiliation and political crisis to the general process which, as elsewhere, provoked the despair of those who rejected the notion of inevitable progress, the growing pessimism of the century's last three decades took that particular form known as the *fin de siècle* spirit—a spirit that would influence more or less strongly all the rest of Europe.[6] The key word was *decadence;* some feared it, others rejoiced in it, but all agreed that it was there. Historical analogies came readily to mind: the last days of Rome, and even more of Byzantium; the end of a civilization marked by anonymous corruption, devoid of all grandeur.

As Mario Praz has noted, "The oft-repeated lament over the downfall of Latin civilizations, the 'Ohé!!! Ohé!!! les races latines!' of Péladan, the conviction of d'Aurevilly that the race has arrived 'à sa dernière heure,' Verlaine's 'Je suis l'Empire à la fin de la décadence'—such things show not so much the terror as the attraction of disaster: the very ideas of Decadence, of imminent Divine punishment like the fire of Sodom, of the 'cupio dissolvi,' are perhaps no more than the extreme sadistic refinements of a *milieu* which was saturated to excess with complications of perversion."[7]

Des Esseintes, the hero of J. K. Huysmans's novel *A rebours* (Against the Grain) espouses the most extreme decadentism before calling down the fires of heaven on the civilization around him. Only what is artificial, languishing, and morbid attracts him; the dying embers of the Roman Empire at its end are the only source of authentic beauty. Des Esseintes execrates the rising bourgeoisie, as does the Duke Charles d'Este in Elémir Bourges's *Le Crépuscule des dieux* (The Twilight of the Gods). In the last scene of that novel, the Duke is in the opera house at Bayreuth for the conclusion of Wagner's *Ring* cycle: on one side, he sees the Jews greeted by the emperor, on the other side the American millionaires: "Yes! The fatal time was approaching. All the signs of destruction were visible over the old world, like the angels of wrath above a condemned Gomorrah."[8]

Is there anything more exemplarily optimistic, on the surface, than the bourgeois society of Victorian England? But in fact, there too there was a constant and powerfully expressed sense of anxiety. Fear of social revolution, boredom and doubt, despair in the face of a henceforth empty sky: "It is an awful hour," wrote clergyman Frederick Robertson in the 1860s, "when this life has lost its meaning, and seems shrivelled into a span; when the grave appears to be the end of all, human goodness nothing but a name, and the sky above this universe a dead expanse, black with the void from which God himself has disappeared."[9] Matthew Arnold's

"Dover Beach," to mention only one famous work among many, expressed the same despair.

This decadent sensibility became exacerbated in England during the last two decades of the century, and especially during the "Yellow Nineties."[10] John Ruskin had just announced the probable disappearance of his country as a major power; Gerard Manley Hopkins endowed the social crisis with an apocalyptic dimension:

> This, by Despair, bred Hangdog dull; by Rage,
> Manwolf, worse; and their packs infest the age.[11]

As for author and naturalist Richard Jefferies, in *After London* he predicted a return to total barbarism and bestiality, a time when London, covered over by a pestilential swamp, would have disappeared without a trace.

This feeling of uncertainy, anxiety, and decline, this all-pervasive sense of unease, was expressed most intensely by Nietzsche in one of his fragments on the "History of European Nihilism": "Disintegration—that is to say uncertainty—is peculiar to this age: nothing stands on solid ground or a sound faith. People live for the morrow, because the day-after-tomorrow is doubtful. All our road is slippery and dangerous, while the ice which still bears us has grown unconsciously thin: we all feel the mild and gruesome breath of the thaw-wind—soon, where we are walking, no one will any longer be able to stand."[12]

What all this would lead to was envisioned in different ways, however. While some could foresee nothing but disaster and an inevitable slow decline, Nietzsche called for the coming of the Superman. Others, like J. K. Huysmans and Léon Bloy, looked for the first signs of an apocalyptic redemption through Christ.[13] Still others, like Richard Jefferies and William Morris, hoped for salvation through the new blood, the blood of the barbarians, a hope that was also expressed by the American historian Brooks Adams in *The Law of Civilization and Decay.* The possibility of salvation through science—and this brings us into the twentieth century—was expressed in H. G. Wells's *Tono-Bungay.* And finally, Zola's *Les Rougon-Macquart,* that immense fresco chronicling a long decline, ends in the vision of a quasi-mythical renewal; the fire that consumes Paris in the closing pages of *La Débâcle* is the fire of purification and rebirth: "Beyond the still screaming furnace, living hope was being reborn in the depths of the great calm sky, infused with a sovereign limpidity. It was the certain rejuvenation of eternal humanity, the renewal promised to him who works and hopes, the tree which sends forth a new and powerful bole after the rotten bole whose poisoned sap was turning the leaves yellow has been cut."[14]

It is against this background, where visions of the end were nonetheless mitigated by hope, that there developed at the same time a wholly new vision: that of the total end of man.

At the beginning of the nineteenth century, to be sure, this vision re- mained tentative. Some early literary works of the century evoke the total end, but always beneath the gaze—neutral, perhaps, but nevertheless present—of the Almighty. This is what we find in Edgar Allan Poe and in Mary Wollstonecraft Shelley, in the "conversation between Eiros and Charmion" as well as in *The Last Man.* This sibylline tale by the author of *Frankenstein* ends with the lines: "Thus around the shores of deserted earth, while the sun is high, and the moon waxes or wanes, angels, the spirits of the dead, and the ever-open eye of the Supreme, will behold the tiny bark, freighted with Verney—the LAST MAN."[15]

It was around the 1850s and 1860s that a noticeable change appeared. With the crumbling of faith in a divine Providence, the Judeo-Christian teleological conception of the end of history also came under question. The theory of natural selection, although it was often identified with the notion of infinite progress, nevertheless saw the destiny of man as the result of chance—whence the possibility that evolution could just as well lead to degeneration as to the increasing perfection of human beings. Furthermore, a vision of future degeneration, decrepitude, and death was consonant with the new physical theories concerning the future of the universe. Thermodynamics put an end to the metaphor of the Divine Clockwork and the Divine Clockmaker. Generally speaking, no sooner had the new positivism lost its first optimistic cast than the way was opened for the scientific possibility of the irremediable extinction of man. And when, in the last two decades of the century, the faith in progress became seriously shaken, when the *fin de siècle* spirit began to envisage the end of a civilization, when the triumphant bourgeoisie perceived the first cracks in the "Crystal Palace," then the scientific theories of the end of man took on a powerful resonance. It was at this time too that there first appeared, in a very attenuated form to be sure, a new element in the prognostics of catastrophe: the destruction of man by science and technology.

If we assess the speculations about the biological future of man that characterized the second half of the century, we find the predominance of two totally pessimistic views: on the one hand, the racial theory of Arthur Comte de Gobineau, which would reappear in various guises in the dec- ades to come; and on the other, the interpretation of Darwin's theories by some of his disciples. Darwin himself remained, on the whole, optimistic about the future of the species. Occasionally, however, he too was shaken by doubt: since the ethical norms of modern society protected the weak and those who could not adapt, did they not threaten to interfere with the process of natural selection and provoke the progressive degeneration of man? "Excepting in the case of man himself, hardly any one is so ignorant as to allow his worst animals to breed."[16] He then goes on to express the hope—but without believing in it too much—that the unadapted will perhaps abstain from reproducing themselves.

For Darwin to postulate the existence of humanity on the restoration of the natural laws of the war of all against all, or else on systematic euthanasia, can be called a temporary weakness of a great mind. As for the French diplomat and man of letters Gobineau, he considered all hope lost. The mixing of races, which was the source of degeneration and death, was too far gone to make any halt in the process of degradation possible; the end was certain, "the last sigh of our species" foreseeable. But the shape of things to come was more depressing still: "What is most saddening about the future is not death; it is the certainty of reaching it in a degraded state; and perhaps even that shame reserved for our descendants might leave us unmoved, were it not for the fact that we feel, in secret horror, that the hands of destiny are already on us."[17]

Are these the marginal considerations of a morose aristocrat threatened by the rise of democracy and the masses? This kind of sociological explanation is inadequate: the biological theories of the nineteenth century, whether those of Gobineau or Darwin, led by a logic of their own to perspectives of catastrophe as well as of progress. To come back to Darwin's circle, Francis Galton, the founder of eugenics, voiced his fear well before Toynbee that man might not be capable of meeting the "challenge" of his environment, and even more of civilization itself. After noting the disappearance of various "savage" races who succumbed to the "pressure of the requirements of an incoming civilisation," Galton adds:

> And we too, the foremost labourers in creating this civilisation, are beginning to show ourselves incapable of keeping pace with our own work. The needs of centralisation, communication, and culture, call for more brains and mental stamina than the average of our race possess. . . . Our race is over-weighted, and appears likely to be drudged into degeneracy by demands that exceed its powers. . . . When the severity of the struggle for existence is not too great for the powers of the race, its action is healthy and conservative, otherwise it is deadly.[18]

For Galton, a single hope remains: eugenics. According to Gobineau, thus, it is the mixing of races that leads to inevitable catastrophe; in Darwin, it is ethical principles which, by interfering with the principle of natural selection, are the source of mortal danger; and as Galton sees it, the evolution of the higher races risks ending in catastrophe because of the widening gap between the increasing complexity of civilization and human potential itself. Finally, according to T. H. Huxley, one of the most

illustrious scientists of the Victorian era and Darwin's most highly respected disciple, there can be no question of ascending evolution except
in a very limited period of time; after that, decline must inevitably set in:
"If, for millions of years, our globe has taken the upward road, yet, some
time, the summit will be reached and the downward route will be com-
menced. The most daring imagination will hardly venture upon the suggestion that the power and the intelligence of man can ever arrest the
procession of the Great Year."[19] There was, according to Huxley, but one
weak hope: as long as men survived, they might perhaps succeed in
attenuating the ineluctable degeneration of the species thanks to the
"ethical principle," which was what made them specifically human.

These theories expounding on the possibility of a total biological degeneration of man found a fertile terrain in the second half of the
nineteenth century, which, as we have already seen, was a period when
theories of decadence and partial degeneration also flourished. If one
looks among historians for further evidence, one finds the famous seventh
chapter of Burckhardt's *The Age of Constantine the Great,* the theories of
Otto Seeck on the end of the Roman Empire, and Hippolyte Taine's
theory of the destruction of elites by the basest elements in society. In the
social sciences, Théodule Ribot and Gustave Le Bon are but the best-
known authors among a whole phalanx of prognosticators of degeneration
(described exhaustively by Max Nordau in his famous work on this subject[20]).

In fact, a parallel series of visions of the future was developed on the
basis of these invariables regarding possible biological degeneration. According to some authors, it was only through an attachment to social
traditions and through the preservation of hereditary elites that one could
hope to contain the explosion of the animal instincts of the masses, an
explosion which would lead only to absolute chaos. According to other
authors, the future depended on the result of a battle between the races:
the race that was defending culture and creativity and the race (or races)
that could only destroy culture and creativity.

As a representative of the first of these two sets of visions of the future,
we may cite Taine. If the traditional elites lost their place, "man, deprived
of the precious legacy transmitted to him by the wisdom of ages, would at
once fall back into a savage condition and again become what he was at
first, namely a restive, famished, wandering, hunted brute."[21] For Taine,
the French Revolution proved the correctness of his analysis; the civiliz-
ing constraints accumulated over the centuries were broken, and the
brute reappeared: "Nothing remains but the primitive animal, the fero-
cious, lewd gorilla supposed to be tamed, but which still subsists
indefinitely."[22] Could we not suggest that Freud's thought acquired some
of its foundations and drew some of its metaphors—both on the level of

explanations concerning individual psychology and on that of enlarged projections concerning society, as in *Civilization and Its Discontents*— from the cultural pessimism of such conservative thinkers at the end of the last century?

As for the second set, the various theories of the struggle between the races, these led to more recent versions that we are only too familiar with. They are apocalyptic theories, since the victory of the Aryans is not certain, whether in the French anthropologist and sociologist Georges Vacher de Lapouge, the Anglo-German writer (and son-in-law of Wagner) Huston Stewart Chamberlain, or, obviously, the Nazis. There is no need for us to linger here over well-known themes; let it suffice to point out that the biological pessimism we have been discussing would become, in a short time, the essential ideological terrain of National Socialism. But let us return now to the more general themes of total biological degeneration.

One of the writers who doubtless contributed the most to popularizing these themes was H. G. Wells, especially in *The Time Machine* and in *The Island of Dr. Moreau*. In *The Time Machine*, Wells describes the forms of human degeneration in a distant future, to be followed, millions of years later, by the end of all life: the future degeneration will be provoked, as Darwin foresaw, by a too cultivated, too perfect, too harmonious society, in which the absence of effort and struggle, the absence of a brutal selection, will bring about the weakening and degeneration of the elites—of the Eloi, who, like children, laugh and play in the light of day. Beneath the earth live the Morlocks, descendents of the proletariat of our time; they are needy, blind, and obscene, but they have been made stronger and more brutal than the Eloi by the back-breaking work in their underground industries. To feed themselves, these inhabitants of the depths surface at night, kidnap some Eloi, and devour them.

The Island of Dr. Moreau, the most terrifying of Wells's allegories, describes man's attempt to overcome his animal nature (in the novel, Moreau tries to transform animals into people, but after a short period as pseudohumans they fall back into their bestiality) and his inexorable relapse:

> And they walked erect with an increasing difficulty. Though they evidently felt ashamed of themselves, every now and then I would come upon one or other running on toes and finger-tips, and quite unable to recover the vertical attitude. . . . I realised more keenly than ever what Moreau had told me about the "stubborn beast flesh." They were reverting, and reverting very rapidly.[23]

On the demonic island, everything perishes forever, or else returns to animality; but the narrator, who barely escapes alive, cannot help noticing that the people in the streets of London bear the same cast and are thus condemned to the same inevitable road to bestiality. Huxley's ethical principle is but an illusion.

These theories of biological degeneration often went hand in hand with visions of geological catastrophe or the slow death of the universe. In Jules Verne, for example, biological degeneration and geological catastrophe might be simultaneous. Already in his earliest works, Verne was haunted by the theme of the mythical Atlantis. Was it an evocation of the past? a presage of the future? "Whilst I was dreaming thus," recounts the passenger of the *Nautilus*, evoking the sudden discovery of the lost civilization in the depths of the sea, "whilst I was trying to fix in my mind every detail of this grand landscape, Captain Nemo remained motionless, as if petrified in mute ecstasy, leaning on a mossy stone. Was he dreaming of those generations long since disappeared? Was he asking them the secret of human destiny?"[24] In the story "L'éternel Adam" (The Eternal Adam), his posthumous message, Verne sought to attenuate the image he had painted of man's ineluctable degeneration after a series of geological catastrophes, but the only consolation he offered was the notion of the eternal return.

Even more than the notion of a past or future catastrophe, however, it was the new theories about the thermal death of the universe that captured many people's imagination. The physicist Sadi Carnot had led the way in 1824, with his *Réflexions sur la puissance motrice du feu* (Reflections on the Motive Power of Fire); he was followed by the physicists R. J. E. Clausius, Ludwig Boltzmann, and William Thomson (later Lord Kelvin), who formulated his famous second law of thermodynamics: a vision of the inevitable disappearance of all life through the accelerating diffusion of energy until the level of absolute zero temperature was reached throughout the universe, leading to "the thermal death of the universe."

This theory had a powerful impact. Darwin referred to it, as did Conrad and Tennyson. It was bound to provoke melancholy, as in Tennyson's verses on the moon in "Locksley Hall":

> Dead, the new astronomy calls her, . . .
>
> Dead, but how her living glory lights the hall,
>   the dune, the grass!
> Yet the moonlight is the sunlight, and the sun
>   himself will pass.[25]

Did the thermal death of the universe imply an absolute end, with no possibility of a fresh start? According to the French astronomer Camille Flammarion, our humanity and our universe are destined to perish, but "others will succeed them. . . . And always there exist in space worlds and stars, souls and suns; and always eternity endures. For there can be neither end nor beginning."[26] For Wells, on the other hand, at the end of his journey through time, there is no such hope: Thirty million years from our own time, there is nothing but icy silence and desolation, and the last living creature dragging its tentacles through a landscape of death.[27]

The notion of the thermal death of the universe, unacceptable to traditional religion, was equally unacceptable to the religion of progress. It is interesting to see how certain positive minds tried to get around the discoveries of physics. Friedrich Engels, for example, could not but admit the probable disappearance of our solar system and other star systems as well:

> Instead of the bright, warm solar system with its harmonious arrangement of members, only a cold, dead sphere will still pursue its lonely path through universal space. And what will happen to our solar system will happen sooner or later to all the other systems of our island universe; it will happen to all the other innumerable island universes, even to those the light of which will never reach the earth while there is a living human eye to receive it.

But—and here is where the mystical faith appears—Engels was convinced that the laws of matter and movement would sooner or later produce the necessary conditions for the creation of new worlds, "even if only after millions and millions of years and more or less by chance, but with the necessity that is also inherent in chance."[28]

If the notion of the thermal death of the universe captured so many imaginations in the latter half of the nineteenth century, it was due to both the inevitability and the strangeness of this vision of the total end. But this was merely one kind of uncontrollable natural catastrophe envisaged in this period. Flammarion himself, in *La Fin du monde*, began by describing the near-annihilation of the earth by a comet.[29] In 1873 the Swiss scientist Alphonse de Candolle, after evoking the possibility of a new Ice Age and the catastrophic consequences of "the diminution of land surfaces and [of] the sinking of elevated regions through the unceasing interaction of water, ice and air," envisaged a strangely modern hypothesis: that of decline through the inexorable depletion of sources of energy. To be sure, the process would not necessarily lead to the end of man; but it would certainly lead to the inevitable collapse of civilizations:

> The oxygen in the air and the unceasing action of human labor have as a result the decrease in the quantity of metals and coal readily available on the surface of the earth. Some scientists of genius will no doubt discover procedures for mining at greater depths, and for exploiting the metallic oxides scattered in the soil. New combustible substances will also be found;

however, they will never be as efficient as those natural substances that we benefit from today, and the scattered metallic dusts will always be harder to reach than the primitive deposits we have now. . . .

There will necessarily be a decrease in the population when the old resources become rare, especially when they become almost inaccessible and eventually run out altogether. The most civilized peoples will then be the most unhappy. They will have neither trains, nor steamboats, nor anything based on coal or metals. Their industries will be considerably reduced when copper and iron are rare. Certain societies, being both sedentary and agricultural, living in warm climates and contenting themselves with little, will then be the best adapted to the general circumstances of the globe. It will thus be around the tropics, and near the large deposits of coal in the United States and in China, that large population groups will remain together the longest. However, the scarcity of metals will be a cause of decadence even in those privileged localities.[30]

Thus, during the second half of the century, the vision of a total end resulting from natural processes, be they biological, geological, or cosmic, haunted men's minds. It was at the turn of the century, however, that a new vision of catastrophe appeared, one which, from its timid beginnings, has come to haunt the imagination of our own time: catastrophe through science and technology, the destruction of man by man.

It has become almost a commonplace to discover, in rereading Jules Verne, the latent and then the explicit pessimism that lurks behind the apparently enthusiastic espousal of science by the author of the *Extraordinary Voyages*. Verne's doubts about science are expressed only very indirectly in his early works; yet even there, in every novel the machine ends up being destroyed or disappearing mysteriously.[31] The most extraordinary technical and scientific discoveries are often reported with a reticence and a reserve that may be there for surprising effect, but that are there nevertheless. What could be more exciting, for example, than the "National Society for Interstellar Communications" founded in the United States after the return of the heroes of the first voyage around the moon? The author, however, ends his narrative with these words: "And as it is part of the American temperament to foresee everything in business, even failure, the Honorable Harry Trollope, and Francis Drayton, magistrate, were nominated, beforehand, assignees in bankruptcy!"[32]

It is in his last works, published posthumously, that Verne's pessimism about the future of science is given full expression. *L'Étonnante Aventure de la mission Barsac* (The Barsac Mission), for example, is none other than the story of man's destruction by uncontrolled technology. If anyone survives, it is only because the novel needs a narrator. As Michel Serres has remarked, "This is the novel of the nuclear age, set in an insular city in the center of Africa."[33] The city founded by Killer and Camaret is totally destroyed; it signifies the end of man through the combined effect of science and political power gone mad. In a different form, this is the same message one finds in H. G. Wells's *The War of the Worlds*. The fact that the invasion comes from Mars is irrelevant; the arms imagined here can, if technology goes beyond certain limits, destroy all of humanity.[34]

In both these works, the end of man is envisaged as the direct result of the use of an unleashed technology by human beings who have lost the sense of responsibility or the use of reason. Other variations are possible. In *L'Île à hélice* (Propeller Island), for example, Verne suggests that the final destruction will be the result of a number of very different converging factors. One is an unleashed, but in the last instance unreliable, technology: "Yes! And now the population no longer has confidence in this artificial ground. . . . To fear at every instant that Standard Island will open up and be engulfed in those abysses of the Pacific that no lead has yet succeeded in plumbing—there's a thought that even the stoutest hearts cannot envisage without flinching." Another is the irresponsibility of men—and specifically of leaders—who, through the misuse of this technology, will lead their people to the edge of the abyss. Finally, the omnipotence of natural forces which appear to be subjugated by technology but which suddenly take their terrible revenge. Thus, Propeller Island, that marvel of the most advanced technology, after being partially destroyed by human madness, is totally destroyed by the cyclone: "And now, of that marvelous Standard Island there remain only scattered pieces, similar to the sporadic fragments of a shattered comet, which float not in space but on the surface of the immense Pacific."[35]

A deep-seated fear, which appears in muted form throughout the novel, becomes altogether explicit in its concluding lines. The floating island, Calistes Munbar claims, will be rebuilt one day. "And yet," the narrator adds, "one cannot repeat it too often: to create an artificial island, an island that moves upon the surface of the seas, is that not to overstep the limits assigned to human genius, and is it not forbidden to man, who controls neither the winds nor the waves, to usurp with such temerity the role of the Creator?"[36]

A novel of the fantastic and a work of science fiction, Wells's *The Time Machine* is above all a quest narrative. This is evident in its general theme, the quest for the limits of time, as well as in the various episodes which mark the traveler's exploration of the world of the Eloi and the Morlocks: the descent into the underworld, the subterranean caverns of the Morlocks, the exploration of the Palace of Green Porcelain, the crossing of the dark forest. The quest for the limits of time ends in the horrifying discovery of a landscape of death and of the last living creature; the partial quests end in the discovery of the monstrous Morlocks and the ruins of civilization, and in the death of a child-woman, Weena, the symbol of gracious innocence. On the level of allegory and symbol, Wells's message here is one of despair. This same message recurs, obsessively, in a great number of different works at the end of the century: the impossible quest for eternal youth in Oscar Wilde's *The Picture of Dorian Gray*, ending in crime and suicide; mad scientific quests and the quest for solitude and aestheticism in Huysmans's *À rebours*, ending in imprecations and calls for divine thunder and fire; and perhaps the most striking quest of all, that of Conrad's hero, Marlow, who penetrates into the heart of darkness. If there is a single exemplary allegory of the mythic quest ending in solitude, darkness, and death, which characterizes the closing years of the nineteenth century, Conrad's novel is undoubtedly the one.

Kurtz, the adventurer employed by the Company, has penetrated to the depths of Africa in order to find ivory, the symbol of all wealth, and in order to spread progress (as his posthumous report indicates). The expedition in which Marlow, the narrator, takes part, discovers Kurtz dying in a hut surrounded by a fence of stakes topped by skulls. Kurtz dies on the way back, uttering his final cry, "a cry that was no more than a breath: 'The horror! The horror!' "[37]

But, one could say, Marlow is the veritable hero of the novel, and he returns to tell his tale. Indeed, Marlow narrates the story one night on the deck of a ship anchored in the Thames, ready for another journey. When Marlow falls still, the author who reports his narrative adds these lines: "I raised my head. The offing was barred by a black bank of clouds, and the tranquil waterway leading to the uttermost ends of the earth flowed sombre under an overcast sky—seemed to lead into the heart of an immense darkness."[38]

That immense darkness, symbol of death: for Marlow as well, there is no hope, just as there was none for Dorian Gray, for Des Esseintes, for the voyager through time, for Prendrick, Moreau, or Camaret, for Dr. Jekyll destroyed in the person of Mr. Hyde in Robert Louis Stevenson's tale, for Aschenbach who sought beauty and love and who dies alone on a beach in Venice, while the sirocco is blowing and the rising mists announce the epidemic in the midst of a city which is itself slowly sinking into the waves. With Thomas Mann's *Death in Venice* we have crossed over into the twentieth century, but the spirit remains the same—a spirit of despair and of the sense of an irremediable end.

One could go on accumulating symbols. Indeed, nothing resembles more the apparent, artificial, mortally undermined youth of Dorian Gray than the obscene old man with the brightly painted face who accompanies Aschenbach on the ferry from Pola to Venice, or than Aschenbach himself, his hair and eyebrows dyed black by a *barbiere*, his lips and cheeks painted red when already death is at hand, when soon afterward that caricature of youth will collapse on his lounge chair on the beach: a society rotting from the inside, a world in decomposition, despite the appearance of youth and strength.

Nor is there any symbol of survival. Even the beautiful young Tadzio seems diseased, as Aschenbach notes in observing the paleness of his skin and the color of his teeth.[39] As for Aschenbach, he is all alone, as are Dorian Gray, Des Esseintes, Jekyll, Camaret, and Marlow. Kurtz hangs on to the precious memory of his fiancée in Brussels, but he dies, and after his death we see her walled up in sadness, nostalgia, and solitude— without a nourishing love, without children, without a future. The heart of darkness, the deserted beach of a condemned city, the vision of horror of a frozen world, or a world in which the ultimate bestiality has reasserted its hold on man, or yet again that silent snowfall burying the earth under an immense shroud, that snow which, at the end of the last story in Joyce's *Dubliners*, covers over everything, "the living and the dead."[40]

And behind this general symbolism of the end, there loom fantasies of destruction: fantasies of the evil demiurge, and the fantasy of the human monster.

The fantasy of the evil demiurge made its appearance in the last decades of the century. The providential God of tradition is here replaced by a human being endowed with semidivine characteristics, thanks to the extraordinary knowledge he has mastered and the quasi-superhuman power this knowledge gives him. But he uses his power blindly and haphazardly, often simply to gratify his demonic hubris. Subject to no moral laws, at times mad, he destroys his creation and himself at the same time.

Already in the early years of the century, one finds a version of this figure in the person of the unfortunate Victor Frankenstein, the creator of the monster who perishes on a ship caught in the polar ice, strangled by his own terrifying creature. But Mary Shelley described this strange demiurge as sensitive and unhappy. A slightly different kind of ambiguity exists in some of Jules Verne's characters, such as the engineer Robur, a master of the most advanced technology, in *Robur le conquérant (The Clipper of the Clouds)*. Robur certainly appears mad; the norms of behavior are no obstacle to him. He is also a monster of pride. And yet, when he unexpectedly saves his two hated rivals, one cannot be sure whether to interpret his gesture as a sign of scientific and technological generosity, or else as a supreme manifestation of pride which can only lead to catastrophe. In the last lines of the novel Verne seems to affirm an optimistic vision of the science of the future, but the ambiguity of the character persists.

On the other hand, Schultze in Verne's *Les Cinq Cents Millions de la Bégum* (The Begum's Fortune) is unequivocally mad and demonic. His city, Stahlstadt, is the very image of the totalitarian city of the future, and he has worked out detailed plans for total war. He perishes, the victim of his own invention; and in death, he appears more frightening than ever: "There was no doubt about it! . . . It was Herr Schultze, recognisable by the frightful grimace of his jaws and his glaring teeth, but a gigantic Herr Schultze whom the explosion of one of his terrible war-machines had asphyxiated; at the same time, a terrible cold had frozen him stiff."[41]

Even here, however, the rendering of the figure is only partial, since the character of Schultze is in some sense annulled by the character of the good Dr. Sarrasin, and the destruction of the horrible Stahlstadt allows the ideal Franceville to develop unimpeded. The political content of the manifest discourse is thus clear, but in the background there still remains the character who seems to fascinate Verne, as he did Verne's contemporaries, by his evil and superhuman powers of destruction.

Whereas Schultze possesses both political and scientific power, Thomas Roch, in Verne's *Face au drapeau* (Facing the Flag), is simply a mad scientist; he is manipulated by gangsters, but at the last minute he takes hold of himself and destroys both his invention and himself. The same dichotomy exists in Verne's *The Barsac Mission*, but the result is somewhat different: Killer, the politician, and Camaret, the scientist, form a team; they are the two components of a possible synthesis whose actualization makes one shudder. At the end of the novel they destroy each other, but in the process they also annihilate the city they have founded in central Africa: "All was over now. Blackland, totally destroyed by the very man who had created it, was a heap of ruins and wreckage. Of Marcel Camaret's admirable but nefarious work, nothing remained."[42]

Finally, there is Dr. Moreau. It is in Wells's novel that the fantasy of the evil demiurge is given its fullest expression—so much so that even today, the reader cannot shake off a feeling of horror.

Moreau creates beings haphazardly, with no moral restraints whatsoever:

> "The thing before you is no longer an animal, a fellow-creature, but a problem. . . . I wanted—it was the only thing I wanted—to find out the extreme limit of plasticity in a living shape."
> "But," said I, "the thing is an abomination—"
> "To this day I have never troubled about the ethics of the matter. . . . I have gone on, not heeding anything but the question I was pursuing, and the material has . . . dripped into the huts yonder. . . ."[43]

In the depths of a cave the monsters learn the law and deify Moreau, but their taste for blood does not disappear, nor does the effect of the tortures that Moreau's experiments constitute. A puma, suffering for weeks under an experiment of transformative vivisection, escapes and tears Moreau to pieces. At that point the system falls apart: Moreau's assistant, the alcoholic Montgomery, also perishes, and the island returns to bestiality. The accursed demiurge thus disappears with his creation: Moreau is devoured by his monsters; Killer and Camaret destroy each other; Frankenstein is killed by the monster he created; Dr. Jekyll is obliterated by Mr. Hyde, who then destroys himself.

Even more than their creator, these monstrous creatures, these humanoid or human monsters, call for destruction, for they are all hybrids, and hybridity provokes horror in the depths of the unconscious. Prendrick feels this horror without being able to explain it to himself at first, when he observes the servant that Moreau has given him—and that he still takes for a human being:

> "He's unnatural," I said. "There's something about him. . . . Don't think me fanciful, but it gives me a nasty little sensation, a tightening of my muscles, when he comes near me. It's a touch . . . of the diabolical, in fact."[44]

This hybridity which provokes horror and destruction manifests itself physically, but this external aspect is only the expression of the total wretchedness of the creature, a creature that struggles to become human and ineluctably fails. This is evident in the narrative of Frankenstein's monster, in Jekyll's struggles with himself, and in the efforts of Moreau's monsters to learn the law. They all succumb to the base part of their being, and all must be destroyed. In fact, in a nineteenth century that was beginning to be haunted by the theme of inevitable decay, they are all symbols of man. They all perish: some by violent death, some by returning to the animal state, some in a setting symbolizing death, calling for their own destruction.

These fantasies, as well as the symbols we have been dealing with, are organized into a clearly discernible mythic sequence: the transgression of a certain norm of knowledge and power, which necessarily leads to punishment and destruction. Nineteenth-century man has penetrated into forbidden territory, overstepped limits considered inviolable, dared to attempt what should not be attempted: he must perish.

One might consider Wagner's *Ring* as a significant mythical expression of this theme—at once the oldest and most modern of themes. The gods, reduced here to the fate of humans, since they are condemned to die, perish in the flames that destroy Valhalla, because Wotan was not able to resist the temptation of absolute power that was offered him (at least so it seemed) by the accursed golden ring. *Die Götterdämmerung*, the last work of the *Ring* cycle, belongs, in fact, both to the visions of a final destruction that escapes any individual will, a destruction present in the very act of creation as soon as the paradisiacal vision of the beginning falls apart, and to the myth of a catastrophic end provoked by the transgression of inviolable norms. Indeed, this work has often been interpreted in the second sense, as an absolute destruction resulting from the will to absolute power by a demonic Reich.

Equally significant, from our point of view, are the stories of transgression told by the novels we have been discussing: the voyage through time, the advance into a threatening heart of darkness, whether in the depths of a wild continent or in the country of the Morlocks; the use of magical means to transform life, as in the case of Dr. Jekyll and Dorian Gray; or the use of scientific means which nonetheless resemble magic, as in the case of Frankenstein and Moreau. In each instance, man penetrates into domains that reveal dark forces, more diabolical than divine, a transgression that can only provoke the worst punishment.

Looked at more closely, this theme of transgression implies either the acquisition of scientific knowledge and technological power that go beyond what man has a right to know and to do, or else the creation or transformtion of life by magical as well as scientific means (and in this instance magic symbolizes a scientific power capable of infinite development); finally, it implies that indefinable but undeniable hubris which, in various ways, was pushing nineteenth-century man to consider himself a god.

In Verne's *Propeller Island*, we recall, the narrator ends his tale with the following question: "To create an artificial island . . . is that not to overstep the limits assigned to human genius, and is it not forbidden to man . . . to usurp with such temerity the role of the Creator?" In fact, this question, this obsessive image of transgression, is present, implicitly or explicitly, in Verne's earliest works. What, after all, could be more optimistic than *From the Earth to the Moon?* There is no punishment there; that novel, like its sequel, *Round the Moon*, celebrates the power of science. And yet the question appears, bringing fear with it: "Was it possible to go to the aid of these bold travelers? No! for they had placed themselves beyond the pale of humanity, by crossing the limits imposed by the Creator on his earthly creatures."[45] There is an evident, if indirect, progression from this first, hesitant question to the destruction of Propeller Island and the annihilation of Blackland, as well as of the man who goes beyond the limits imposed by the Creator: Marcel Camaret.

And what about the voyager through time? Does he in fact return? No, he disappears forever, suffering the fate of all those who too brashly cross the frontiers of the inviolable: Kurtz, Moreau, Jekyll, Gray. Among these transgressors, the most terrible punishment destroys, as we have seen, those who came closest to usurping God's role by creating life or by transforming its acceptable forms: they are killed by their monstrous creations (Frankenstein, Moreau, Jekyll). The closer the nineteenth century came to certain limits, the more fear it generated: Were we not on the verge of disrupting the very norms of the universe and life, of violating the most sacred of taboos? Every violation of a taboo calls for death, and the violation of an absolute taboo calls for absolute destruction.[46]

Two American writers, Edgar Allan Poe and Herman Melville, expressed this theme of transgression and catastrophe with particular force. Consider, for example, Poe's "MS. Found in a Bottle," published in 1833. The narrator, whose terrifying adventure becomes known only through a massage he threw into the sea, is carried off by a tempest on a rudderless ship in the direction of the southern pole. Like Kurtz and Marlow fifty years later, or like the voyager through time, he penetrates into the heart of darkness after a gust throws him from the deck of his own ship onto what appears to be a kind of phantom vessel. It is at that point that we read the sentence which could serve as an epigraph for these pages, and for this chapter as a whole: "It is evident that we are hurrying onward to some exciting knowledge—some never-to-be-imparted secret, whose attainment is destruction."[47] Moreover, there remains little else to read: the manuscript ends two paragraphs later with the fateful words: "going down!"

It is within this same American tradition, which, in Harry Levin's words, concentrates on "the dark other half of the situation,"[48] that Herman Melville presents, in *Moby Dick*, the very essence of the theme of transgression and destruction. But what exactly is, on the level of the myth we are discussing, the transgression in question, and who is the agent of punishment?

As concerns the character of Ahab, the accursed captain, the meaning of the transgression is clear: driven by a "fatal pride,"[49] Ahab seeks to conquer and to eliminate every manifestation of the divine. Melville repeatedly emphasizes the divine character of the white whale, the mysterious Leviathan of the Book of Job, Moby Dick, whose supernatural whiteness is the very sign of his belonging to the supraterrestrial world. As Jean-Jacques Mayoux has noted, "Melville's whale is not only a cosmic manifestation, it does not merely bear the mark of god; rather, it comes from god. . . . Melville's whale is thus *angelic:* a terrible messenger from the Almighty, as is already indicated by the sermon devoted to Jonah's whale which is the veritable opening of the novel."[50] But it is after one has admitted as much that the genuine questions arise: Does Moby Dick emanate from the world of goodness and light, or is he a fallen angel? And is the divinity that Ahab defies a divinity of darkness? For the whiteness of the whale is not necessarily a sign of brightness and purity; it is also the "visible absence of color," "the intensifying agent in things the most appalling to mankind."[51]

And if that is the case, then Melville's message is hardly one of hope. Ahab may not be the model of "modern man," but his rejection of the divine, his Promethean spirit, express something of the very essence of modernity: the pride, the boundless energy—and the madness. Ahab is destroyed. Only Ishmael, the narrator, remains alive. Some have spoken of a message of ultimate redemption. "The only one in the tale," writes James E. Miller, "to achieve a balance of intellect and heart, knowledge and love, Ishmael is the single survivor."[52] But, for others, Ishmael partakes in Ahab's madness and in the captain's understanding of the ultimate indifference of God. As Lawrence Thompson has pointed out, the motto of the Epilogue, taken from the Book of Job ("And I only am escaped alone to tell thee"), puts Ishmael in the role of the messenger who remains to tell the story. And what would be the message transmitted to the reader? "The entire voyage," writes Thompson, "enabled Ishmael to arrive at that catastrophe, and at that lonely opportunity to confirm his worst suspicions; to coffin-meditate on the paradox of God's simultaneous malice and indifference."[53] And if this is the message, the final images have something premonitory concerning human fate: The *Pequod*, that microcosm, that reduced model of humanity, has disappeared; hostile nature has engulfed man under the gaze of an indifferent God: "Now small fowls flew screaming over the yet yawning gulf; a sullen white surf beat against its steep sides; then all collapsed, and the great shroud of the sea rolled on as it rolled five thousand years ago."[54]

It might be objected that some of the literary works discussed in these pages express not so much the scientific theories about evolution and natural selection as the social foundations of the visions of the end that were described. Thus in *The Time Machine*, the Morlocks symbolize the mortal menace that the working classes, buried in their underground factories, represented for the hegemony of their bourgeois exploiters; in *The Picture of Dorian Gray*, one finds some horrified allusions to the vile proletariat; in Hopkins's poem quoted at the start of the chapter, the initial theme is the misery of the unemployed and their resentment. One could cite numerous other examples to show that by the end of the century the triumph of the bourgeoisie appeared less certain: the social edifice was cracking, assassination attempts became more frequent, and a general feeling of uncertainty more widespread. According to this interpretation, the visions of total catastrophe were but the direct or indirect expression of these social transformations.

If one adds to that the factors already mentioned—the radical questioning of faith in a providential God, the evolutionary theories heading in uncertain directions, the second law of thermodynamics, the disquieting aspects of modern science and technology—then the intellectual context of the visions of the end comes together with and reinforces their social context.

And yet, the general impression produced by the works we have cited is that these visions of a total end plunge their roots into a deeper ground than that of the social tensions or the scientific theories of the period. We can discern here the surfacing of archaic fears, fears provoked by the overstepping of the limits prescribed to man. But in that case, in a century where, notwithstanding references to the "limits imposed by the creator", faith was disappearing, who was the agent of punishment? What was the source of the menace that weighed on man guilty of transgression? Although the fear was mythical and vague, one can nevertheless discern an image behind it.

The ocean rolling over the *Pequod,* over Ahab and his crew, gives us the answer: the agent of punishment was nature itself. The same answer is suggested by *Frankenstein,* by *Dr. Jekyll and Mr. Hyde,* by *The Picture of Dorian Gray,* by *Propeller Island:* the forces of nature have been unleashed and are taking their revenge. Similarly, what is the vision of the ineluctable degeneration of man, or of the thermal death of the universe, if not the verdict of an indifferent nature that eliminates man like an ephemeral parasite? In fact, with the disappearance of faith in Providence, under the gaze of an indifferent Divinity, man finds himself once again face to face with what Philippe Ariès has called "savage nature" and he imagines it as the agent of his destruction. Even the sense of an end to civilization fits in with this general view: civilizations are born, reach their apex, and die according to a kind of biological, natural necessity.

Thus, at the very moment when man appears to have tamed nature and utilized it for his own ends—becoming all-powerful, no less than God himself—at the very moment when man affirms that unlimited progress will put an end to the natural movement of civilizations, a fear develops: the fear that nature will take its revenge and destroy man, who denies its laws and transgresses the limits imposed on him.

Perceived in this light, the causes of the end imagined in the nineteenth century transcend man and pertain to a fundamental antagonism between man and the cosmos—an antagonism of which man, in the end, can only be the victim. But in reality it is a distant and quasi-theoretical end that is envisaged here, even if some of the fantasies reveal a hidden obsession with imminent destruction.

It is only in the works of Wells and Verne, at the turn of the century, that one sees for the first time the great theme of the end which will dominate the twentieth century: the destruction of man by man. What was a transcendent cause of the end will become immanent to society and to human beings; what was distant will become close; what was abstract, concrete; and a theme that was only minor and incipient, the theme of our destruction, will invade the imagination of our own time.

NOTES

Unless otherwise indicated, all translations from the French are by Susan Rubin Suleiman.

1. Quoted in H. G. Schenk, *The Mind of the European Romantics* (London: Constable, 1966), p. 32.

2. Ibid., p. 33.

3. Fritz Stern, *The Politics of Cultural Despair: A Study in the Rise of Germanic Ideology* (Berkeley: University of California Press, 1961).

4. On apocalyptic thought in Vollgraf, Lasaulx, and Burckhardt, see Hans Joachim Schoeps, *Vorläufer Spenglers. Studien zum Geschichtspessimismus im 19. Jahrhundert* (Leiden, 1955). See as well Jacob Burckhardt, *Weltgeschichtliche Betrachtungen* (published posthumously), trans. *Force and Freedom: Reflections on History* (London, 1943).

5. Quoted in Carl E. Schorske, *Fin-de-Siècle Vienna: Politics and Culture* (New York: Alfred A. Knopf, 1979), p. 8.

6. As concerns pessimism in France, see in particular A. E. Carter, *The Idea of Decadence in French Literature 1830–1900* (Toronto: University of Toronto Press, 1958); and Koenraad W. Swart, *The Sense of Decadence in Nineteenth-Century France* (The Hague: Martinus Nijhoff, 1964).

7. Mario Praz, *The Romantic Agony*, trans. Angus Davidson (London: Oxford University Press, 1933), p. 381.

8. Elémir Bourges, *Le Crépuscule des dieux* (Paris: Stock, 1912), p. 33.

9. Walter Houghton, *The Victorian Frame of Mind: 1830–1870* (New Haven: Yale University Press, 1957), p. 73.

10. On some aspects of the decadent literature in the England of the "Yellow Nineties," see Richard Gilman, *Decadence: The Strange Life of an Epithet* (London: Secker & Warburg, 1979), chap. 4.

11. Quoted *in Jerome Hamilton Buckley, The Triumph of Time* Cambridge, Mass., Harvard University Press, 1966, p. 66.

12. Friedrich Nietzsche, *The Will to Power,* in *The Complete Works of Friedrich Nietzsche,* ed. Oscar Levy, 18 vols. (Edinburgh, 1909–1930), vol. 14, p. 55.

13. During the nineteenth century, traditional visions of the end flourished as never before. The majority have been familiar with astronomical calculations and the marvels of electricity; in order to end the world, they proclaimed, the divine wrath would use a comet or else proceed to a general electrocution: see Perry Miller, "The End of the World," in his *Errand into the Wilderness* (Cambridge, Mass.: Harvard University Press, 1976), p. 229 ff.; and Paul Vuillaud. *La Fin du Monde* (Paris: Payot, 1952), p. 176. On a different level of spirituality, men like Joseph de Maistre, and F. R. de Lamennais, J. K. Huysmans, and Léon Bloy called for the descent of heavenly fire; see Léon Bloy's *La Femme pauvre* (Paris, 1897).

14. Émile Zola, *La Débâcle,* 2 vols. (Paris: Fasquelle, 1957), vol. 2, p. 654.

15. Mary Wollstonecraft Shelley, *The Last Man,* 3 vols. (London: Henry Colburn, 1826), p. 352.

16. Charles Darwin, *The Descent of Man and Selection in Relation to Sex*

(London: John Murray, 1873), p. 134. For an interesting discussion of Darwinism and the future of man, see Frank E. Manuel and Fritzie P. Manuel, *Utopian Thought in the Western World* (Cambridge, Mass.: Harvard University Press, 1979), pp. 773 et seq.

17. Arthur Comte de Gobineau, *Essai sur l'inégalité des races humaines,* 2 vols. (1853–55; Paris: Firmin Didot, 1933), vol. 2, pp. 562–64. In a later work, *Renaissance,* published in 1877, Gobineau does evoke the possibility of a way out, thanks to the saving action of an elite.

18. Francis Galton, *Hereditary Genius: An Inquiry into Its Laws and Consequences* (London, 1869), p. 345.

19. Thomas H. Huxley, *Evolution and Ethics and Other Essays* (London: Macmillan, 1894), p. 85.

20. Max Nordau, *Entartung,* 2 vols. (Berlin: Duncker, 1893), Eng. trans. *Degeneration* (New York, 1895).

21. Hippolyte Adolphe Taine, *The Ancient Regime* (*L'ancien régime* [Paris, 1876]) (New York: Henry Holt & Company, 1876), p. 208. Quoted in K. F. Helleiner, "An Essay on the Rise of Historical Pessimism in the Nineteenth Century," *Canadian Journal of Economics and Political Science* 8:4 (November 1942), 534.

22. Taine, *The French Revolution,* trans. John Durand (New York: Henry Holt & Company, 1878), vol. 1, p. 248; quoted in Helleiner, "An Essay on the Rise of Historical Pessimism in the Nineteenth Century," 534. Helleiner sees similarities between Taine's theories and the views expressed by the English social scientist and critic Walter Bagehot in *Physics and Politics* (1872), as quoted in ibid., 534–70.

23. H. G. Wells, *The Island of Dr. Moreau* (London: William Heinemann, 1896), pp. 202–203.

24. Jules Verne, *Twenty Thousand Leagues Under the Sea,* trans. I. O. Evans (New York: Thomas Y. Crowell Co., 1873), p. 249.

25. Quoted in Jerome Hamilton Buckley, *The Triumph of Time: A Study of the Victorian Concepts of Time, History, Progress, and Decadence* (Cambridge, Mass.: Harvard University Press, 1966), p. 66.

26. Camille Flammarion, *La Fin du monde* (Paris: Flammarion, 1894), p. 385.

27. H. G. Wells, *The Time Machine* (London: William Heinemann, 1898), p. 97.

28. Friedrich Engels, *Dialectics of Nature,* trans. and ed. Clemens Dutt (New York: International Publishers, 1940), pp. 20, 22.

29. The popular literature abounds in stories of this kind, and they are even more frequent in the early years of the twentieth century. One of the most famous novels in the genre is M. P. Shiel's *The Purple Cloud* (1901; London: Victor Golancz, 129). The same theme can be found in Sir Arthur Conan Doyle's *The Lost World* (1904; London: John Murray, 1952).

30. Alphonse de Candole, *Histoire des sciences et des savants depuis deux siècles* (Geneva: Georg, 1885), pp. 190–91.

31. Marie-Hélène Huet, *L'Histoire des Voyages extraordinaires. Essai sur l'oeuvre de Jules Verne* (Paris: Minard, 1978), p. 8.

32. Jules Verne, *Round the Moon*, ed. Charles F. Home (New York: F. Tyler Daniels Co., 1911).

33. Michel Serres, "Le Savoir, la guerre et le sacrifice," *Critique* 367 (December 1977), 1068.

34. This is also I. F. Clarke's interpretation in *Voices Prophesying War 1763–1984* (London: Oxford University Press, 1966), p. 98.

35. Jules Verne, *L'Île à hélice* (Paris: Humanoides Associés, 1978), pp. 311, 315. See also Verniculus, "*Histoire de la Fin du Monde ou la Comète de 1904*" [Bibliothèque populaire de la Suisse Romande] (Lausanne: Jaunin, 1882).

36. Verne, *L'Île à hélice*, p. 324.

37. Joseph Conrad, *Heart of Darkness* (New York: Bantam, 1969), p. 78.

38. Ibid., p. 132.

39. Thomas Mann, *Der Tod in Venedig* (Frankfurt: Fischer Verlag, 1977), p. 34.

40. James Joyce, "The Dead," in *Dubliners* (New York: Viking Press, 1968), p. 224.

41. Jules Verne, *Les Cinq Cents Millions de la Bégum* (Paris: Hachette, 1966), p. 277.

42. Jules Verne, *L'Étonnante Aventure de la mission Barsac* (Paris: Roux, 1919), 439.

43. Wells, *The Island of Dr. Moreau*, pp. 116–17.

44. Ibid., p. 52.

45. Jules Verne, *From the Earth to the Moon*, ed. Charles F. Home (New York: F. Tyler Daniels Co., 1911), p. 150.

46. This same theme reappears as well in the popular literature of the end of the nineteenth century and the beginning of the twentieth; see J. H. Rosny Aîné, "La Mort de la terre" [1910], in *Récits de science fiction* (Verviers: Éditions Gerard, 1973); also Robert Hugh-Benson's *Le Maître de la terre* (1907; Geneva: S.A.R.I., 1955).

47. Edgar Allan Poe, *Complete Tales and Poems* (New York: Vintage Books, 1975), p. 125.

48. Harry Levin, *The Power of Blackness: Hawthorne, Poe, Melville* (New York: Alfred A. Knopf, 1958), p. 7.

49. Herman Melville, *Moby Dick* (New York: New American Library, 1961), p. 487.

50. Jean-Jacques Mayoux, *Melville par lui-même* (Paris: Éditions du Seuil, 1958), p. 74.

51. Melville, *Moby Dick*, p. 196.

52. James E. Miller, Jr., *A reader's guide to Herman Melville* (New York Farrar, Straus and Cudahy, 1962), p. 117.

53. Lawrence Thompson, *Melville's Quarrel with God* (1952; Princeton, N.J.: Princeton University Press, 1973), pp. 237, 239.

54. Melville, *Moby Dick*, p. 535.

5

APOCALYPSE AND THE
MODERN

Frank Kermode

IN FASHIONABLE USE, THE WORD *APOCALYPSE* HAS NO
very precise meaning, only vague connotations of doom; and to in-
quire into the relevance to modern literature of such a formless concept
would be largely a waste of time. Elect, alienated from his contemporaries, convinced of imminent catastrophe and abandoning the comfort
and support of a known past, the typical great Modern makes cruel jour-
neys into the depths of the isolated self, voyaging, in Baudelaire's words,
"au fond de l'inconnu pour trouver du nouveau." "Make it New!" cries
Pound; "Nothing is good save the new," echoes W. C. Williams. This
millennial New is their version of the future, and it may remind us that
other enthusiasts, perhaps more gregarious, less self-absorbed, have likewise foreseen a future beyond an imminent disaster, defied the common
wisdom of their contemporaries, and abjured the past as dead or irrelevant to the uniqueness of their moment at the great turning point of time.

But we shall need more than these resemblances to justify our speaking of the Modern as apocalyptic. Let us select, out of the thousands of
enthusiastic millenarians, heralds of a new age, that history offers, two
examples: the Emperor Constantine in the fourth century A.D., inau-
gurating a new age by reciting (in a Greek translation) the Fourth *Eclogue*
of Vergil; and a fervid Ranter of the 1650s, to whom the old world is
irrelevant, its laws and even its Testaments entirely superseded, for he
makes his own laws, and the Spirit speaks in him. What have the Emperor and the Ranter in common with Kandinsky and D. H. Lawrence? It
is natural that people should look from the evils of the present, brought to
them by a deplorable past and now reaching what may seem an intolerable pitch, to a better future; that they should conceive of theirs as a
between-time, with decadence before it and renovation to follow. As
Shelley remarked, when he recalled in *Hellas* the millennial prophecies

of Isaiah and Vergil, the "ardent spirits" of such men "overlap the actual reign of evil which we endure and bewail," already seeing "the possible and perhaps approaching state of society in which the 'lion shall lie down with the lamb.'" To label all such aspirations and predictions "apocalyptic" would be to try to compress the history of a desperate human situation into the confines of a literary genre.

Yet it is true that expressions of hope and despair, of desires to have done with the old and welcome the new, must have their literary and rhetorical history. Constantine hailed the new with a prophecy already centuries old; the Ranter condemned the superseded Bible in language that owed everything to it; Shelley's types of the utopian temperament are ancient Hebrew and Latin poets. The proclamation of new world orders is an old proclamation; the language and forms of the new must always remember their history. That history is written down; and every enthusiast, whether an untutored mechanic or a learned poet, must have read at least one of the books in which it is recorded. He will stand on his uniquely important and terrible ridge of history, descrying from that privileged place the transformation of the world, perceiving history, or an epoch of it, approaching its end; and he will be required to understand the relation between his own time of transition and the world that is past, as well as the world that is to come. He must map the past, know the courses by which the world came, in his time, to the great moment of crisis. But he will know that the relation has been understood before, the map drawn before, the world seen before at its unique moment of crisis. He will know all this because of the apocalyptic tradition.

I shall suggest in this essay that there is, after all, a reasonably precise sense in which we may speak of an apocalyptic strain in modern literature; that we find in that literature transformations of a variety of apocalyptic traditions. Some of these may be traced directly to the canonical apocalypses, some to the interpretative accretions that those apocalypses have, over the ages, been so ready to bear along with them. The existential crisis of the human being, arbitrarily placed in history and making fictive sense of it, must be prior to all his acquisitions from the cultural record; but they enable him to speak as he does, provide him whether he wills it or not with the syntax and the figures of his new eschatology.

A strict scholarly definition of *apocalypse* would be, for the present purpose, much too rigorous; it would apply to a peculiar literary genre, crystallizing, during the two centuries preceding and the century or two following the beginning of the Christian era, a specialized expression of certain sectarian eschatologies.[1] On the other hand, it would be self-defeatingly licentious to allow the word to be used of any futuristic utopia.

For my purposes it will be convenient, and sufficiently restrictive, to use the word as follows. I shall allow myself to speak of an apocalyptic "set"—a state of affairs in which one can discern some sociological predisposition to the acceptance of apocalyptic structures and figures. By "canonical apocalypse" I intend Daniel, Revelation, and the other apocalyptic passages of the New Testament. "Interpretative apocalypse" will refer to material other than the strictly canonical which became attached to it in the course of its transmission. The history of apocalyptic thought is the history of the interaction of these three elements.

The first of these categories—the "set"—has nothing necessarily to do with written apocalypse. We should very reasonably call some South American Indian beliefs apocalyptic, since they have many of the necessary features: confidence that a new time is about to begin, a prophecy of a golden world, with some harrowing experience (a migration, for example) to come first. Investigators of Melanesian Cargo cults note that the social conditions conducive to their flourishing are usual enough: discontent with low wages, the need to endure the insulting discipline of apparently omnipotent colonialists, and so on. This present misery, it is believed, will be ended by the arrival of a cargo (formerly by sea, latterly by air) containing whatever it is that makes the white man rich and happy. The cult has its ritual, its charismatic leader, and a narrative myth embodying its beliefs.[2] The New Guinea society studied by Peter Lawrence exhibits several different phases of the cult; older, indigenous myths are overlaid by the apocalyptic teaching of Christian missionaries. The cult develops its original expectations in conformity with the new scheme, and there ensue practices reminiscent of the behavior of many earlier fundamentalist movements in Europe; for example, the elect no longer observe the old rules governing sexual conduct (fancying themselves in the same position as some early Christians reproved by Saint Paul), and get themselves into a muddle about the Heavenly City; just as Norman Cohn's proletarian apocalyptics in the Middle Ages took any large city for Jerusalem, so the Melanesians confound Sydney, Rome, and Heaven.[3] Repeated disappointment has now given some of these cults a certain this-worldliness and some of the characteristics of an institution; they have taken on political and nationalist colorings, and desire to expel the oppressor by ordinary force. Political and military action, work, replace the magic of the cargo.

The Cargo cults are simply an instance of the manner in which the canonical apocalypse impresses itself upon communities of whom it can be said that they have an apocalyptic "set." Indeed, the history of the Christian apocalypse itself illustrates the point. The first Christians, imagining themselves at the great crisis of history, indeed at its end, were not alone in their conviction—the Jewish sect at Qumran, for example, was also apocalyptic in character. In neither case did the imminent end of the world prevent the sectaries from writing about how it felt to be about to experience it, and their writings were conditioned by existing apocalypses, notably that of Daniel.

Of course their expectations were disappointed. As John Gager neatly expresses it, "Millenary movements fail by definition."[4] When the end fails to happen, they are left with a difficult problem of "cognitive dissonance" (Leon Festinger's formula).[5] There are various ways of resolving the dissonance: one can argue that the event occurred, but in an unexpected form, or one can recalculate one's predictions; or one can overcome disappointment by practicing what Festinger calls "group reinforcement." The isolation of the disappointed prophet and his elect is reduced by proselytizing. The movement survives the end, and passes from charismatic to institutional. Within the institution work replaces magic, and the end waits upon the completion of missionary activity.[6]

Early Christianity followed this pattern; and the most hectic of its apocalypses became something of an embarrassment to it. Revelation was the last of the New Testament books to be accepted into the canon; though once in, it was protected by the authority of the institution and circulated by the missionaries. It has always been something of a powder keg in the basement of an institution that was no longer as willing as it formerly was to think of itself as existing on the very brink of the end, an institution tending to grow conservative, as all do that make the transition from charismatic to institutional. This can be seen from the history of successful enthusiastic sects; for example, American Pentecostalism, when the ecstasy subsided, moved toward social and political reaction;[7] and in *The New York Times* for August 17, 1980, there was a front-page story on the emergence of "ultraconservative" evangelical movements as "a new political force" to be reckoned with in the elections the following November. Enthusiasm gives way to institutions, and institutions in their nature distrust change and value orthodoxy.

Of the original Christian enthusiasm there remain, however, the apocalypses that were written down and made canonical. They share with the other books of the canon the esteem and veneration properly accorded to inspired writings; and over the centuries they are particularly welcomed by men and women of an apocalyptic "set"—people whose hope of finding some tolerable place for themselves in the world and in its history takes the form of supposing that they are living through a time of privation and anguish that must issue in a new age. The entire process, and the figures under which that new age can be imagined, will derive from the apocalyptic works so sedulously publicized by word or mouth and by the circulation of the books themselves. The new version of the world and time must in some measure derive from those early apocalypses which taught us how to eschatologize history.

It is, however, of great importance that the original writings have been subject, for 2,000 years, to the devoted attention of interpreters. Written, in the first instance, for elect groups who could read their allegories and enigmas, they offer quite exceptional scope to exegetes who have lost access to those original senses. The modern scholar is trained to Revelation as he would any other ancient book, and his efforts are devoted largely to the recovery and rational interpretation of long-lost allusions and secrets, all conceived as relevant only to the moment of composition. But such interpretative assumptions, though they seem natural enough to the learned of our own time, did not bind the great majority of their predecessors, and for that matter do not bind the majority of their unlearned contemporaries. The tropes and numbers of apocalyptic prediction were enigmas to be solved in ways that were important to the interpreter at his special moment in history. That the Beast was Nero and his number, 666, a cipher for that name—that the writer of Revelation was playing a game that also interested Suetonius[8]—was not the kind of answer most interpreters sought. Each remade the original prophecy in the interest of some later theory of history and some later crisis. The mysterious numbers are a key to history; in the Protestant tradition the Whore is the Roman Catholic Church; and so on. A predisposition to apocalypse allowed the Cargo believers to adapt the canonical apocalypse to their own needs; the canonical apocalypse is in its turn modified by interpretative apocalypses.

The accretion of secondary elements is endless, and the subject of endless studies. For our purposes it is sufficient to mention a few of the most important and enduring additions. They come from Sibylline writings about Rome's destiny, from the legends of the medieval Alexander, and from many other sources.[9] Among the apocalyptic legends which have had powerful historical consequences are those of the Last World Emperor, the ultimate conversion of the Jews, and the Everlasting Gospel. The Emperor of the Last Days will, before the reign of Antichrist, lay down his crown on the Mount of Olives, presumably his remote original is the Hinderer or Restrainer, the person who would limit the ravages of Antichrist, in II Thessalonians 2:7. The Everlasting Gospel, one of the most important and effective elements in the interpretative tradition, is essentially a vast gloss on the *euangelion aionion* of Revelation 11:6 where the words imply not a book but news of the impending end.

I shall have more to say of the Everlasting Gospel; meanwhile it may be noted that the other themes, the Conversion of the Jews and the Last Emperor, had an effect on secular literature never yet fully explored. The

Arthurian cycle is influenced by the Last Emperor myth[10] and so is Spenser's *The Faerie Queene*, of which the First Book is a Protestant apocalypse with Una as the Woman Clothed with the Sun, Duessa as the Whore (and the Roman Catholic Church), and Arthur as the World Emperor, though part of his role is played by the Red Cross knight, a familiar apocalyptic figure and related to the knight faithful and true of Revelation. That the Jews were to be involved in some important way in the events leading to the establishment of the millennium was a belief that unfortunately outlasted many others, occurring not only in the fantasies of revolutionary fanatics but in the murky apocalyptic program of the Third Reich.

For we are not discussing mere historical or literary curiosities. The Last Emperor not only animated the wild prophets of the medieval apocalyptic movements described by Norman Cohn, but figured also in the propaganda of the Emperor Charles V and Elizabeth I. That he was able to do so in these and many other instances was in large part owing to his association with the most important single interpretative transformation of the canonical apocalyptic themes, which was the work of a twelfth-century Calabrian monk. Apocalyptic thinking is often commended as the begetter of the Western philosophy of history;[11] but Joachim of Fiore, who died in 1202, was the man responsible for converting the original insights into schemes capable of directing the imagination of the future. If the Emperor survived to assume grotesque parodic forms in the Duce and the Führer, he did so because he was associated with Joachim's philosophy. It divided history into three epochs, one for each person of the Trinity, and ordained a period of transition between each. It was a meliorist philosophy: the world progressed from an age of Law to an age of Love, and from that to an age of the Spirit; the three ages were typologically related, but each represented an improvement over its predecessor. Whoever subscribed to this view of history might suppose himself to be standing at the moment of transition between the second and the third age or *status (Reich)*. And this was as true for the supporters of Frederick II in the thirteenth century as for Moeller van den Brück in the twentieth. The Last Emperor became associated with the establishment of the third *status*, an earthly millennium. As we have seen, he influenced political as well as literary history. The other great Joachimite invention, the Everlasting Gospel, was no less influential in both respects. We must reflect a little more on Joachim before considering some modern developments of the triadic structure of history, of epochal transition, and of the Everlasting Gospel.

Joachim himself was a pacific personality, on good terms with the authorities, and expecting, in 1250, a third age characterized mostly by monastic meditation. But his interpretation of apocalypse made a strong appeal to visionaries and activists, who habitually conceive of themselves as standing on the brink of a new order of history. The germ of his thought is, of course, in the beliefs of the earliest Christians, who supposed themselves to be existing in a between-time; the end was upon them, and a new order about to break in. Theirs was the archetypal period of "now-already-not-yet," of the great transition, usually thought of as a time of terror. The philosophy of Joachim, by instituting a second transition, made it possible for other seers to think of themselves as poised at a similar but later moment, looking back at a past that included the earlier *transitus* upon which theirs was modeled.

Where Joachim got his ideas—apart, of course, from the canonical apocalypses—is doubtful; perhaps some derive from a heterodox cabalistic tradition.[12] What is not in doubt is that they provided a uniquely manageable scheme for subsequent apocalyptic history. The typological relations between the two transitional periods, and the three ages, provided the means whereby the structure of a coming age could be predicted through its predecessors (each, for example, would consist of the same number of generations, and the *transitus* would always be of the same length, calculated from the numbers in Revelation). As each age was presided over by a person of the Trinity, so each had its characteristic book; the book of the Third Age was to be the Everlasting Gospel. It is to Joachim, or rather to Joachimitism, that we owe this Gospel, which will supersede the New Testament as the New superseded the Old. Just as the New Testament spoke more plainly of mysteries which were expressed only as types and shadows in the Old, so the third testament would be more perspicuous than the New, clear of all darkness, *sine enigmate et sine figuris*, face to face, as Saint Paul said. A document called the Everlasting Gospel, put together from the works of Joachim and his followers, was condemned in 1263; but it is in the nature of the Everlasting Gospel that it should assume no permanent form; rather will it be constantly renewed by the inspiration of a new *transitus*. For, of course, the precise predictions of Joachimitism are disappointed like all the others; but the scheme of three ages, transition, and gospel is unaffected. The transition from first to second age lies in the past; the second transition falls within the lifetime of any succeeding generation; and the Third Age is very congenial to all millenarian idealists, of whatever stamp. The identity of the Emperor will change, and so will the content and character of the Gospel. But the patterns of history and prophecy remain constant.

Marjorie Reeves detects the first political use of the historical triad in the 1240s.[13] Since then it has not been forgotten. Frederick II, as Last World Emperor, meant to institute the Third State and purge the Church. So Joachim, even at this early date, became an instrument of imperial propaganda, and made his contribution to the Ghibelline myth of the future Emperor; Dante's imperialism was in some measure Joachimite. Charles VIII of France, descending on Florence in the late fifteenth century, and Savonarola, who met him there, were aware of the prophecy; and its employment in imperial causes extends to the sixteenth century (as we have seen) and beyond, to the Elector Frederick, who married the daughter of James I, and was to be the Protestant Emperor who brought in the new age of peace, and to the Rosicrucian Enlightenment whose English and Bohemian history Frances Yates has discovered. Charles I, Frederick's brother-in-law and the last British king to be given anything like the full imperial treatment, was another Last World Emperor.[14]

The same myths were potent in far less exalted circles, as the studies of Norman Cohn, E. J. Hobsbawm,[15] Frank Manuel, and Marjorie Reeves attest. The proletarian movements also associated the coming of the new age with an apocalyptic leader. And many of them also entertained some version of the new, and Everlasting, Gospel.

It may seem strange that the age of vernacular translations and of print, which as we know was an age of popular bibliolatry, should also have seen the arrival of sects which regarded the Bible as superseded. But of course the philosophy of supersession, given such sharp definition by Joachim, is founded in the primary supersession of the Old by the New Testament. (It does not necessarily involve the total elimination of what is superseded; that is the strength of the typological approach.) And the hope of a third testament transcending the second seems to have originated, as one would expect, among the learned.[16] But it became scandalous because of its adoption by extreme Protestant sects, notably the Anabaptists. Thomas Müntzer preached that Lutheran literalism was a servitude to the flesh.[17] Free of the Church and its Testaments, a man might now himself be Christ.[18]

The greater freedom allowed to enthusiasts under the English Commonwealth encouraged the activity of sects convinced of the great transition and devoted to the Everlasting Gospel. The Ranters (who, according to Christopher Hill, got their notions from the Familists and Jakob Boehme) believed that the Bible had been "the cause of all our miseries and divisions."[19] The New Testament, like the Old before it, belonged to ages now past, like the rules governing marriage and property. On the brink of a new age, the sectarians found themselves between the world of these old laws, and the old books, and a new world where neither had any force. Their position had a precedent in the earliest Christian congregations, but they had no Paul to stabilize them. Yet they had more staying power than might have been expected. Blake, who produced his own Everlasting Gospel, learned from the Ranters;[20] Muggletonians were still preaching in London at the end of the eighteenth century.[21] For a moment, in the late 1640s, it was possible for a man as learned as Milton to entertain ideas not altogether remote from those of the Ranters and Muggletonians;[22] but as time went by, and the king came back, men of reason came to hate and fear enthusiasm, though the canonical foundation of apocalypse was hard to forget. In the hands of the unruly laity the time of apocalypse was (and is) always now; periods of great political disturbance and oppression, such as the years of the Napoleonic Wars, were particularly rich in revolutionary millenarianism, charismatic leaders, and substitute gospels.[23]

Curiously enough, Joachim was again to find favor with the learned. Lessing, who believed in an archaic gospel in Aramaic that must have been the source of the ones we have, discovered Joachimite thought, with its imaginary Gospel, which would in turn replace those canonical gospels. From Lessing the Saint-Simonians learned about these matters and passed on their knowledge to Comte, who admitted the influence of Joachim on his three-stage theory of history.[24] George Eliot, a close student of Comte, seems to have done some research into Joachimitism for her novel *Romola* (1863), which has among its characters Savonarola, another disciple of the Abbot of Fiore ("the Abbot Joachim prophesied of the coming time three hundred years ago, and now Fra Girolamo has got the message afresh"). The Eternal Gospel was kept alive in America, but I know little of its transatlantic provenance. Emerson seems to have had it in mind in the Harvard Divinity School Address, when he spoke of the need of a new revelation and urged his clerical auditor to be himself "a newborn bard of the Holy Ghost."[25] The theme recurs in his essay on Goethe: "We too must write Bibles, to unite again the heavens and the earthly world." Whitman referred to his work on *Leaves of Grass* as "the Great Construction of the New Bible," and the strain survived at least until the death of Wallace Stevens. For what is Steven's Supreme Fiction but the poet's Everlasting Gospel? It is a new revelation; if it could ever be articulated there would be no need of another; the "war between the mind and sky" would be over. But it cannot be articulated. Among the requirements of that Fiction is that "It Must Change". Certainly, like the original *evangelium aeternum*, it must be "absolute," transparent, liberated from stale tropes and rhetorical opacities, "Seeming, at first, a beast disgorged, unlike, / Warmed by a desperate milk." But also it must change: "The freshness of transformation is / The freshness of a world. It is our own, / It is ourselves, the freshness of ourselves."

Less freshly, more obscurely, the tradition survived as part of that body of occult and semioccult lore, so attractive to men of imagination who distrusted science, which flourished in the nineteenth century and fed the fancies of the *fin de siècle*. It frequently happens that the myths of renovation and decadence are strong at the ends of centuries ("centurial mysticism" as Henri Focillon called it).[26] Other apocalyptic traditions contributed to the strange mood of the time—astrological, hermetic, founded in comparative religion or offbeat liturgical research or even the bogus medicine of Nordau's *Degeneration*. But there was to be a new age; the time was a time of transition; and the prevailing literary sect of Symbolists had as its hero the poet Mallarmé, who said that the whole world exists to culminate in a Book *(pour aboutir à un livre)*.[27] This is the book of the new order, the Everlasting Gospel of the Modern.

Like almost everybody else, "modernist" authors are likely to have had some instruction in or early acquaintance with the biblical apocalypses. Beyond that, they are more likely than most to have encountered interpretative apocalypse, and to have observed its various effects on literature. The great romantics, fathers of the Modern, showed how the fervent desire for apocalypse, disappointed in the course of history, might be internalized, so that revelation and renovation become functions of the individual imagination.[28] Between them and the moderns there runs also that tradition of antipositivism so congenial to many literary minds. Science was changing the map of world history; a simple beginning and decisive end looked less and less a matter of fact as geology and evolutionary biology lengthened the epochs of the earth; and the apocalyptic arithmetic and predictive allegory of the interpretative tradition withered as fundamentalist conviction weakened in educated men and women. But as all students of the prehistory of the modern are aware, there was, among artists, a backlash against that new rationalism. The scientists were dividing the mind and the sensibility; as Blake cursed Newton for ruining England by destroying the imagination, so Yeats, echoing him, banned Huxley and Darwin. To such minds, magic, mystery, pseudoscience, apocalypse, afforded considerable occult satisfaction; if that satisfaction was called Decadent, then the artist accepted the insult as a mark of honor. But the real Decadence, he thought, was the work of the men who imposed on the world what Blake called "single vision." And he gloried in the possession of forms of knowledge incompatible with those prevailing in a world from which he, to his joy and pain, was alienated.

When the learned divide, and elect conflicting modes of understanding the world, the dissenter who has abandoned the common sense of his peers may find himself (often gratifyingly) closer to traditions that have continued among the uneducated. If this was true of Freud when, despite his veneration for the criteria of the physical sciences, he differed from his colleagues on the meaning of dreams, how much more will it apply to artists, who, in sophisticated reaction from the poetry-destroying styles and opinions of contemporary science, actively seek to share the primitive wisdom of the people! In matters apocalyptic, they will find themselves more in sympathy with the naive enthusiast than with the rational professor of theology. Consequently we find among writers essential to our notion of the Modern, expressions of belief which link them more closely to popular millenarian beliefs than to the official wisdom of their time; and we could count among the forebears and congeners of the modern many popular sects, some dead of the failure of their prophets, like the Millerites and the Southcottians, some flourishing as institutions, like the Mormons and Seventh-Day Adventists. The raw literalism of modern Californians who daily expect the Rapture as a fulfillment of Paul's prophecy in I Thessalonians 4:7 has much more in common with D. H. Lawrence than might have been expected.

The basis of this measure of conformity is obvious enough. The artist shares with the proletarian sect a conviction that he exists at the end of an epoch, in a time of transition, on a ridge of history from which the contours of the whole are visible. That vision of the design of history, of the outcome of the great narrative plot, cannot be an innocent vision; it must be influenced by the existing schemata. Just so, at their moments of crisis, the Cargo believers reshaped to their own ends the fundamentalist teaching of the missionaries; just so the *profetae* of Norman Cohn's book led the faithful to the conquest of astonished cities, and Thomas Müntzer, touched like other radicals by the revolutionary implications of Joachim's Third Estate, brought his peasant following to the disaster of Frankenhausen.[29] But the disasters of artists are less likely to be military, just as their successes are less likely to found institutions. They may, on occasion, speak as prophets, advocate political action, lay down rules for the governance of the Third State or for dealing with the emergency of Transition; but we are less likely to attend to these practical provisions and recommendations—written, as Milton put it, with the left hand—than to the works they and we agree to assign to the right-handed category of art. It is among the products of the right hand that we should seek the book, the modern equivalent of the Everlasting Gospel of the new order.

So far as I am aware, no twentieth-century writer has so fully accepted and expounded a Joachimite version of apocalyptic thought as D. H. Lawrence. Born in 1886, he was just the right age to feel the apocalypticism of the *fin de siècle* in its most characteristic form. His generation was perhaps exceptionally conscious of itself as a historically privileged group, living, as Ernst Fischer said, "in the abyss between two times."[30] In revolt against the mannered Decadence of the previous generation, they passionately sought renovation and welcomed the purgative experience that must precede it. The war of 1914–18 provided that experience, constituted the terrible transition. Some who survived it brought their dedication, their commitment to a new age, into politics, often into

fascism. Born at the turn of the times, they did not forget the old apocalyptic themes: the Emperor, the Eastern hordes, the stumbling block of
the Jews.[31] Others, working with the right hand, remembered the Gospel, always yet to be written.

Lawrence's intellectual audacity is very striking. Though of working-
class origin, he quickly achieved a social position as near as possible
classless, and was on easy terms with the intellectual and even the political leaders of his society. But although he shows signs of being, perhaps
against his will, somewhat gratified by such acquaintance, he used his
freedom to think confidently along lines that had, from early youth, been
open to a man of his formation, but were always closed to such superb
products of upper-class educational arrangements for getting the best out
of the best as Russell and Keynes. There seem not to have been any kinds
of thought that Lawrence ruled out as too fanciful or too absurd or too
déclassé to bother with. And he was well aware that the religion of his
youth continued to affect him, not least the apocalyptic strain of it, the
evangelical hymns and sermons. His interest in Revelation began when
he was a small boy.[32] Somehow it blended with the "cranky" utopianism of
early British socialism and with the gentle bohemianism of his early adult
years, which included for a time an interest in the apocalypse of Wagner's
Ring cycle, then enjoying its first period of fanatical adulation among the
educated British. And indeed it is characteristic of Lawrence that he
could read the books and assimilate the prejudices of the society he had
joined without abandoning the intellectual luggage he had brought with
him. With a touch of absurdity he makes Aaron, in *Aaron's Rod*, a flute-
playing collier who leaves the pit and at once joins the orchestra at Covent
Garden; yet he himself did something of the kind, penetrating English
intellectual life with educational equipment that would have struck many
people (as it did T. S. Eliot, for instance) as extremely amateurish, were it
not that they felt the prophetic power of its owner.

Strong tides of apocalyptic feeling were running in Europe, and they
affected the arts; it was an age of artistic sects, of manifestos for a new age
in painting, music, and poetry as well as in politics. In England the sense
of change, of transition, was less programmatic, and its manifestation in
the arts largely confined to the European-style movement led by Wyndham Lewis. Yet Lawrence brought to the intellectual life and the literature of the period an apocalypticism more naked, more literal than that of
any of his contemporaries. History obliged him; some kind of new age *was*
beginning, and for Lawrence as for so many others (though none expressed so powerful, indeed so hysterical, a sense of them) the Great War
represented the Terrors. The Joachimite pattern would be complete if
one could provide an Everlasting Gospel

Lawrence's thought took so strongly Joachimite a form that even he, with all his boldness and arrogance, saw that it invited a skeptical response; he was much given to undercutting his own literalism by calling himself "a great bosher" or the like, and affirming that the letter of apocalypse did not matter except as a vehicle of imaginative truth. But obviously, in some perfectly valid sense, he believed it all. Kandinsky seems to have held very similar views in a manner almost equally simple—that we are on the threshhold of a Third Age, epoch of the Holy Spirit, and that the new abstract painting announced—was the gospel of—this new age.[33] But Lawrence went beyond him, spoke more defiantly and with more detail; if the Gospel was the work of the right hand, the left could still make imperious prophetic demands, and elaborate detailed programs for the new world coming into being.

I have written elsewhere of Lawrence's preoccupation with apocalyptic "signs," for instance, the star that falls from heaven in *St. Mawr,* the Lamb and Flag of *The Rainbow* (which ends with the sign of the new covenant), the zeppelin among the Terrors of the "Nightmare" chapter of *Kangaroo;* and, with others, I have discussed the radical apocalyptic schemes of *Women in Love* and the intimate relation of *Lady Chatterley's Lover* to Lawrence's final thoughts on Revelation in the posthumous book *Apocalypse.*[34]

At the height of his apocalyptic fervor he even cast himself as Emperor: "I shall change the world for the next thousand years," he proclaimed.[35] He saw history in terms of the Joachimite transition, though he added his own coloring, representing the end of one state as death, and the rise of its successor, after the terrible interval, as rebirth—a strong infusion of Pauline theology, boldly dechristianized and boldly personalized. He believed, as *Apocalypse* most fully explains, that the canonical Revelation was itself a version (degenerate) of something that preceded it, a mystery religion enacting death and rebirth; and the interpretation of Joachim, which in turn overlaid the original Christian version, appealed to him as affording a more intelligible scheme of history. Joachim helped him, in Yeats's expression, to "hammer his thoughts into a unity."

Lawrence spoke of the epochs of Law and of Love, and the reconciliation of them in a third epoch of the Comforter, now approaching. The secular agent of this reconciliation was sometimes what he called Consummate Marriage (for he associated Law with women, Love with men; the present unhappy relations between the sexes, with women—as mothers—dominating, would end in the new age, to be succeeded by a tense union of separates). And sometimes it was Art, and specifically the novel.

The war was proof that we had reached the Great Pause of Revelation, and were experiencing the "ghastly sickness of dissolution." We were far gone in corruption, led by the Jews, who were particularly prone to female domination (followed quite closely by the English); but the flow of corruption and that of regeneration were reciprocal and contemporaneous, and except in his most frantically depressed moods Lawrence saw the first as proof of the presence or imminence of the second. So the war, anyway at first, gave some cause for hope. But the continuing and growing horror of it compelled a change of mood between *The Rainbow* and *Women in Love*. The precise apocalyptic expectation was disappointed; and in *Lady Chatterley's Lover* the "bad time" is still to come. *Women in Love* (a war novel, though it never mentions the war) was a "purely destructive" book. Sometimes Birkin's new world has no people in it, only animals, perhaps only grass (a despair mocked by Ursula, who often voices the skepticism Lawrence kept in reserve for his own opinions). Yet if there was a human future, it needed organizing. He would work, with Bertrand Russell, to "give a new Humanity its birth," or found a utopian community of elected brothers and sisters. The relation of the sexes would be transformed; there would be a leader demanding absolute obedience. Even in his schoolbook, *Movements in European History* (Joachim is its presiding genius), Lawrence tells the children that there will be "a great chosen figure . . . supreme over the will of the people." And as time went by the left-handed doctrines took a stronger and stronger hold over the work of the right hand; male dominance and the Leader in *Aaron's Rod*, a peculiar Australian fascism in *Kangaroo*; the adaptation of these and similar concerns to an invented mystery religion in *The Plumed Serpent*. The ideas were destroying the novels.

Lawrence knew well that this could happen; the novel was "the one bright book of life" only when it was not "subdued to a metaphysic"[36] though it must contain one. Metaphysic played the role of Law, fiction that of Love; the conflict between them was what must issue in the Third State of the Spirit, and the site of the conflict and the reconciliation was the novel. That *The Rainbow* and *Women in Love* really are books which do much more than merely talk about the change of the times, the new age with its transformed sexuality, and so forth, is the reason why most will accept that they are his greatest works. They proclaim and advise; but they also enact the reconciliation, they *are* manifestations of the Spirit, the Comforter. The characters do not achieve the new age, and *Women in Love* is deep in the flow of corruption; but the book, for all its destructiveness, is meant to show forth the new age, to be an image of its tensions and its beauty, the Gospel of the Third State.

Lawrence is very much of the tradition in that he assimilated to the apocalyptic schemata many new interpretations, but the old ones remained central to his imagination and controlled his view of world history and his hopes for the future. When his hopes were disappointed, as such hopes must be, he did what enthusiasts have always done; said that the changes, the Terrors, the new life, still lay in the future, that things, however intolerable, were still not bad enough to get better, that he had miscalculated. When prophecy fails, sects are either forgotten or become institutions. Lawrence has himself become an institution in the only way open to a writer: he is protected by the academies, allowed into the secular canon, expounded according to its exegetical rules and within the limits of its proper interests. It is a nice historical irony that certain aspects of his work, for all their enormous prominence, are hardly ever discussed; they are the apocalyptic aspects. Institutions do not find themselves easy with enthusiasm or with imminent ends. Nor do we care to think of a hero of modernism as less sagacious, less moderate and guarded, than ourselves. The most explicitly fundamentalist apocalyptist of them all, the author of book after book intended to be, rather than merely discuss, the new gospel, is everywhere read and taught; but not as an enthusiast or evangelist; and not as an ideological cousin of the Ranters and of Hitler.

Yeats, too, was heir to the apocalypticism of the Decadence, always sensitive to the trembling of the veil and awaiting the annunciation of some savage god. Behind him lay the occult tradition in which Joachim had found a place, and his early story "The Tables of the Law" demonstrates his acquaintance with the Three States. It also supposes that a copy of the original Everlasting Gospel has survived: "It has swept the commandments of the Father away . . . and displaced the commandments of the Son by the commandments of the Holy Spirit."[37] His historical and prophetic diagram and figures have something in common with Joachim's *figurae;* but Yeats's apocalypticism is at once more general, more colored by magical tradition, and more peculiar than that of Joachim, or indeed that of Lawrence, and it is cyclic instead of linear and progressive. Generally one might say that he was a transitionalist and, from aesthetic as well as magical conviction, a believer in the Book; to that extent he was Joachimite. But so, to some extent, were all the other artists who thought the times critical and saw themselves, in the midst of dismay and corruption, shaking off a past and preparing a new age. Their manifestos, Futurist, Vorticist, Surrealist, and so forth, prove it; and the archetypal modernist movement, Dada, is an equivalent in the arts of Ranterism. Among the ideas most often heard was the view that in the present unprecedented state of the world only the poet could find language for its complexity, and offer what men required to live well, now that religion and its testaments were obsolete. This is a view held by persons as disparate as Hofmannsthal and I. A. Richards.[38] Heidegger and Wallace Stevens, in their own ways, also treat poetry as gospel, though Stevens understood that its everlastingness depended upon its power to change.[39] Occasionally a poet might prefer an institutional view of the matter, as T. S. Eliot, acutely conscious of living in a time-between, accepted the direction of the Church of England, and thought of the present as a time to be patiently lived through, with some faith in renovation; though *The Waste Land,* with its Babylon and its Whore, its desolation and hooded hordes from the east, borrows the colors of apocalypse.

We might expect that in such a time (say, the first quarter of the present century) all versions of apocalypse would find a place to flourish; the "set," no one doubts, existed. We have seen that the Joachimite version had special appeal, and not only to artists—Jung came upon it with the same kind of interest shown long before by Lessing,[40] and the ideologues made careful use of it. But it was among the artists that the idea of the Everlasting Gospel flourished. The waning of orthodoxy, the long development of a view of art as the occult savior, gave the artists of this period a particularly poignant sense of their responsibilities at the time of transition, and at the very moment when the world was swamped as never before by artifacts and writings of no spiritual value, mere commodities and instruments of a despised social system, endowed their work with a special kind of sacredness, such that only the renewed world, to which it truly belonged, could understand it; or such that only a band of the elect could understand it.

Art was the gospel of the New; it announced the terrible sterility of the old order, its sexual debility and corruption, the collapse of its cities, its evil communications. Sometimes it offered formal imitations of these terminal conditions; but always with a sense that they would be replaced by something new, and that, however much the artist might also support programs of social action advocated by Maurras or Mussolini, arrayed in black or brown or blue shirts, dedicated to the reform of education or to eugenics, or to some other panacea, the agent and symbol of regeneration was the book, the work of art. That work would stand apart, outside the dirty flux of life and time—dead, as Wyndham Lewis insisted, or at any rate somehow transcending time, inhabitant of a transformed future and, in a manner proper to itself, eternal and, in its own way, a gospel.

In conclusion I should try to draw out some of the resemblances between apocalyptic and modernist thinking, and stress the affinity between the Everlasting Gospel and the sacred Book of the Modern.

If we consider the options open to the artist, we shall have to agree that although he may have no more chance than his remote cousins the millenarian enthusiasts of avoiding disappointment, he cannot hope to substitute for the certainty of an immediate apocalyptic transformation the less hectic satisfactions of institutionalization. He will rarely send out missionaries; there will be no group reinforcement because, as a rule, there is no group. The sects of modernism, especially perhaps the most obviously apocalyptic like Dada, tend to be extremely fissile and ephemeral; if, like Surrealism, they show signs of organization and stability, they may be tempted to merge with sects of a different sort, possessing programs more suitable to proselytizing, like the Communist Party. There are apocalyptic loners who see the danger of such accommodations; Antonin Artaud was briefly attracted by Surrealism, but left the movement out of dissatisfaction with its political optimism and went his own way.[41] Our society has ways of expressing its respect for such solitary and tragic enthusiasts, but it also has ways of cutting them down to size, and of reducing their gospel to a mere cultural interest. Artaud's new age has not dawned.

It is true that the Modern has been accommodated by and given institutional status in the universities (and that this occurred at about the time Modernism was losing its early force), but secondary, academic modernism also ends in disappointment, as Lionel Trilling memorably complained in his essay "On the Modern Element in Modern Literature."[42] At the present moment institutional modernism has taken a form that is especially hostile to older modernist assumptions about the Book, and about the artist as prophet. The "archaeology" of Michel Foucault, it must be allowed, has a certain Joachimite character; it sharply divides history into discontinuous epochs and supposes that the present moment is a moment of transition between two of them. But the epochs are not typologically related and they have no gospels (unless the hidden *episteme* is a gospel). Learning is not crystallized in a Book, but atomized and reconstituted in relation to its occult epochal source. The new epoch is expressly not utopian; it is what comes after Man. And, in the same philosophy, the Author is already dead. There are many modernisms, as there are many Cargo cults; the academic variety is a late one, and has little to do with the kinds of art and prophecy associated with the earlier and purer type, which was distinguished by its desperate confidence in the Book as unique, and the work of the unique Artist.

Lawrence believed that the varying conditions of the struggle between "tale" and "metaphysic" must make every true novel an absolutely new form, unlike that of any novel preceding it; he did not believe that there were ways of making novels that could be learned from, say Arnold Bennett. We, the institutional scholars, are usually ready to demonstrate the impossibility of such uniqueness (and Lawrence in fact did learn from Bennett), but nevertheless reserve our highest degree of respect for those works which seem to be brought in like the Everlasting Gospel, as if by another angel flying in the midst of heaven—as Lawrence himself saw Melville's *Moby-Dick*, with its unique plotting of the world and its evangelical proclamation of the death of the white consciousness. These unpredictable, unimaginable works of art—the prophecies of Melville, Proust, Joyce, Musil—are plots of, or against, the world and time.

Stories originally occurred in myth time. The strange variant of story called the novel took on the responsibility of representing the time of the real world, plotting it as apocalypse plotted history. At first it retained the old full ending of mythical narrative; but eventually that came to seem, in a world that continued to withhold endings, dishonest. Novels began to avoid the full close, and sometimes appeared simply to halt in the middle of the time sequence. (*The Rainbow* ends; *Women in Love*, and many later works of Lawrence, simply halt.) And other novels were founded on the difficult understanding that there are ends other than ends in time, ends which derive from a sense of formal completion. For example, those *anachronies* (to use Gérard Genette's expression for interruptions of ordinary chronological sequence[43]) which had been only expository devices needed for the recounting of more than one sequence of events, in the same temporal continuum, became instruments of form and diffused the sense of endings throughout whole works. Conrad's *Lord Jim* has many expository anachronies, but Jim dies on the last page and that is the act of completion; Conrad's *Under Western Eyes* might have ended with the death of Razumov, but it does not. Lily Briscoe's final brushstroke may be, chronologically, the last event to be described in *To the Lighthouse* but it produces an end other than that of a temporal sequence by conferring, for the first time, order and structure upon a canvas which is in itself an emblem of the book that contains it, a unique formalization of the world and time. The whole of *Le Voyeur* tries to disappear, swirling through the hole in the middle of it, the confusions between the words of the book and the events of the world at last totally confounded—all reality, such as it is, dealt with, disposed of, explained insofar as explanation is not false or absurd. Much might be learned from a comparison of Robbe-Grillet's novel with Conrad's *The Secret Agent*, half a century or so earlier; Conrad's novel also has a hole in the middle, during which the assault on time—the attempt to blow up Greenwich Observatory, the point from which arbitrary world-time is measured—takes place. Conrad's book has the confidence to fill up that hole; Robbe-Grillet's, the nihilistic confidence Conrad reserves for his anarchist professor at the end. For him the relation between fiction and the time of the world is quite illusory, and he destroys it; he belongs to a future Conrad prophesied but could not join, a future which might have no place for the book as gospel.

What we think of as truly Modern or Modernist is always relatively apocalyptic. Cézanne plotting against his world mountain, Kandinsky deserting appearances in favor of his abstract proclamations, the novelists with their unique plots against time and reality, all are apocalypticists and in their measure Joachimite. They honor the *transitus*, announce new orders, restructure the world, utter their once-only but Everlasting Gospels. In their own estrangement they are one-man sects, their books the modern equivalent of the scrolls at Qumran or of the "fiery flying roll" of the Ranters,[44] annunciations of a new order superseding the old law and the old book: every artist his own gospel. When we have some notion of the scope and terror of their efforts, we venerate such artists, considering their courage, inquiring into their heroic illnesses, seeing in them images of ourselves extended to a heroic scale; for in an age when every apocalypse, however trivial, must be personal, when every man's suffering and death are finally his own business only, all ends are insignificant except when transformed by the huge effort of art.

We are now accustomed to thinking of Modernism as a historical period, like Romanticism. That may account for the fact that the cult of the book as gospel, associated in the literature of the period with the conviction that a great historical change was imminent, is no longer of much interest, at any rate to the cultivated. The great war and its aftermath divided the times. Insofar as the old doctrines took political forms, for example, in Communism—*The Communist Manifesto* is certainly a millenarian document, a gospel for a crisis, even perhaps a Joachimite book—one might expect to find, in the literature of the thirties, some form of the old cult. And, to give but one instance, one can find it in the early Auden over and over again, especially in such poems as the Prologue to *Look, Stranger!* (written in 1932), "Out on the lawn I lie in bed" (1933), and, above all, *Spain* (1937). But Auden was soon to disown or rewrite these poems. His sense that the world-historical Day was upon him gave way to a conviction that the true crisis-event was the Incarnation; the anguish of the world became a personal anxiety, a religious and not a political or an aesthetic issue. It now seemed presumptuous for a poet to aspire to "hold in a single thought reality and justice." The oracular, the magniloquent, are exorcised; at one point Auden went so far as to declare that a Christian ought to write only in prose. Sagacious, witty, skillful as ever, he was through with poetry as the evangel of the transition and the new age.

The war of 1939–45 qualified at least as well as the earlier one for the description "apocalyptic"; the Last Days might not be very different. But the English school of "Apocalypse" achieved little more than a hectic revival of the most offensive habits of Romanticism; and the New Age that was to follow it was largely the matter of propaganda posters. For the time being, the apocalyptic, certainly in Western literature, is out of fashion, and the Gospel is not being written. Meanwhile the institutions which took over the Modernists expounded them only as a preparation for their present task of demythologization and deconstruction. Popular fundamentalist apocalypticism thrives,[45] but the educated, the heirs of Joachim of Fiore and his heirs, have given it up. Deconstructors write no gospels. But it is hard to believe there will never be another.

NOTES

1. An example of rigorous definition: "Apocalypse is a genre of revelatory literature with a narrative framework, in which a revelation is mediated by an otherworldly being to a human recipient, disclosing a transcendental reality which is both temporal, insofar as it envisages eschatological salvation, and spatial insofar as it involves another, supernatural world." John J. Collins, "Apocalypse, the Morphology of a Genre" *Semeia* 14 [1979], 9.

2. Peter Lawrence, *Road Belong Cargo* (Manchester: University Press, 1964). And see Peter Worsley, *The Trumpet Shall Sound: A Study of "Cargo" Cults in Melanesia* (London: MacGibbon & Kee, 1957).

3. Norman Cohn, *The Pursuit of the Millennium* (London: Secker & Warburg, 1957); Lawrence, *Road Belong Cargo*, p. 77.

4. John G. Gager, *Kingdom and Community: The Social World of Early Christianity* (Englewood Cliffs, N.J.: Prentice-Hall, 1975), p. 35.

5. Leon Festinger, Henry W. Riecken, and Stanley Schachter, *When Prophecy Fails* (Minneapolis: University of Minnesota Press, 1956).

6. Bryan R. Wilson, *Magic and the Millennium* (London: Heinemann, 1973; London: Paladin, 1975), p. 494.

7. Robert Mapes Anderson, *Vision of the Disinherited: The Making of American Pentecostalism* (New York: Oxford University Press, 1979), pp. 194, 231.

8. J. A. T. Robinson, *Redating the New Testament* (London: SCM Press, 1976), p. 235.

9. See Bernard McGinn, *Visions of the End: Apocalyptic Traditions in the Middle Ages* (New York: Columbia University Press, 1979); and Bernard McGinn, trans., *Apocalyptic Spirituality* (London: SPCK, 1980). For Alexander, see Andrew R. Anderson, *Alexander's Gate, Gog and Magog and the Inclosed Nations* (Cambridge, Mass.: Medieval Academy of America Publications, 1932); and George Carey, *The Medieval Alexander* (1956; Cambridge: Cambridge University Press, 1967). For the whole tradition as influenced by Joachim of Fiore, see Marjorie Reeves, *Joachim of Fiore and the Prophetic Future* (London: SPCK, 1976; New York: Harper & Row, 1977).

10. V. M. Lagorio, "The Apocalyptic Mode in the Vulgate Cycle of the Arthurian Romances," *Philological Quarterly* 57 (1958), 1–22. Lagorio argues that the Arthurian world has an apocalyptic structure. Elements include an ending in the Last Days, pseudonymous revelations, esoteric prophecies, the division of history into world ages, a Last World Emperor, and an Antichrist (Mordred, King Arthur's treacherous nephew). Sir Thomas Malory has Arthur crowned as Holy Roman Emperor by the Pope. For other medieval literary examples of apocalyptic

writing, see Morton W. Bloomfield, *"Piers Plowman* as a Fourteenth-Century Apocalypse," in *Interpretations of Piers Plowman,* ed. Edward Vasta (Boston: D. C. Heath, 1968), pp. 348–52. One literary allusion of some interest occurs in the seventeenth century in Andrew Marvell's "To His Coy Mistress." The lover, had he world enough and time, would be willing to spend ages wooing his mistress; he would carry on till the conversion of the Jews (a signal for the end of time). But since he cannot wait so long, he urges her to join him in anticipating time's end; let them tear their pleasures "with rough strife/ Thorough the iron gates of life." These gates puzzle commentators, but they are probably the iron gates supposed to have been built by Alexander to confine the Scythians, the tribes of Gog and Magog (Revelation 20:1–7) behind the Urals. At the coming of Antichrist, these tribes were to break through the gate and descend on civilization. If the lovers cannot, like Joshua, make time stop, at least they can hasten its end (and shorten their own waiting time). Marvell's glancing allusion shows how available such information must have been. His was an age of intense apocalypticism; Oliver Cromwell readmitted the Jews to England in order to speed the end, and the career of the Jewish Messianist Sabbatai Zvi, across the narrow seas, was observed with keen interest.

11. For example, by Frank E. Manuel, *Shapes of Philosophical History* (London: Allen & Unwin, 1965), and by Ernst Käsemann, ("it was apocalyptic which first made historical thinking possible within Christendom"—quoted by Klaus Koch, *The Rediscovery of Apocalyptic,* translated from the German *Ratlos von der Apokalyptik* [1970] by Margaret Kohl [London: SCM Press, 1972], p. 76).

12. Frank E. Manuel and Fritzie P. Manuel, *Utopian Thought in the Western World* (Cambridge, Mass.: Harvard University Press, 1979), p. 55.

13. Reeves, *Joachim of Fiore and the Prophetic Future,* pp. 27–28.

14. See the section on Savonarola in McGinn, *Visions of the End;* also see Frances Yates, *The Rosicrucian Enlightenment* (London: Routledge & Kegan Paul, 1972; Boulder, Colo.: Shambhala Publications, 1978), p. 35; and Ernst Kantorowicz, "Oriens Augusti-Lever du Roi," *Dumbarton Oaks Papers* 17 (1963), 119–77.

15. E. J. Hobsbawm, *Primitive Rebels* (Manchester: Manchester University Press, 1959).

16. See J. S. Preuss, *From Shadow to Promise* (Cambridge, Mass.: Harvard University Press, 1969), p. 57 ff.

17. Manuel and Manuel, *Utopian Thought in the Western World,* pp. 186–89.

18. Keith Thomas, *Religion and the Decline of Magic* (London: Weidenfeld & Nicolson, 1971; London: Peregrine Books, 1978), p. 158 ff.; and Christopher Hill, *The World Turned Upside Down* (London: Temple Smith, 1972).

19. Hill, *The World Turned Upside Down,* pp. 118, 210.

20. A. L. Morton, *The Everlasting Gospel* (London: Lawrence & Wishart, 1958).

21. E. P. Thompson, *The Making of the English Working Class* (London: Victor Gollancz, 1963; London: Penguin Books, 1968), p. 52.

22. Christopher Hill, *Milton and the English Revolution* (New York: Viking Press, 1977).

23. Thompson, *The Making of the English Working Class;* J. F. C. Harrison, *The Second Coming: Popular Millenarianism 1780–1850* (London: Routledge & Kegan Paul, 1979).

24. Reeves, *Joachim of Fiore and the Prophetic Future;* Manuel, *Shapes of Philosophical History,* chap. 2. According to the Manuels (*Utopian Thought in the Western World,* p. 613), it was Saint-Simon who first gave a dialectic character to the triad. See also p. 722 on Comte and 1848, and p. 752 on Sorel's apocalyptic General Strike.

25. Ralph Waldo Emerson, "The Divinity School Address, delivered before the Senior Class in Divinity College, Cambridge, Sunday evening, July 15, 1838," in Frederic I. Carpenter, *Ralph Waldo Emerson: Representative Selections, with Introduction, Bibliography, and Notes* (New York: American Book Company, 1934), p. 88.

26. Henri Focillon, *The Year 1000,* trans. Fred D. Wieck (New York: Harper & Row, 1971).

27. Stéphane Mallarmé, "Le Livre, instrument spirituel," *Oeuvres Complètes* (Paris: Éditions Gallimard, 1956), p. 378.

28. M. H. Abrams, *Natural Supernaturalism* (New York: W. W. Norton Company, 1973).

29. Manuel and Manuel, *Utopian Thought in the Western World,* pp. 196–99.

30. Quoted in Robert E. Wohl, *The Generation of 1914* (London: Weidenfeld & Nicolson, 1979), p. 229.

31. Wohl, *The Generation of 1914.* For the "generationalist" aspect of Joachimitism, see M. W. Bloomfield, "Joachim of Flora: A Critical Survey of His Canon, Teachings, Sources, Biography, and Influence" *Traditio* 12 (1957), 249–309.

32. D. H. Lawrence, *Apocalypse* (1966; New York: Viking Press, 1977), p. 3 ff.

33. Vasily Kandinsky, *Essays über Kunst und Künstler,* ed. M. Bill (Bern-Bümpliz: Benteli-Verlag, 1963).

34. Frank Kermode, "D. H. Lawrence and the Apocalyptic Types," *Modern Essays* (London: Fontana, 1970), pp. 153–81; Frank Kermode, *D. H. Lawrence* (New York: Viking Press, 1973).

35. Edward H. Nehls, *D. H. Lawrence: A Composite Biography,* 3 vols. (Madison: University of Wisconsin Press, 1957–59), vol. 1, p. 162.

36. Harry T. Moore, ed., *Collected Letters of D. H. Lawrence,* 2 vols. (New York: Viking Press, 1962), vol. 1, p. 204.

37. W. B. Yeats, "The Tables of the Law," *Mythologies* (London: Macmillan, 1959), pp. 293–307, cited by Reeves, *Joachim of Fiore and the Prophetic Future,* p. 171.

38. See Carl E. Schorske, *Fin-de-Siècle Vienna* (1979; London: Weidenfeld & Nicolson, 1980), p. 317; I. A. Richards, *Science and Poetry* (1926; 1935; New York: W. W. Norton & Co., 1970).

39. Heidegger's essays on Hölderlin are translated in Martin Heidegger, *Poetry, Language, Thought,* trans. Albert Hofstadter (New York: Harper & Row, 1975), and in Werner Brock, *Existence and Being* (New York: Henry Regnery Co., 1949).

106   FRANK KERMODE

40. Reeves, *Joachim of Fiore and the Prophetic Future*, pp. 167–69, 173–74.

41. See Susan Sontag, "Antonin Artaud," in *Under the Sign of Saturn* (New York: Farrar, Straus & Giroux, 1980).

42. Lionel Trilling, "On the Teaching of Modern Literature," in *Beyond Culture: Essays on Literature and Learning* (1965; London: Secker & Warburg, 1966), pp. 3–30.

43. Gérard Genette, *Narrative Discourse: An Essay in Method*, translated from *Figures* III (Paris: Éditions du Seuil, 1972) by Jane E. Lewin (Ithaca, N.Y.: Cornell University Press, 1980), p. 40.

44. For Abiezer Coppe's *Fiery, flying roll*, a Ranter publication of 1649, see Hill, *The World Turned Upside Down*, p. 170.

45. Hal Lindsey, *The Late Great Planet Earth*, an extremely fundamentalist work published in 1970, had by 1977 sold over 8 million copies (Grand Rapids, Mich.: Zondervan Publishing House, 1976). See Patrick Henry, *New Directions in New Testament Study* (Philadelphia: Westminster Press, 1979), p. 242 ff.

PART II

6

TECHNOLOGY-RELATED CATASTROPHES: MYTH AND REALITY

Harvey Brooks

THE NEXT TWENTY-FIVE TO FIFTY YEARS REPRESENT A critical transition in the evolution of human societies on earth. The world is at some sort of turning point—a transition from which we either descend toward disaster of unprecedented magnitude or move forward to a new plateau of material and social well-being. For perhaps the first time in human history, mankind has the technical tools with which poverty and deprivation could in principle be eliminated entirely, yet at the same time man's ability to manipulate nature contains the seeds of possible disasters without historical precedent. This chapter seeks to examine and assess some of these potentials for disaster that arise directly or indirectly out of man's technical prowess.

To do this we must distinguish among three levels of technology-related catastrophe: disasters which threaten the whole fabric of civilization, or even of human existence itself; those which threaten a severe and rapid regression from the material and social standards of well-being we have achieved already; and those which may result only in large localized losses in human life or well-being but do not threaten the survival of civilized society as a whole. Failure to distinguish among these three levels has often been a source of confusion in public discussions about the fate of mankind.

Each of the three types of catastrophe may in turn be subdivided into three categories according to the character of the threat: traumatic events which impact the physical environment of large numbers of people within a short time; creeping crises which slowly erode man's relationship with nature and the physical world so that large numbers of people may be adversely affected cumulatively and severely over time periods possibly extending for generations; and social crises which lead to the deterioration of human relations, rather than, as in the first instance, the destruction of man's physical surroundings.

Obviously these three subcategories—traumatic events, creeping crises, and social crises—can be closely interrelated. The deterioration of man's physical environment may be the result primarily of social decay which prevents the timely deployment of available technical means that could preserve and enhance his environment without sacrifice to his material standards. Conversely, competition among different human groups for dwindling resources could be the trigger for social disintegration or expanding conflict that could be the source of immediate disaster. Indeed, social and environmental deterioration could result in scarcity of resources, competition for which could increase the level of social conflict and thus further erode availability of and access to resources. Or the competition to exploit a deteriorating physical environment could trigger conflict on a scale that could truly wipe out civilization in a short time.

Despite these potential interactions, the distinctions outlined above are still useful to keep in mind. For example, it is important to understand whether we are faced with an imminent actual scarcity of resources needed to sustain our material civilization for the next few decades, or whether our problem lies in our inability to organize human relations in such a way as to develop and exploit the resources that we require. Similarly, it is important to understand the degree to which it is possible to meet our material aspirations while preserving the more intangible social and political values which alone may make the material standards humanly satisfying. These are complicated questions, and we can only hint at possible answers in most cases, although we shall attempt to provide our own considered judgments.

Our discussion deals first with catastrophe in terms of the character of the threat—traumatic events, creeping crises, and social crises—and under each of these we shall try to analyze selected examples of suggested catastrophes and indicate the extent of their possible or likely human impact. In this last connection we can then divide the impacts into the three categories of civilization-threatening catastrophe, severe and universal welfare regression, or localized disasters. In the end we shall conclude that thermonuclear war dominates other events both in terms of the level of its impact and the probability of its occurrence. Indeed, the various creeping and social crises that we shall also consider must be viewed primarily not in terms of their direct effects, but rather in terms of their influence on the future development of conflicts that could ultimately eventuate in the accidental or intentional use of nuclear weapons.

Thermonuclear Conflict

The overwhelming threat from modern technology that dwarfs all others is the threat of large-scale thermonuclear conflict. While it is doubtful whether even the largest nuclear exchange possible with current weapons stockpiles would wipe out all human life on earth, or completely destroy the world ecosystem, the face of the earth would be so altered that it is improbable that any form of civilized society would survive. Although it is possible to make reasonably good estimates of the immediate effects of a nuclear exchange by assuming various plausible targeting scenarios, it is much more difficult to imagine the indirect effects of the destruction of most of the infrastructure of civilized society. For example, it is virtually certain that any significant thermonuclear exchange would totally paralyze the capacity of the medical system to alleviate either immediate medical problems or subsequent starvation, disease, and injury.[1] Similarly, while it is possible to estimate long-range health and ecological effects in areas distant from those targeted in the nuclear exchange, the indirect human psychology, physiology, and behavior in the face of death and destruction of this magnitude in the targeted areas can only be speculated about.[2] An estimate made in 1963 suggests that more than 2,000 megatons of nuclear weapons reaching nonmilitary targets in the United States would raise "insuperable" obstacles to the recovery of American society.[3] With 10,000 megatons available on both sides, it seems almost certain that at least 2,000 megatons would fall on nonmilitary targets. Lesser exchanges might leave viable societies, but how leaders would react after even this degree of destruction is completely problematic. It seems at least likely that, once begun, any nuclear exchange would be difficult to contain until most of the weapons on both sides had been expended. Nor could civil defense, even if politically feasible in a democracy, provide much protection for the population. Civil defense would represent a reasonable strategy only for nontargeted countries, such as Sweden or Switzerland, whose viability following an attack on neighboring countries could be considerably enhanced by a shelter program. While a shelter program that included blast shelters could improve survival even in targeted countries, it is doubtful whether the improvements in immediate survival would make much difference to the longer-term social disintegration which would follow a thermonuclear attack in or near the targeted areas due to the destruction of so much of the societal infrastructure.

Recently new estimates of the physical consequences of major nuclear exchanges have been published which suggest that they could be considerably more severe than those estimated during the 1960s and 1970s.[4] The new severity arises from a reestimate of climatic effects resulting from the blackout of solar radiation by dust and smoke as well as the suppression of photosynthesis. The same climatic effects also result in increased exchange of air between the Northern and Southern Hemispheres and hence in considerably greater severity of radioactive fallout in the Southern Hemisphere than estimated earlier. These findings are still rather preliminary and have not been tested by wide scientific criticism to the degree that would be necessary to consider them as definitive. However, in my opinion, these calculations probably do not alter any of the earlier conclusions as to the catastrophic nature of a nuclear exchange. Their only policy significance lies in the fact that some decisionmakers may be more persuaded by calculable physical effects than by the arguments related to social disintegration following a nuclear attack mentioned in the preceding paragraphs. Thus while the new estimates may not much alter the objective reality, they may have a profound effect on the perception of this reality by key decisionmakers and the public. For the purposes of the present discussion they merely reinforce the conclusion that nuclear war is a catastrophe beside which all other doomsday predictions are trivial.

So devastating is even the most limited nuclear war, its effects would far outweigh in importance any direct adverse effects induced by other social or technological developments. For example, if it could be shown that the rapid worldwide deployment of fission breeder reactors would reduce the probability of nuclear wars caused by conflict over energy resources, breeders would be a good bargain even if they were many times less safe than experts believe them to be. Unfortunately, whether abundant nuclear energy would increase or decrease the chance of nuclear war is an issue of political prediction rather than technology, and so almost impossible to resolve by expert analysis.[5] In fact, one's emotional disposition for or against nuclear energy appears to determine one's political expectations about the effects of nuclear power on the probability of nuclear war, rather than the more logical converse.[6]

As a consequence of such dominance of nuclear war over other possible catastrophes, any discussion of other technology-related threats to the survival of humanity or civilization has an aspect of rearranging deck chairs on the *Titanic*. In reality, such other threats ought to be analyzed not in their own terms but in relation to their influence on the probability of conflicts which could ultimately escalate into a nuclear exchange. Unfortunately, nuclear war and its sequelae are so "unthinkable," and the effects of other technical and political events on its likelihood so speculative, that projections of possible world futures tacitly neglect this possibility. Rather we tend to make "surprise-free" extrapolations based on existing economic and technical trends, leaving more probable but less predictable traumatic events out of consideration. This might be justified if there were no interaction between our smooth extrapolated trends and the probability of nuclear war, but this is almost certainly not the case. For example, the evolution of the world economy and the level of competition it generates for resources, especially energy, will strongly influence the probability of outbreak of conflicts potentially leading to use of nuclear weapons. Nevertheless, because almost anything connected with nuclear war is so speculative, most of the remaining sections of this chapter will tend to sweep it under the rug; if this were not done, there would be little more to say, and we could stop at this point.

Civilian Nuclear Power

Probably no potential disaster has occupied as much public attention and expert analysis as civilian nuclear power. Concerns have ranged from the effects of reactor accidents through the difficulties of radioactive waste disposal to the possible relation between a worldwide nuclear power industry and the acquisition of nuclear weapons by terrorists or "irresponsible" national leaders. In the view of most experts, this last problem—nuclear proliferation—is probably the most serious and real but also the least possible to deal with "scientifically." Its seriousness, however, arises less from its direct impact than from its ability to trigger a chain of political developments culminating in nuclear conflict. The prevention of the spread of nuclear weapons is basically a political and institutional problem, not a technical one, and there is very little that can be agreed upon in the way of purely technical measures to reduce the threat. For example, the elaborate international technical study initiated by the U.S. government under the Carter administration, known as the International Fuel Cycle Evaluation (INFCE), concluded that there were no promising "technical fixes" which would make civilian nuclear power less susceptible to the hazards of proliferation;[7] even the abandonment of nuclear power, were it possible on a worldwide basis, would not close off other cheaper and easier routes to a nuclear weapons capability for a nation or political faction sufficiently intent on achieving it. This is a conclusion with which most people who have thought about the problem agree.

One of the greatest fears associated with the proliferation problem is that security measures required to prevent the theft or diversion of fissionable materials, or the sabotage of nuclear reactors, would lead to the erosion of civil liberties and the subversion of democratic safeguards.[8] Indeed, this may be the real, and perhaps most justifiable, reason underlying much of the political opposition to nuclear power and the close emotional kinship between the antinuclear demonstrations of the 1970s and the antiwar and civil rights movements of the 1960s. The extent of the threat to civil liberties is difficult to assess because it is so closely related to public perception of the dangers of theft or sabotage. A few well-publicized incidents might cause a panic leading to draconian security measures. Yet, objectively, the number of people who would have to be subject to security measures is far smaller than the number who are affected by the measures used to deter the hijacking of commercial aircraft. The difference would be that if actual theft of fissionable material were suspected, security measures might be extended to innocent bystanders in contrast to aircraft passengers who, in principle, have a choice. On the other hand, many people believe that the existence of widely dispersed nuclear weapons, albeit under the control of the superpowers, is a bigger danger than the existence of a reasonably well-monitored commercial trade in reactor plutonium, since the probability of weapons being stolen or hijacked may exceed that of the theft of plutonium and fabrication into weapons.

It may well be that the most serious threat to society represented by nuclear power would be the political reaction to a nuclear accident. From the standpoint of radioactive hazards, both actual and potential, the accident at Three Mile Island in 1979 was very minor, yet the political and economic impact worldwide was enormous and came as a considerable surprise to most people who had been thinking about or planning for reactor accidents. In the case of an accident that actually caused injury or death to a few dozen people, the social reaction could be overwhelming, even resulting in many people being injured or killed by panic, and almost certainly resulting in extensive shutdown of operating reactors. If the percentage of electric power generated in nuclear plants worldwide increases as now projected, the disruption that would result from a severe political and psychological reaction to an accident, even one not much worse than Three Mile Island, might approach the dimensions of a disaster, with shutdown of vital services and severe trauma to the political process. The political repercussions would probably be much greater in the industrial world than elsewhere, however. The sudden energy shortages that might develop could precipitate competition for alternate energy resources that would generate new world tensions.

The area of nuclear technology that arouses the most public apprehension is probably that of high-level waste disposal, and yet this is a problem that rates as rather minor in the thinking and planning of most nuclear experts. To the public, ionizing radiation is mysterious and impalpable, and there is little appreciation of the actual kinds of scenarios that might accompany malfunctioning of waste management systems. The failure of waste disposal systems is, at worst, a very gradual process that leaves time and scope for deliberate countermeasures; the radiation exposures that can be experienced would be usually a small fraction of background radiation levels, and under the worst imaginable circumstances only a small multiple of background, less than the exposures permitted to radiation workers. The most likely contingency—contamination of groundwater connected to water supplies—might cause widespread inconvenience for a long time, but would not be life threatening. The worst threat might occur to some future society unfamiliar with radiation and less technically sophisticated than ours; but such a regressed society would probably be subject to many other environmental threats much more serious than a slight enhancement of natural background radiation.[9]

Another potential disaster connected with widespread use of nuclear power would be the spread of radioactivity arising from conventional weapons attacks aimed at nuclear power installations or nuclear fuel cycle facilities such as chemical processing plants. This possibility has received increased discussion since the Israeli air attack on the Iraqi research reactor.[10] Because of the heavy shielding required for nuclear facilities, they are probably intrinsically less vulnerable than other industrial installations. Thus a serious extra hazard is likely to be presented only in case of a deliberate selective attack against reactor facilities, rather than an accidental attack that was part of a more extensive raid. The radioactivity hazards associated with large-scale conventional warfare between nations with sophisticated weapons and numerous nuclear power facilities have not received as much attention or analysis as other civilian nuclear hazards, although they may represent a more probable social threat than most of the accident scenarios analyzed in great detail in connection with nuclear power. However, it appears that the loss of life from this cause would probably not be large compared with the loss of life from the war itself, although there might be more lingering aftereffects, such as contaminated areas and delayed cancers in the surrounding population.

Direct nuclear attacks aimed specifically at nuclear reactors and fuel cycle facilities could be much more serious disasters. The amount of radioactivity dispersed as a result of a direct hit could be much larger than that caused by fallout from the weapon itself. On the other hand, unless the nuclear attack were selectively concentrated on nuclear facilities, it seems probable that the additional loss of life from this cause would be small compared with the loss of life from the nuclear war itself. It would thus not seem sensible to forgo the use of civilian nuclear power for this reason alone.

Thus, except for the triggering of a general nuclear war by proliferation or diversion of fissionable material, and possibly the dispersion of radioactivity from deliberate conventional attacks in wartime on nuclear installations, nuclear power by itself does not represent even a remote threat to the survival of civilizations. It does not lend itself to any doomsday scenario, but should be considered only in its relation to the possibility of nuclear war. The political problem of management of civilian nuclear power in a manner acceptable to democratic societies presents a far more difficult problem than any objective threat it presents to human health or safety.

Natural Disasters

Natural disasters are technology related because their effects depend on the distribution of populations and levels of technology available. Higher population concentrations mean that natural hazards such as earthquakes, hurricanes, or floods could affect many more people than in the past. However, the loss of life in industrialized countries from storms and floods has declined dramatically since the beginning of the century because of better warning and communications systems, sturdier structures, and greater technological capacity to organize relief and rescue measures— using helicopters, for example. On the other hand, the value of real property losses from natural disasters has steadily increased. This does not imply we could not do much better; for example, the repeated resettlement of floodplains results in unnecessary hazards to people. Improper management of watersheds and wetlands has increased the severity and frequency of floods, especially in heavily populated areas. Nevertheless, the basic trend is unmistakably toward reduced hazard to life and limb from severe storms.

The situation for earthquakes is harder to assess, since their occurrence in highly industrialized areas has been so infrequent. A major earthquake in the Los Angeles basin would undoubtedly result in great loss of life and enormous property damage, not to mention traumatic political repercussions. Improvements in structures for earthquake resistance have been made, but probably have not kept up with the threat, and seem unlikely to because of the infrequency and uncertain location of the events. Facilities such as gas and oil pipelines or hydroelectric dams are not fully designed against earthquakes and could cause serious floods or fires with large loss of life. Great fear has also been expressed with regard to nuclear reactors and associated spent-fuel storage facilities, although probably more care has been devoted to earthquake-proof design of nuclear reactors than for any other type of industrial or commercial facility. Indeed, some analysts have suggested that in a major earthquake in an industrialized area, nuclear power may be the only thing still operational. Much less attention has been given to earthquake-proofing of oil and natural gas storage facilities or dams.

In fact, as a general matter, much less attention has been given to the analysis of major accident possibilities for nonnuclear industrial and energy installations than for nuclear power. This may be partly due to the fact that what is a low enough probability to be ignored in the case of a nonnuclear installation is considered worthy of attention when ionizing radiation is involved. Most attention to nonnuclear accidents has been focused on the type of accident involving transportation or storage of liquified natural gas, particularly the siting of such facilities close to populated areas. Here the possibilities seem comparable to or more severe than those associated with nuclear power, at least in terms of the number of lives affected. Similarly, major fires in oil tank farms could not only be very destructive but could produce severe air pollution episodes over a large area, possibly with subsequent delayed deaths. Nevertheless, the scale of all these accidents is such that, while they may be socially and politically very traumatic, they are far from threatening whole communities or whole societies. Nor under present circumstances are they likely to produce a political reaction that would be as severe as that attending a comparably destructive accident involving radiation. Perhaps the largest threat to human life comes from the combination of large industrial installations with natural disasters, the prime example being dams in seismic areas. Estimates for at least one large dam in the western United States have identified circumstances in which the number of lives lost would run to a quarter million; these would be immediate deaths, and the numbers would be comparable to the largest estimates made for nuclear reactor accidents. (However, in the latter case most of the deaths would be delayed cancers. There is room for a large difference of opinion as to whether a large number of delayed deaths, representing only a small statistical excess in a much larger population, is more serious than the same number of prompt deaths. Some argue that it should be the total population at risk, rather than the cumulative number of deaths, that should be the appropriate measure of the social damage represented in an accident.)

Natural disasters in the poorer parts of the world represent a greater threat in terms of lives lost and suffering created than natural disasters in more industrialized societies. Increasing population densities and urbanization with primitive infrastructures, but above all the increasingly precarious balance between resources and population, may tend to amplify the consequences of natural disasters in the developing world. This will probably not be fully offset by the greater capacity of modern transportation and communications to mobilize assistance. The balance will clearly be close, however. What can be said is that there is a close interaction between poverty and the degree of trauma arising from natural disasters, and consequently a potential synergism between such disasters and the various kinds of "creeping crises" that we deal with below.

Biological Disasters

Another type of traumatic event that is frequently discussed is an epidemic arising from a new type of pathogenic organism—virus or bacteria—which might sweep through large nonimmune populations. Indeed, the elimination of some of the classic epidemic diseases in large parts of the world is frequently suggested as a source of vulnerability to new biological disasters. Genetically engineered organisms resulting accidentally or deliberately from recombinant DNA experimentation are only one suggestion in this regard, but an epidemic resulting from spontaneous mutation of a natural organism is usually thought to be much more probable. It seems rather unlikely, however, that epidemics comparable to the Black Death of medieval Europe could occur under modern conditions, given the many medical techniques available. Only if serious social disintegration had preceded the appearance of the epidemic does it seem likely that it could affect an appreciable fraction of the population. On the other hand, it is interesting to note that in the famous swine flu affair of 1974 medical experts were sufficiently fearful of the recurrence of something like the 1918 influenza epidemic, possibly on an even larger scale due to rapid dispersion by air travel, that preparations were made for a multimillion-dollar mass immunization program on an unprecedented scale. In fact, modern air transport does create the possibility of much more rapid spread of infection than in the past, offset, of course, by the availability of antibiotics and an increasing number of antiviral agents. Critics of the 1974 swine flu panic also point out that the large mortality from the 1918 flu epidemic arose primarily from secondary bacterial infections which today would be susceptible to treatment with antibiotics. On the other hand, it could be argued that strains of bacteria resistant to antibiotics are appearing with increasing frequency and that over time the rate of evolution of pathogens may overtake advances in antibacterial technology, giving rise to a recrudescence of the epidemics of the past. The appearance of strains of the malaria parasite that are resistant to antimalarial drugs is often cited as a parallel for what might eventually occur with many bacterial or virus diseases as well. It is also frequently pointed out that in tropical countries diseases such as tuberculosis, which respond to therapy in temperate climates, are much more resistant to treatment. Could this foreshadow an evolving vulnerability to major epidemics in a world much more intimately connected by modern technology—in this instance, rapid transportation—than in the past?

It seems that the threat of biological catastrophe would be greatest in situations where it arose as a by-product of some other man-made catastrophe, for example, nuclear war, or a large-scale and prolonged breakdown in social and political organization over a significant fraction of the world. A biological disaster could also be initiated by biological warfare. Either the attack itself could decimate large populations, or the organisms might escape the target areas and affect other populations. Should genetic engineering techniques be used to develop new artificial pathogens for biological warfare, the threat of human extinction might conceivably become real, though in my view the potential is probably not as great as for thermonuclear war.

CREEPING CRISES

Most recent public discussion has focused on slowly developing crises rather than traumatic events that destroy large numbers of people within a matter of months or less. Creeping crises include those arising from resource depletion, environmental pollution, or the failure of food production to keep up with population growth—what might be termed the "limits to growth syndrome," after the Club of Rome–sponsored book which most recently popularized this idea in the early 1970s. The scenario involved in the various creeping crises is usually a gradual deterioration of the quality of life characterized by declining life expectancy, rapidly declining material living standards, rising incidence of malnutrition, and disease.

During most of the twentieth century, life expectancy, material living standards, and even nutrition have been improving on the average and for most of the world's population. While it is true that the number of people in absolute poverty may have increased recently, contributing to the widening income gap between rich and poor in some countries, they still constitute a declining fraction of the poor. Reversal of these generally improving trends would be a distinctively new event, deserving the label of crisis. It is also true that life expectancy has been declining in the last decade in a few countries, the most notable example being the Soviet Union, but there is little evidence to indicate that this portends the beginning of a new trend. Just how abrupt the reversal predicted by some of the models would be is a matter of some dispute among the authors of such Malthusian scenarios.[12] What they have in common is the belief that present world levels and rates of growth of economic activity are unsustainable and hence inherently unstable. In their view also, an asymptotic approach to a steady state based on extrapolation of current trends is not a feasible possibility. Any asymptotic level would entail a decline from the present per capita consumption levels of the developed countries, and hence a fairly drastic equalization of world income.[13]

Resource Depletion

The idea that the world's base of renewable and nonrenewable resources could not support the continuing growth of population and/or industrialization is a very old one, and has been put forth many times during the last two centuries, only to be belied by technological progress.[14] As in the past, literary intellectuals and nature lovers have embraced the predictions of the latest Malthusian computer models, while almost all economists and most scientists and engineers have scoffed at them, frequently with considerable emotional intensity.[15] In view of past predictions that have proved wrong, the central question is what is new and different about the current world situation which might make the current predictions of crises more plausible than the earlier ones. There were enough defects and questionable assumptions in the various computer models to provide ample ammunition for critics, but these difficulties tend to add uncertainty rather than definitively to refute the models. Most of the criticisms, in fact, show only that there are equally plausible assumptions that can lead to almost any final result the modeler would prefer. Both the larger number of variables involved and the uncertainties about the nature and rate of future technological developments provide scope to support almost any projection about the future. Thus the personal temperament and political preferences of the modeler tend to determine the outcome more than any objective reality that can be pinned down.[16]

Despite the complexity and uncertainty surrounding the topic, a few general conclusions can be drawn.[17] For almost any one of the sources of instability in the models, it seems possible to imagine technological developments not violating any natural laws that could overcome the physical or biological limits on economic growth, provided world population growth levels off before the middle of the twenty-first century. In the case of nonrenewable resources, for example, it is important to understand that the resource base for industry is not a fixed stock but is constantly changing as a function of new technology in the extraction and use of resources, changes in relative price, and the discovery of ways to exploit and use materials not hitherto regarded as resources at all. The question is thus not so much whether this can happen technically or economically, but whether it can happen fast enough and diffuse on a large enough scale to keep pace with the growth in demand for the human and material services that resources provide. In this view, it is not so much the level of resource consumption or of population which is limiting as their rate of change.

Because both the compounded rate of population growth and, until recently, the compounded rate of economic growth have been without precedent in human history, at least when measured on a world-aggregated basis, the population-resource problem has been transformed from a physical problem into a sociopolitical one. Can the human race organize itself to identify, develop, and deploy the technologies necessary to circumvent projected resource scarcities in a sufficiently timely manner? Equally important, can the social mobilization necessary to achieve a technical solution of the resource-availability problem be achieved in a manner compatible with other social, political, and ethical values? Although the growth of demand to which technology must adapt is unprecedented, the technological capacity that can in principle be mustered to solve problems is also unprecedented, since the number of scientists and engineers—or, more broadly, the number of technical, professional, and managerial people of all varieties—has been growing at more than twice the rate of the general population for at least two centuries. Against this fact we have to offset the inherent problems of managing complexity, of orchestrating the wide variety of skills and specializations that are necessary, and of understanding and dealing with the increasing interactions between different problem areas. We know from recent experience that a technological solution to one problem often gives rise to other problems in apparently unrelated areas, which in turn require new technical or managerial solutions. Do all these interactions and cross-linkages between skills and solutions generate impediments to progress, making the whole less than the sum of the technological parts? Do the very specializations required to tackle one problem efficiently make it more difficult to identify and anticipate all the systemic and long-term ramifications of the solutions? In short, we cannot be certain whether technological progress is a convergent or divergent process—whether the new problems generated by technology will proliferate faster than the solutions. It is almost impossible to assemble evidence on such an overarching question. Opinions seem to be based on intellectual temperament, illustrated by selective anecdotal evidence which is amply available to support either an optimistic or a pessimistic position.

In addition, there is a skewed distribution of technical and managerial capacity. Most of it is concentrated in the developed world and is organized to cope with developed-country problems. There is great uncertainty about the extent to which it can be redeployed successfully to address the problems that are mostly concentrated in the developing world, even if the political will existed to do so. Thus, although the aggregate world capacity may be adequate, the problems of mobilizing it may be insurmountable because of geographical separation, political fragmentation, national pride, or a local cultural and political situation that frustrates the potential benefits of the technology transferred.

Let us examine the case presented by C. Marchetti in an interesting pamphlet which attempts to demonstrate that the world could support a population of a trillion (10^{12}) people at a material standard of living better than that of the most affluent countries. In appearance it would be a very different world than the one we are accustomed to. Two-thirds of the human population would inhabit artificial islands in the world's oceans, and the remaining land dwellers would be packed at a density about five times that of the present Low Countries (Belgium, Luxembourg, and the

Netherlands), already the most densely inhabited area of the world. Structural materials would be based on iron, aluminum, and magnesium—all essentially infinitely available in the earth's crust or oceans—or on oxides, nitrides, or carbides of abundant elements like silicon, calcium, and aluminum, or on synthetic polymeric materials of carefully crafted properties. Per capita energy use would be comparable to that in North America today, and would be based on a combination of nuclear (fission and fusion breeders) and solar technologies generating both electricity and fluid fuel carriers such as hydrogen distributed in global networks from centralized sources. With this level of energy consumption the earth's heat balance would be preserved by "albedo engineering," the modification of the reflectivity properties of the earth's surface over large areas to compensate for extra energy dissipation. Food would be produced chemically with the aid of solar energy rather than by dispersed agriculture. None of this would involve implausible extrapolation from potential scientific and technological capabilities we can identify in the laboratory today. It would not violate any fundamental physical or biological principles.

This thought experiment illustrates the fact that it is not technical but social feasibility that is limiting; no blueprint can be given for how to get from where we are now to such a state. Nor is any value judgment implied as to whether this technological dream is a nightmare or a utopia. It does tend to refute the conventional belief in a human predicament fenced in by inherent physical or biological limits, however.

Energy

If we turn to a shorter time horizon, we can find an analogous projection for energy made in a recently published study of the Energy Systems Program Group of the International Institute for Applied Systems Analysis, a multinational research institute including Eastern and Western scholars headquartered in Queen Maria Theresa's former summer palace in Laxenburg, Austria. The conclusion of this study is summarized in the following words:

> Based on the analysis of technological and economic factors, we conclude that with technologies at hand or potentially at hand, and using the world's resources as perceived today, it is possible to provide enough energy for a world of eight billion people in the year 2030. It could be done! This is not a trivial statement, given the degree of cultural pessimism that one often encounters.

This optimistic conclusion is tempered by the observation:

> What has emerged quite starkly from our study is that any way of balancing

supply and demand, whether high, medium, or low, would lead to some form of hardship.[19]

Furthermore, the hardships would fall differently on different groups and individuals, depending on which future path toward a balance of supply and demand was chosen. These differential hardships imply that the choice of path has a large political dimension and that at the same time any smooth transition will require a high degree of political consensus among highly disparate groups likely to perceive their own self-interest quite differently. This is a point to which we will return later.

Carbon Dioxide

A number of future "creeping crises" with regard to environmental deterioration have received intensive discussion recently. One concerns the buildup of carbon dioxide (CO_2) concentrations in the earth's atmosphere due to the continued combustion of fossil fuels, and probably also to the clearing of the world's forests, particularly in the tropics. As a result, the global climate may warm at a constantly accelerating rate accompanied by a drastic but largely unpredictable (at present) redistribution of rainfall and agricultural productivity over the earth's major agricultural regions. More recently, attention has also been directed to other trace gases released into the atmosphere as a consequence of human activity. It is estimated that these could augment the influence of carbon dioxide alone by as much as 50 percent owing to an additive "greenhouse effect."[20] The principal culprits are nitrous oxide (N_2O, from agriculture and combustion), methane (CH_4, from agriculture and wastes), fluorocarbons, and additional water vapor. There are many uncertainties in the climatic part of these predictions owing to the existence of complex feedback mechanisms, both positive and negative, which exist in the earth's coupled ocean-atmosphere-glacier systems, and are difficult to model.[21]

One of the serious aspects of the problem is that an irreversible basis for climatic change might be laid before the change is actually detectable in weather and climate observations. This is in part because of several inherent time lags in the system and in part because of the superposition of large natural fluctuations on secular trends of anthropogenic origin. In addition, some mechanisms have been proposed that could result in rapid changes of sea level (in a matter of a few years) resulting from rapid movements of the Western Antarctic ice sheet triggered by polar warming. What is more uncertain in all these predictions than the environmental changes themselves is the human response—the capacity of society to adjust in a timely manner. If the present slowdown of the rate of growth in worldwide energy use continues, the climatic changes might not become significant until after the middle of the twenty-first century, by which time the capacity of the world to alter its food production system on a time scale of decades may be enormously greater than it is today. In all probability this technological capacity will grow in rough proportion to the growth of energy use, so that if the carbon dioxide problem appears sooner as a result of higher energy growth, our ability to adjust to it will emerge sooner as well.[22] Here again, the skewed distribution of technical and managerial capacity may be a more serious limitation than the absence of potential tools for adaptation. If the most severe adverse changes occurred in the regions where the greatest technical capacity for adjustment existed, the problem would be minimized, but if the adverse effects fell (as seems more likely) on the already marginal regions with the least technical capacity, the adjustment might prove impossible. Moreover, the problem of adjustment to climatic change, like that of adjustment to resource depletion, is more likely to be limited by sociopolitical than technical considerations. Conflicts arising from the social repercussions of alternations in patterns of agricultural productivity are likely to be much more threatening to human survival than the more direct and obvious consequences of these changes.

If all the available fossil fuel resources in the world were consumed, the ultimate increase in atmospheric carbon dioxide concentration would be between five and eight times preindustrial levels,[21] and there is little question that the resulting environmental and climatic effects would be catastrophic, though they might take several centuries to arrive. This shows that it will be important to replace fossil with nonfossil energy sources well before the fossil resources run out, but this does not appear to offer any insurmountable technical difficulties. The replacement could be largely completed by the end of the next century, which might be soon enough if there is sufficient slowing of energy growth. This is by no means certain, however.

Stratospheric Ozone

Another environmental crisis that has received much discussion recently concerns stratospheric ozone. The intensity of the debate has apparently been stimulated by the extremely esoteric nature of the effect. Several human activities—the production of fluorocarbons for propellants, refrigerants, and other uses; the increased release of nitrous oxide due to agricultural and industrial expansion; possibly the release of bromide compounds—are of a magnitude sufficient to change the natural ozone content and distribution of the stratosphere and thus to alter the amount of biologically dangerous solar ultraviolet radiation which penetrates the earth's atmosphere to the earth's surface. Even more than in the case of carbon dioxide, the time lag is inherently long, so that an irreversible commitment can be incurred before any detectable adverse effects appear.[24] The most dramatic effect of the altered ozone layer would be the predicted increase in the incidence of skin cancer (and, more doubtfully, malignant melanoma) among light-skinned people, but from the standpoint of "crisis" consequences, the possible impact on agricultural productivity and natural ecosystems is likely to be both more significant and more difficult to counteract. However, there are many uncertainties, which become greater as one moves from the prediction of physical effects to the prediction of their ecological and human consequences. In the case of nitrous oxide—potentially the most difficult problem in terms of its controllability—the magnitude and even the sign of the effect is still a matter of some dispute. Moreover, there are uncertainties about the actual magnitude of any biological impact due to the fact that the ozone depletion has a complex seasonal and latitude dependence, so that seasonally averaged biological effects may be much smaller than simply the annual average depletion of the ozone above a given point on the earth's surface.[25] On balance, it seems unlikely that ozone depletion should be classified among the potential creeping disasters resulting from technology, especially since the largest effects are those associated with the industrial activities that are easiest to control (fluorocarbons). However, one cannot be completely confident of this conclusion at the present time. Interestingly enough, the one exception to this statement may be the ozone depletion that could result from a large thermonuclear exchange between the United States and the Soviet Union.[26] Thus even in this case, we come full circle, back to the threat of nuclear war.

The Biosphere

Far more threatening than either the carbon dioxide buildup or stratospheric ozone alteration would be the gradual deterioration of the biosphere as a result of the accumulation of a large number of environmental insults and stresses due to overexploitation. Two serious consequences would entail the loss of soil fertility due to erosion and to depletion of humus, and the loss of genetic diversity on which may depend the future capacity of food crops to resist pests and pathogens. Even in the highly productive North American continent, possessing the most advanced and sophisticated agricultural technology in the world, there is major uncertainty and debate as to whether present cropping systems can be sustained, how much of the present rate of soil loss is due to erosion, and what level of soil erosion can be tolerated indefinitely because of regeneration through fertilization and good agricultural practice.[27] Nor is the future vulnerability of increasingly extensive homogeneous monocultures well understood. Moreover, soil loss and desertification in the Third

World, especially the tropics, may be much more severe than in the temperate zone.[28] Intensive cultivation methods are just beginning in many of these areas, and we have much less basis for predicting their consequences than in temperate-zone agriculture.

On the other side of the coin, the emergence of a number of potentially powerful new biological technologies, such as recombinant DNA, offers hope of new tools to deal more flexibly with increased agricultural productivity and various side effects. The possibilities for much more efficient application of irrigation water and fertilizers (with much reduced consumptive use) and pesticides to crops are just beginning to be developed and exploited.[29]

If the future sustainability of renewable resource production in the United States is in doubt, the uncertainty is much greater for the rest of the world. At present rates of population growth only high-input agriculture requiring rapid growth in the use of chemical fertilizer, pesticides, and intensive cultivation of monocultures promises to keep up with food demand. Because of cartelized world oil prices, the competition between energy and food for renewable resources is a new feature which is increasing the stress on a system already stressed by food demands alone.[30]

Yet, difficult as it is, sustaining the productivity of the biosphere is probably not an insurmountable problem from the technical standpoint. Economists who have analyzed the world agricultural situation have concluded that there is gross underinvestment in agricultural research in relation to the demonstrable social and economic rate of return on such research.[31] Furthermore, the capital investment (including investment to counteract environmental and soil deterioration) necessary to implement the results of such research is probably modest compared with that required in several critical industrial fields such as energy production. Again, the problem is mostly sociopolitical. The technological choices, however, may be harder to define precisely than in some other areas. The world food system is highly dispersed and decentralized, and adaptation to idiosyncratic local conditions is often very important. Hence the diffusion of innovations encounters great obstacles of both an institutional and a technical nature. Since individual producers are scattered, the dissemination of information to them forms, or should form, a much larger fraction of the necessary effort expended in agricultural research and its implementation than in most industrial fields. In addition, the disjunction between individual and social incentives in agriculture is often unusually large. Even in North America the individual farmer may feel impelled to overexploit the land at the expense of its long-term productivity, while high value-added industrial and residential use of land may result in the withdrawal of the most productive land from agricultural use, since such land is frequently close to already developed urban areas. Environmentally sound practices in the use of land are frequently more costly in the short run than current or traditional practices.

Toxic Chemicals

Another area of environmental concern, toxic chemical wastes, has received considerable public attention because of several dramatic incidents such as the one at Love Canal. The character of the threat, again like that postulated for carbon dioxide and fluorocarbons, lies in the possibility that the threat can become well established before overt human consequences are apparent. Carcinogenic or genetic effects of chemicals are manifested only after time delays or "induction periods" of many decades. Thus, in theory at least, it is possible for large segments of the population to be exposed over a period of time to hazardous substances in food[30] or the environment or in occupational situations without any detectable health effects warning of danger. This possibility has been emphasized by several examples of exposure in the workplace to toxic substances such as asbestos and vinyl chloride, where serious health damage or premature death has become statistically significant only many decades after the original exposure. As another example, most hazardous waste dumps are at least twenty to thirty years old, and were established at a time when there was much less public awareness of the hazard and often very little scientific knowledge of how wastes would move in the soil, enter the water table, or affect health.

Fortunately, the populations involved in these various incidents were small, so that they had little impact on overall health statistics, but the matter is nevertheless of concern because of the vast expansion in the last thirty years of the use of chemicals not previously found in nature and to which the human organism may thus not have become adapted by natural selection. These chemicals could, collectively, constitute a "time bomb" which could manifest itself in a rapid increase in the incidence of cancers, or of genetic or developmental defects, in large human populations at some time in the future. That this has not occurred so far except in very small occupationally exposed or localized populations (such as residents in the Love Canal housing development) is regarded as no guarantee that it could not occur over increasingly extensive areas in the future.

Long-lived radioactive wastes raise similar problems, but much more is generally known about their biological hazards, monitoring methods for the environment are more sensitive and reliable, and radioactivity, unlike many of the chemicals of concern, is already present in the background. In fact, the chief function of the public debate over radioactive waste management may have been to sensitize both public and experts to the hazards of waste disposal in general. My own view is that the radioactive waste problem gives considerably less cause for concern than the chemical waste problem, and that feasible technical solutions are more nearly in hand, despite widespread public impressions to the contrary.[33]

Chemical wastes, like so many of the other creeping crises discussed above, may pose much more a rate-of-change problem than one arising from the absolute level of industrial activity. The proliferation of legislation such as the Toxic Substance Control Act, the Resource Conservation and Recovery Act, and the superfund bill is likely both to slow the rate of introduction of new chemical entities and to stimulate the deployment of anticipatory monitoring and control measures. Supporters of such legislation point out correctly that the investment required to avoid future damage from improper disposal of chemicals is almost always minuscule compared with the costs of remedying or compensating victims for the damage after it has occurred.[34] In the long run, therefore, the system of chemical manufacture and disposal will probably become sufficiently self-correcting so that while it may not satisfy the most stringent criteria of risk avoidance that an increasingly sensitive society would prefer, it is unlikely to produce any time bombs of sufficient severity to reverse long-term overall trends in the improvement of health statistics. Undoubtedly there will be some localized crises and panics, but they will not be important in the aggregate.

In general, creeping crises of a physical or biological nature are not by themselves likely to be critical in the sense of producing a reversal of long-term trends toward improvement of physical or biological measures of the quality of life. This is not to say that expectations or aspirations may not exceed actual achievements, but there will continue to be objective, if not subjective, improvement. If a reversal does in fact occur, it will most likely be mediated through some sort of social, political, or institutional breakdown not directly related to technology though perhaps indirectly derived from technological complexity. However, this conclusion must not be taken as implying that technical-economic and sociopolitical considerations can be so cleanly distinguished. Clearly, the two interact in a complicated way. For example, competition for resources such as oil is likely to increase stresses on the international political and economic system. The OPEC (Organization of Petroleum Exporting Countries) cartel and its political sequelae would probably not have been possible without the saturation of U.S. oil and gas production in the early 1970s. Environmental deterioration and rapid technical changes both tend to increase social stresses, while at the same time social deterioration and fragmentation of interest groups tend to decrease the capacity of the world as a whole to deploy its human and natural resources wisely and efficiently—by decreasing the capacity to generate and assimilate technological change, by decreasing the capacity for efficient division of labor and resource sharing across national boundaries, and, not least, by diverting an increasing proportion of scarce technical and managerial talent toward the preservation of both internal and external security.

SOCIAL CRISES

The Widening Gap

Perhaps one of the greatest social crises produced at least indirectly by technology is the growth of income inequalities between nations. This has a number of societal implications. While income inequalities have generally declined within industrialized nations, inequalities between nations, and within most developing nations, have increased as the modern sectors move ahead of the traditional sectors of their economies. Within less than a century the difference in average GNP (gross national product) per capita between what is now the "developed" world and the countries now making up the "developing" world has grown from about three to one to about twelve to one and shows no sign of decelerating, except for a few "newly industrializing" countries representing less than 10 percent of the global population.[35] During the period since the end of World War II economic growth in both the developed and developing world has been faster and more continuous than in any corresponding historical period, but the acceleration of population growth in most of the developing world has largely offset economic growth in these countries. In contrast, decreasing population growth in the industrialized countries has had an opposite effect, so that the per capita income gap between developed and developing countries has a doubling time of less than thirty-five years.[36]

Public health measures, technical advances in agriculture, and improved transportation and communications have all contributed to declining mortality rates in the developing world, while fertility has hardly been affected, or in some cases has even increased.[37] Advances in communications have also brought the poorer parts of the world increasingly into the orbit of material aspirations characteristic of the developed countries, creating the "revolution of rising expectations" which is probably a major source of political disequilibrium both in the international system and inside the developed and the developing countries themselves. In the developed countries, legal and illegal immigration from developing countries, combined with high natural increase rates among immigrant groups, has begun to contribute to income and social inequalities in the industrialized world. This trend could grow spectacularly in the next few decades, contributing to problems of governance even in the most stable and affluent nations.

Social Decay

There are growing symptoms of alienation and social deterioration even within the most prosperous countries—rising crime rates, erosion of family life, failures in the socialization of children and youth, inflation and unemployment, disaffection and alienation in the labor force, acrimonious conflict between interest groups, and difficulties in reaching political consensus on how to cope with burgeoning problems such as energy, environment, and inflation.[38] This deterioration is occurring in an increasingly closely articulated and interdependent world society, where social disruption, or even individual acts of violence or sabotage, have ever wider and more severe systemic ramifications.[39] In our discussion of physical, environmental, and biospheric resources we have indicated the increasing necessity for cooperative exploitation of these resources through "interdependence" and through coordinated technical progress. Yet such cooperation and coordination appear ever more elusive. What some consider cooperation others perceive as exploitation, a situation which is exacerbated in the presence of income and status inequalities. In addition, it is possible that the rapid modernization which may be necessary in the Third World if the material conditions of life are not to deteriorate may result in the acceleration of social disintegration, as appears to have happened in Iran. This paradox has led some to propose a radical restructuring of society and technology pointing toward emphasis on self-sufficiency, reduction of interdependence and the division of labor, and a much reduced level of consumption of energy and materials and hence of goods and services that are materials and energy intensive, such as personal mobility.[40] There is serious disagreement even as to the physical feasibility of such a radical lifestyle change, given present levels of world population. An extended period of negative population growth might be one answer, but this would require a worldwide consensus on values, which seems even more remote than that required by even the changes in lifestyle proposed. In addition, the mode of life implied by the "soft path" will surely be regarded as highly restricting by a sufficient segment of the world's population as to make it politically infeasible without heavy coercion, even if it should prove technically feasible.

The debate could perhaps be summarized in terms of two visions of the future. One entails continuing evolution in the direction of interdependence, technical progress, and social complexity, with gradual diffusion of present Western material standards to the rest of the world's population

within a century. Such an evolution is probably technically and economically feasible, but its political feasibility is open to doubt in view of
some of the trends we have identified in contemporary society. In the
minds of its critics, such an evolution would place impossibly great demands on psychological adjustment, managerial competence, and political institutions; the symptoms of this "human overload" are claimed to be
already apparent. In the other direction the simplified, decentralized
civilization envisioned by the prophets of "appropriate technology" is of
more dubious technical feasibility, though perhaps not out of the question.[41] If achievable, it might indeed reduce psychological and social overload, but there are grave doubts as to whether evolution toward such a
social system could ever occur through the spontaneous and democratic
change of social values that proponents hypothesize. Short of dividing the
world into two self-sufficient areas with differing lifestyles and permitting
free migration between the two,[42] it is hard to see how such a transformation could occur without the use of coercive measures and force,
with chaos and conflict the likely result.

Vulnerability

The social disintegration that appears to be afflicting industrial societies
on both sides of the Iron Curtain is rendered more dangerous by the
proliferation and accessibility of technologies which make it much easier
for individuals or small groups to cause disproportionate damage to our
highly integrated sociotechnical systems. The hijacking of aircraft has
been precariously contained only at rather high cost, and this delicate
balance could be upset at any time by a minor technical innovation or by
the offer of sanctuary to terrorists or criminals by a few uncooperative
countries. The problem of theft or the simple appropriation of nuclear
weapons now spread around the world is a constant threat. The capacity
of "industrial action" on the part of a few people to paralyze whole
societies has been amply demonstrated in a variety of contexts—air traffic
controllers, public transportation employees, coal miners, post office
workers, fire and police workers, health personnel, power plant
operators. The incident at Three Mile Island and numerous transportation and industrial accidents have illustrated the large effects that can flow
from minor errors of judgment and nonmalevolent incompetence. It is
unlikely that any technological system can be rendered immune to human
error.

In the United States, growing deterioration in educational achievement, especially in scientific and technical matters, is occurring at a time
when more and more technical competence at lower and lower job levels
is required to keep the machinery of our technological society running

smoothly and safely. Rule-of-thumb on-the-job training is not sufficient to insure that minor mishaps do not escalate into major technological failures. People must be able to diagnose troubles and use their understanding of the system to manage malfunctions, often with improvisations devised on the spur of the moment, based on a fundamental understanding of the functioning of the system. What is worrisome is whether in the future we can look forward to reliance on a work force capable of operating and repairing the complex systems on which our society depends, a work force that has to be both highly motivated and capable of continually acquiring new skills. Our technology is too ubiquitous for us to be able to count on trained engineers to manage every aspect of it. It must be capable of being run by ordinary people who have a high enough level of both technical education and motivation to do it. The fact that the school achievement of the young people in some societies—notably Japan—is much higher on the average than in the U.S. is something that could be a harbinger of our future inability not so much to innovate and invent new technology as to commercialize and maintain it in good functioning condition.

What is not clear in all this is the degree of connection between our technological and economic progress and the symptoms of social breakdown and loss of morale which many observers profess to see developing in advanced industrial societies, especially in the U.S. Do technological civilizations contain the seeds of their own self-destruction, not through technology itself or its ecological side effects, but through slow deterioration of the quality of people at all levels? Do technological societies place ever-increasing demands on the intelligence and dedication of their members at the same time that they create a social ambiance that causes people to become slack, sloppy, and unmotivated? A part of the social deterioration may consist of the loss of a willingness and capacity to adapt to changing environments and to look forward rather than backward. It is sometimes said that nothing fails like success, that success in any endeavor generates rigidities and an unwillingness to undertake new risks similar to those that led to success in the first place, and hence to adapt to constantly changing external circumstances whether they be changes in world markets, international power distribution, or environmental or resource problems.

If the human prospect proves to be as dim as the prophets of doom would have it, the cause will lie not in the direct consequences of technology but in the complex interplay between technological development and the evolution of individual and social character. There are almost certainly workable technical solutions to all the problems and dilemmas of the next hundred years. The question is whether humanity can summon the collective wisdom and consensus necessary to implement these solutions without compromising other social and moral values that we also hold dear. Or will the implementation of solutions require so much social coercion that they are not really solutions in the larger human sense? Finally, of course, the huge stockpiles of nuclear weapons and the dedication of enormous managerial and technical skill, as well as capital investment, to the building of an ever-escalating destructive capacity continue to be the principal threat of doom, perhaps the only one that seems to this commentator, at least, to be fully credible and real.

NOTES

1. See, for example, the special articles on "The Medical Consequences of Thermonuclear War" in *New England Journal of Medicine* 266:22 (May 31, 1962), especially Victor W. Sidel, H. Jack Geiger, and Bernard Lown, "II. The Physician's Role in the Postattack Period," 1137–45.

2. A. O. Nier, et al., *Long-Term Worldwide Effects of Multiple Nuclear Weapons Detonations* (Washington, D.C.: National Academy of Sciences, 1975). For a short summary of the literature on the effects of nuclear war, see *F.A.S. Public Interest Report, Journal of the Federation of American Scientists* 34:2 (February 1981); also U.S. Congress, Office of Technology Assessment, *The Effects of Nuclear War* (Washington, D.C.: Office of Technology Assessment, 1979).

3. Sidney G. Winter, Rand Report RM-3436-PR (Santa Monica, Calif.: Rand Corporation, 1963).

4. R. P. Turco, O. B. Toon, T. P. Ackerman, J. B. Pollack, and Carl Sagan, "Nuclear Winter: Global Consequences of Multiple Nuclear Explosions," *Science*, 222:4630 (December 23, 1983), 1283–92.

5. For a summary of the arguments see National Research Council, *Energy in Transition 1985–2010*, Report of the National Research Council-National Academy of Sciences Committee on Nuclear and Alternative Energy Systems (San Francisco: W. H. Freeman & Co., 1980), pp. 326–38.

6. A. S. Manne and R. G. Richels, "Probability Assessments and Decision Analysis of Alternative Nuclear Fuel Cycles," chap. 15 in Robert G. Sachs, ed., *National Energy Issues: How Do We Decide?*, American Academy of Arts and Sciences Series (Cambridge, Mass.: Ballinger Publishing Company, 1980).

7. Gerard Smith and George Rathjens, "Reassessing Nuclear Nonproliferation Policy," *Foreign Affairs* 59:4 (Spring 1981), 875–94.

8. *Energy in Transition 1985–2010*, p. 325.

9. Ibid., pp. 311–14.

10. Bennett Ramberg, *Destruction of Nuclear Energy Facilities in War: The Problem and the Implications Revisited* (Berkeley: University of California Press, forthcoming 1984). This book is a paperback revision of Ramberg's 1980 Lexington

Books hardback, *Destruction of Nuclear Energy Facilities in War: The Problem and the Implications* (Lexington, Mass.: Lexington Books, 1980).

11. See Lester R. Brown, *World Without Borders* (New York: Random House, 1972), chap. 3; Dennis L. Meadows, et al., *The Limits to Growth: A Report for the Club of Rome's Project on the Predicament of Mankind* (New York: Universe Books, 1972); and "Poverty, Growth, and Human Development," chap. 4 in *World Development Report 1980* (Washington, D.C.: The World Bank, August 1980).

12. Jay W. Forrester, *World Dynamics* (Cambridge, Mass.: Wright-Allen Press, 1971).

13. Dennis L. Meadows, et al., *The Dynamics of Growth in a Finite World* (Cambridge, Mass.: Wright-Allen Press, 1974).

14. Mogens Boserap, "Fear of Doomsday, Past and Present," *Population and Development Review* 4:1 (March 1978), 133–43.

15. Harvey Brooks, "Technology: Hope or Catastrophe?," *Technology in Society* 1 (1979), 3–17.

16. The widespread debate, and the spate of countermodels and critiques, spawned by the publications of Forrester, Meadows, and their associates have been reviewed in a balanced and critical way by M. Greenberger, M. A. Crenson, and B. L. Crissey in *Models in the Policy Process* (New York: Russell Sage Foundation, 1976), pp. 159–82.

17. Harvey Brooks, "Can Technology Assure Unending Material Progress?," in *Progress and Its Discontents*, ed. Gabriel A. Almond, Marvin Chodorow, and Roy Harvey Pearce (Berkeley: University of California Press, 1982), pp. 281–300.

18. C. Marchetti, *On 10^12: A Check on Earth's Carrying Capacity for Man*, Research Report RR-78-7, International Institute for Applied Systems Analysis (IIASA), Laxenburg, Austria, May 1978.

19. Wolf Häfele, Program Leader, *Energy in a Finite World*, vol. 1, *Paths to a Sustainable Future*, Report by the Energy Systems Program Group, International Institute for Applied Systems Analysis (Cambridge, Mass.: Ballinger Publishing Company, 1981), p. 171.

20. W. C. Wang, et al., "Greenhouse Effects Due to Man-Made Perturbations of Trace Gases," *Science* 194:4266 (November 12, 1976), 685–90.

21. H. Flohn, *Possible Climatic Consequences of a Man-Made Global Warming*, Research Report RR-80-30, International Institute for Applied Systems Analysis, Laxenburg, Austria, December 1980.

22. Thomas C. Schelling, et al., letter report of the *ad hoc* study panel on economic and social aspects of CO_2, Climate Research Board, National Research Council, April 18, 1980.

23. Harvey Brooks, "The Energy Problem," in *Technology and Society*, Oak Ridge Bicentennial Lectures, ORNL/PPA-77/3, Oak Ridge, Tennessee, July 1977, pp. 101–18.

24. Harvey Brooks, "Potential and Limitations of Societal Response to Long-Term Environmental Threats," in Werner Strumm, ed., *Global Chemical Cycles and Their Alterations by Man*, Physical and Chemical Sciences Research Reports No. 2 (Berlin: Dahlem Konferenzen Berlin, 1977).

25. M. B. McElroy, N. D. Sze, and S. Wofsy, "Reports by the U.S. National Academy of Sciences and the U.K. Department of the Environment on the Im-

pact of Chlorofluorocarbons on Ozone: Comparison and Critique," unpublished paper, March 1981.

26. Nier, et al., *Long-Term Worldwide Effects of Multiple Nuclear Weapons Detonation.*

27. "Long-Range Threats Stalk U.S. Farming," *Conservation Foundation Letter*, August 1980; and Norman Berg, "The Adequacy of Agricultural Land—Future Problems and Policy Alternatives," paper for conference sponsored by Resources for the Future, Washington, D.C., June 19–20, 1980.

28. M. S. Swaminathan, "Past, Present, and Future Trends in Tropical Agriculture," chap. 1 in Commonwealth Agricultural Bureau, comp., *Perspectives in World Agriculture* (Farnham Royal, Eng.: Commonwealth Agricultural Bureau X, 1980), pp. 1–47.

29. National Research Council/National Academy of Sciences, *Science and Technology: A Five-Year Outlook,* Report to the National Science Foundation from the National Academy of Sciences (San Francisco: W. H. Freeman & Co., 1979), pp. 116–33.

30. Lester Brown, "Food or Fuel: New Competition for the World's Cropland," *Interciencia* 5 (November/December 1980), 365–72.

31. R. E. Evenson, "Comparative Evidence on Returns to Investment in National and International Research Institutions," in *Resource Allocation and Productivity in National and International Agricultural Research,* ed. T. M. Arndt, D. G. Dalrymple, and V. W. Ruttan (Minneapolis: University of Minnesota Press, 1977), pp. 237–64.

32. The rapid increase in the consumption by young children of diet drinks containing saccharin was cited as one of the reasons for regulation of saccharin as a food additive, despite its being rated as only a weak carcinogen. See National Research Council/National Academy of Sciences, *Saccharin: A Technical Assessment of Risks and Benefits,* Assembly of Life Sciences, National Research Council, National Academy of Sciences, Washington, D.C., 1979.

33. *Energy in Transition, 1985–2010,* pp. 296–318, 447–50; Committee on Science and Public Policy, National Academy of Sciences, *Risks Associated with Nuclear Power: A Critical Review of the Literature,* Steering Committee for the Nuclear Risk Survey, Committee on Science and Public Policy, chap. 26 (Washington, D.C.: National Academy of Sciences, 1979), pp. 96–111.

34. Douglas Costle, Administrator of the U.S. Environmental Protection Agency, Lecture at the Arco Forum, Kennedy School of Government, Harvard University, Cambridge, Mass., April 2, 1980. Costle also pointed out that within a few years of the passage of implementing legislation 90 percent of industries were in compliance with the requirements of the Toxic Substances Control Act.

35. Brown, *World Without Borders,* chap. 3.

36. Nathan Keyfitz, "World Resources and the World Middle Class," *Scientific American* 235:1 (July 1976), 28–35.

37. Nathan Keyfitz, et al., "The Demographic State of the World," chap. 1 in *Outlook for Science and Technology: The Next Five Years,* National Research Council, National Academy of Sciences (Washington, D.C.: National Academy of Sciences, April 1981), pp. 21–66.

38. Andrew Hacker, *The End of the American Era* (New York: Atheneum

Press, 1970); Michel Crozier, Samuel P. Huntington, and Joji Watanuki, *The Crisis of Democracy: Report on the Governability of Democracies to the Trilateral Commission* (New York: New York University Press, 1975).

39. Harvey Brooks, "Remarks on Technological Forecasting in the Next Decades," in *Technology Forecast for 1980*, ed. Ernst Weber, Gordon K. Teal, and A. George Schillinger (New York: Van Nostrand Reinhold Company, 1971), pp. 3–16.

40. Hugh Nash, ed., *The Energy Controversy: Soft Path, Questions and Answers* (San Francisco: Friends of the Earth, 1979); Laura Nader, et al., *Supporting Paper 7: Energy Choices in a Democratic Society,* Committee on Nuclear and Alternative Energy Systems, National Research Council, National Academy of Sciences (Washington, D.C.: National Academy of Sciences, 1980).

41. Harvey Brooks, "The Technology of Zero Growth," Daedalus Conference on No-Growth Society, October 21–22, 1972, *Daedalus* 102 (Fall 1973), 139–52; and Harvey Brooks, "Critique of the Concept of Appropriate Technology," in Franklin A. Long and Alexandra Oleson, eds., *Appropriate Technology and Social Values: A Critical Appraisal,* American Academy of Arts and Sciences Series (Cambridge, Mass.: Ballinger Publishing Company, 1980).

42. Häfele, *Energy in a Finite World,* pp. 174–75.

7

BIOLOGICAL ESCHATOLOGY

Robert S. Morison

A LTHOUGH THE NOTION OF LAST THINGS HAS A VERY
long history, the word *eschatology* itself, as I discovered in the
Oxford English Dictionary, is surprisingly young. The first attribution
dates from 1844, but the citation from 1879 is the more informative:
"Eschatology, the science of the last things, is, as a science, one of the
most baseless." For our present purposes, such an interpretation has the
great merit of allowing anyone to play, even though some, of course, may
be more baseless than others.

The definition one finds, refers, strictly speaking, to "the four last
things": death, judgment, heaven, and hell. In the Judeo-Christian tradition, however, the major preoccupation is not really with the end states
themselves but with the means for avoiding them. Beginning with the
difference between Christians and Jews over whether the Messiah has
already arrived or must be looked for in the future, and continuing
through the debates on faith versus works and predestination versus free
will, almost every mode of escape from the less desirable last things has
been disagreed about, has been branded as heretical, or has served as the
cause of a particularly devastating war. Equally incongruous is the confusion of hope and fear. Thus, on the Day of Wrath ushered in with trum-
pets and the thunder of kettledrums, one fears the worst but is suddenly
relieved to hear that "we shall all be changed"; and the change will clearly
be for the better. The word that springs to mind, in fact, is *incorruptible*.
This optimistic text provides those who like to find the roots of the present in the past with sound religious precedent for the secular idea of
progress. Those who prefer revolution to the slower improvements of
reform can cite Scripture for the belief that the hoped-for change will
come about "in the twinkling of an eye."

An important theoretical distinction is often drawn between "individual (personal) eschatology" and "collective (social) eschatology." In
practice, however, the two are difficult to untangle. Nevertheless, if our
purpose is to scrutinize this "baseless" science from a scientific base, it

may simplify things to accept the assumption of a difference between individual and social last things. Furthermore, it may be useful to postulate a difference between the living and the nonliving worlds. Although one can think of scenarios in which the biological and physical worlds end simultaneously, there are many more in which the physical will stride majestically on to its final bang, long after life as we know it has slipped feebly away with barely a whimper. Life is simply too demanding in regard to such things as temperature, humidity, and energy gradients. This chapter, therefore, is limited to the living world. It will, moreover, concern itself only with the most surely identifiable of the four last things: death as an individual human phenomenon.

DEATH MAKES BIOLOGICAL SENSE

What then do the life sciences have to say about the last stages of human beings (or any other beings, for that matter)? The short answer is "relatively little." Biology has been primarily interested in such matters as fertilization, reproduction, growth, and development, all characteristics of youth. The one great biological generalization—the theory of evolution—is based on the differential capacity to produce offspring. Once an organism reaches the point at which reproduction is no longer possible, it ceases to be of evolutionary significance (except to those who are interested in such esoterica as kinship selection for "altruism"). Aging and death may then be assigned an important though uncomfortably negative role—a mopping-up operation to remove organisms no longer capable of contributing to the great drama of evolution. Indeed, there is some evidence that planned obsolescence was not "designed" into living things until the appearance of sexual reproduction with its potential for rapid evolution through genetic mixing. Until that time, reproduction presumably occurred by simple division, so that all members of a given cell line were much alike. Before sex, we all belonged to "clones"—to use a word that has suddenly become commonplace. In theory at least, such cell lines are potentially immortal. In practice, of course, time and chance happen to them all. But there is no reason to suppose that their finitude was built into them as it is now believed by some students to be built into the cells of sexual species. Thus, although most biologists have difficulty equating sex with sin, the thesis of the Book of Genesis, that we paid for sex by becoming mortal, may have a sound biological base.

For most biologists, except for those in the new specialty of gerontology, the death of an individual, especially one past his or her reproductive prime, is a matter of no great moment. Certainly it is no mystery. It is the inevitable corollary of a system dedicated to change. Some commentators may have been a little too ready to assume that evolutionary change is always for the better. Although Darwin himself was usually careful to avoid outright value judgments on this point, some nineteenth- and many twentieth-century studies assumed that the net result of evolutionary change is an improvement of some kind. Undeniably, living things have tended to become more complex, able to respond differentially to more kinds of stimuli and to adjust to more kinds of environment. Your orthodox, value-free scientist, if he still survives, prefers not to say whether this complexity is better or worse than the simplicity that preceded it. Such judgments must be left to the humanities, whose business it is said to be.

The answer is of some interest to the eschatologist since the death that is the last thing for one individual becomes the opportunity for some new thing for another. By carrying our eschatological research east of the Levant we encounter a quite common view that the essence of one individual may be transferred to another. Whether or not the next in line is an improvement or not depends on a number of factors which I must leave to the specialist, but one can read the doctrine of transmigration of souls as an early metaphor for the Darwinian origin of species. In each case, the fate of the individual yields in interest to a continuity of individuals extending over time. In both instances, there is a certain ambiguity about whether things are getting better or worse overall. In any case, there may always be an extremist wing that rejects the merging of the individual either into the unidirectional evolutionary stream or the recurrently revolving wheel of life, and that hopes, instead, to rise again as incorruptible individuals.

For secular individuals, however, death is indeed the last thing. The material progress of the last century ensures that for the most part it comes at a late stage of our lives, when we have done most of what we were able to do, and in any case have lost the ability to do much more. Now that it steals away only a few infants per thousand per year and cuts down in the prime of life but a fraction of those that it used to reap so regularly, death has lost much of its arbitrary character and most of its mystery. Thus it has become much easier to view death as the sensible biological necessity that it probably is.

THE ART OF DYING AND ITS REVIVAL

A change in attitude toward death and dying can be traced in what is now an enormous literature. The act of dying, which for the first half of the century was almost taboo as a topic for discussion, is now the subject of innumerable books, workshops, seminars, and even high school courses. This is not the first time, of course, that people have given thought to dying well. The Roman Stoics had a good deal to say on the subject, with

Seneca being particularly eloquent about death as the ultimate guarantee of freedom from the tortures and coercions which he felt closing in around him. A recent book on *The Craft of Dying*[1] traces the modern literary tradition to the fifteenth century, when an unknown author produced the *Tractatus artis bene moriendi* at the behest of the Council of Constance.

This earlier literary tradition is, of course, heavily influenced by the Christian interest in immortality and salvation. Nevertheless, because of its emphasis on how-to-do-it and its acceptance of death as part of some sort of plan, however inexplicable, this exposition may be regarded as the forerunner of such modern treatises as those produced by Elisabeth Kübler-Ross and her many imitators. There is much less precedent, and to me much less excuse, for the existentialist characterization of death as an "intolerable scandal" against which we can only rage, with Dylan Thomas, in an orgy of indiscipline.

Another difference, and one much more in tune with the times, is the tendency to turn the craft of dying into a full-blown technology. Thus the psychological states of the dying person are carefully analyzed and sorted into categories, each with its characteristic signs requiring appropriate action by the technical experts in attendance. Naturally enough, even greater attention is given to the physical arrangements. The large general hospital has been tried and found wanting as a good place to die, and another venerable institution, the hospice, has been revived to take its place. Even more surprising in a time when the family seems to be rapidly disappearing as a center of social action, the home or private house been discovered, in an extension of Le Corbusier's famous definition, to be an excellent "machine" for dying as well as living in.

TO BE OR NOT TO BE: A CLASH OF TECHNOLOGIES

Unhappily the technology of dying often finds itself in direct conflict with other technologies designed to extend life as long as possible. In practice, then, the art or craft of dying is no longer simply a matter of adjusting oneself to the inevitable with dignity and grace. Paradoxically, the inevitable no longer happens by itself, or as the result of forces transcending human control. In all too many cases something must be done to let or even to make the inevitable happen. The difference between "let" and "make" is the difference between negative and positive euthanasia and is currently the subject of discussion in legal, medical, and philosophical circles of an intensity and subtlety that would do credit to an Abélard or a Duns Scotus. We need not detain ourselves with even a brief review of what has been so thoroughly presented elsewhere. In summary, just about everyone agrees that there are times when further efforts to prolong a life are likely to do more harm than good. The arguments are about details. For example, who should decide—the doctor, the patient, the family, all of the above, or none of the above? The last possibility is, unhappily, much more real than a sensible person might imagine, and there are a growing number of cases in which the employment of even extraordinary means has been terminated only by court order.

SANCTITY AND UTILITY: WHAT ARE WE HERE FOR?

All of the arguing about procedure serves to conceal, rather than clarify, a basically frightening question: When is a life no longer worth living? Most of the elaborate discussions of euthanasia actually evade the issue by limiting the possible cases to patients who are almost certain to die anyway in a matter of days or weeks and where there is clear evidence of pain and suffering on the part of such patients or those around them. Indeed, a not inconsiderable effort has been made to avoid the problem entirely by limiting termination of treatment only to those who can reasonably be defined as already dead. Thus, much thought has gone into reformulating the criteria for pronouncing a person dead. The classical "signs of life"— heartbeat and respiration—no longer serve the purposes of either medicine or the law since they can so easily be supported by machines. In search of more appropriate criteria, attention has focused on the nervous system, for which the computer has not yet provided an adequate substitute. For a brief moment it appeared that nervous-system death as defined by a Boston committee would solve the problem, but the criteria were so conservative as to leave the profession no way of dealing with many of the most disturbing cases, of which perhaps Karen Quinlan provides the archetype.

A much more radical example of the taxonomic approach is provided by those who speak of psychological or social death. Perhaps the most specific and clearly thought-out proposal has been put forth by the Episcopal theologian Joseph Fletcher in a detailed set of criteria for "humanhood." The implication, of course, is that once an individual loses his or her humanhood the problem of terminating life has been defined away. The proposal has not received as much discussion as it probably deserves, perhaps because a similar line of reasoning was once used to justify slavery, and more recently as a defense of the even more appalling events in Auschwitz and Dachau. There are easily detectable differences between Karen Quinlan and the victims of Auschwitz just as there are between Joseph Fletcher and Heinrich Himmler. Lines can and must be drawn if ethics is to have any meaning; and the slippery-slope argument must be seen for what it is, the last infirmity of philosophic minds. Indeed, it has never been as compelling as it sounds. The absolutists of the past no sooner annunciated the sacredness of all human life than they set about elaborating the defense of war, the execution of criminals, and the burning of heretics as an "act of faith." Where was the slippery slope then?

Nevertheless, what I have called the taxonomic approach does imply something like clear boundaries between classes. On one side is the completely human being with all his rights and privileges; on the other, a nothing. The trouble is that God was neither a mathematician nor a Platonic "realist" reaching into clearly marked boxes to get the parts with which to create the world. On the contrary, everything grades into everything else. It is up to us to draw such boundaries as we find useful.

We may now come to the point and assert that sooner or later men of goodwill are going to have to face up to making life-and-death decisions on their individual merits. Joseph Fletcher pointed out many years ago in his book *Situation Ethics*[2] that persons and circumstances differ so much from one another that attempts to apply general rules result, all too often, in disastrous consequences. The brand of consequentialism which he proposed to mitigate the cruelties of the prevailing deontological schools proved too extreme for most observers. In the first place, it underestimated the role of ethical rules in economizing time and energy. An extreme consequentialism, which regards every new situation as unique, leaves the seeker after virtue with little time to do anything else but struggle to find the right path. A more common criticism is the theoretical possibility that without rules or guidelines the unprincipled are too likely to feel that "anything goes."

Recently an even more awkward problem has surfaced. The old confidence that people in positions of responsibility would discharge their duties in a reasonably ethical manner has given way to distrust and hostility. There may well be some justification for this, but the reason and causes are far too complex to be considered here. The fact is that increasing distrust of authority figures has led in the last few years to increasing attempts to control their behavior and to enforce "good conduct" by legal means. As law becomes more and more concerned with ethics, it naturally seeks for general principles that can be turned into general rules. This preference for the deontological is all too obvious if a little surprising in an Anglo-Saxon system of justice that prides itself on having evolved from an accumulation of individual cases. However that may be, a seemingly endless series of laws and administrative regulations is being developed to regulate the way doctors do experiments, what drugs they may give their patients, how long they can keep them in hospital, and what procedures may or may not be used to aid a sterile woman to have a much-wanted child. One of the least happy possibilities is to take decision regarding the treatment of some gravely ill patients out of the hands of doctors, family members, and even the patients themselves and give them over to lawyers.

Oddly enough, very few people really wanted it to turn out this way.

Physicians have always recognized that there comes a time when it makes no sense to fan the fading spark of life. Ordinary men and women, once the shock of facing up to the inevitable death of a loved one is over, usually recognize that the end came as a relief or even a "blessing." It is only when we try to get a nice, neat philosophical justification for our crude common sense that we run into trouble. Thus, those who wished to make implicit practice into explicit doctrine by organizing euthanasia societies, promulgating the texts of "living wills," or passing legislation favoring death with dignity may have defeated their own ends. With the best intentions in the world, they have unfortunately aroused the passions of those who think the world is simpler than it is and given unforeseen opportunities to those scribes and pharisees who see a personal advantage in hewing to the letter of the law.

What then must we do? Slowly but surely we should work toward a mode of making life-and-death decisions based on some reasonable criteria for determining what makes an individual life worth living. This should gradually take the place of the present practice of regarding all lives as equally sacred and therefore equally bound to be prolonged unless something quite "extraordinary" lifts the burden from us. It is not a question anyone likes to face. In the first place, it implies the necessity of judging other people's lives. Even more unsettling, it implies that other people may judge us. Worst of all, perhaps, is the horrid possibility that it cannot be demonstrated that life is really worth living under any circumstances. There is also the undeniable biological fact that, like all living organisms, human beings are programmed to value survival in an almost automatic, entirely uncritical way. The degree to which such biological programming actually controls human behavior is, of course, a subject of lively and not always polite debate. The difference of view turns on the unusual degree of plasticity built into the human nervous system, which is thereby more subject than most to the influence of culture. More often than not, culture and nature are not really at odds, and most cultures reinforce rather than weaken the basic biological preference for life.

The Judeo-Christian culture in America is characterized by an unusual concern for life in its most minimally definable state. For most of us raised in this dispensation it is hard to realize how parochial we are in our stated belief in the sanctity of any and all life. As our knowledge of the socioeconomic systems that preceded settled agriculture grows, it becomes clear that many if not most of them had schemes, conscious and unconscious, for limiting the number of defective children and adjusting the size of populations to the means of production. These included abortion and infanticide at one end of life and studied neglect of the elderly at the other. Indeed, in some systems it was part of the cultural heritage for the elderly to remain behind when the tribe broke camp under short rations or to wander away from the family on a particularly cold night. Nor were such customs simply the last resort of savages. The ancient Greeks and Romans, whose claims to civilization are unquestioned, were entirely complacent about exposing infants who failed to meet certain criteria and were not above employing infanticide as a device for population control. Indeed, the great nineteenth-century British historian of European morals William Lecky, who could not conceal his admiration for many aspects of the ancient civilizations, especially their tolerance for ideological deviation, found a clear superiority for Christianity only in its effort to abolish infanticide and the gladiatorial games. Those who have since studied the mortality rates in the foundling homes conducted by the religious orders in later centuries may well wonder whether they were in fact monuments to Christian charity and the right to life, or simply another example of the tribute vice pays to virtue. In any event, Lecky never seemed sure whether the nominal abolition of infanticide or even interdicting the games made up for the future horrors of the Inquisition and the religious wars.

As noted above, learned men early recognized the necessity of elaborating defenses for the execution of criminals and heretics, but there are other more surprising rents in the seamless web of sanctity that was supposed to cover all human life. As is well known, a man like Thomas More, fully prepared to die for the faith, could in the sixteenth century explicitly raise the question of euthanasia in strikingly modern terms under the metaphorical cover of his Utopia. Interestingly, the Utopian patient offered the choice of euthanasia is given the further option of starving himself to death or of what we would now call assisted suicide. Whatever More's own view of the matter really was, and whether he is being serious or satirical, the passage demonstrates that even in an intensely religious age it was possible to discuss the termination of life in an objective way.

The satirical and the serious are not antithetical, of course. Indeed, satire and humor are normally used as a kind of cover to make it possible to deal with topics too painful to attack head-on. Such appears to have been the case with the valedictory address delivered at Johns Hopkins University by William Osler in 1905. To at least two generations of American physicians, Osler was as much of a man for all seasons as Sir Thomas and very nearly as worthy of canonization. In his address, Osler devoted two longish paragraphs to the subject of retirement, referring to the accepted impression that most men have done most of their best work by age forty and little or nothing after sixty. Then, with his tongue pushed how far into his cheek it is impossible now to say, he referred to Anthony Trollope's "charming novel 'The Final Period' [with its] admirable scheme of a college into which at sixty men retired for a year of contemplation before a peaceful departure by chloroform." In this case the cloak of humor proved inadequate to cover the nakedness of the suggestion, and Osler was subjected to several weeks of abuse from the press. Though Osler was clearly embarrassed and upset by the incivility of the reaction, he never fully retracted the basic idea. His biographer Harvey Cushing,[3] who as a neurosurgeon was only too well acquainted with death and disinclined to joke about it, leaves us with the impression that Osler did really wish to raise a subject he felt to be of increasing importance. In the event, he misjudged the intensity of the public disinclination to think about last things.

Osler's address is important to us since it takes the question beyond the sickroom where death already hovers in the wings. Furthermore, it explicitly assumes that life is not an end in itself, some absolute essence that must be preserved simply because of its absoluteness. What is important is the opportunity life gives us to do something significant. "Take the sum of human achievement in action," he says, "in science, in art, in literature,—subtract the work of the men above forty, and while we should miss great treasures . . . we would be practically where we are today." The remainder of the two paragraphs simply expands this notion with references from Osler's store of classical literature, points out some of the "calamities that befall men during the seventh and eight decades," and finally attributes to the sexagenarians "nearly all the great mistakes politically and socially, all of the worst poems, most of the bad pictures, a majority of the bad novels, [and] not a few of the bad sermons and speeches."

Osler was deliberately exaggerating the sins of sexagenarians, but we should not allow this to obscure his unquestioned confidence in assessing a person's worth by counting his accomplishments in bettering the human condition. At the time he spoke, the idea was not as unchristian as it might seem now, since there were many who remembered that Christ himself recommended judging a tree by its fruits, and Calvinists were taught to look for outward and visible signs of inward and spiritual grace. Now, however, the religious have given first place to another text, "Judge not, that ye be not judged," while the secular philosophers answer with the Kantian antiphony, "Each man is an absolute end in himself." These dicta, coupled with the uncritical egalitarianism of our time, make it very hard indeed to stand back and even consider the possibility that some lives may be more worth living than others after age eighty, let alone the Oslerian sixty.

Trends and Terrors: Arranging the Appointment in Samarra

In spite of the obvious difficulties and embarrassments, there are signs that the obligation to decide is recognized for what it is, if as yet, only indirectly. Perhaps most instructive is the change in attitude toward suicide. No longer in any U.S. state is suicide regarded as a crime. Even in ecclesiastical circles, much of the previous stigma has been removed, and many suicides are now eligible for Christian burial. The increasing suicide rate among the young is, of course, generally deplored and properly regarded as a serious indictment of a society that offers its youth such inadequate opportunities for the achievements extolled by Sir William Osler. But suicide of the elderly, especially those who have completed their life work, discharged remaining obligations, and now face a life of loneliness threatened perhaps by debilitating illness, is increasingly and sympathetically understood.

It is unclear just how far and fast public discussion of the suicide option will proceed. But the pressures are in favor of something approaching deliberate speed. Everyone by now must know that the proportion of elderly in our society is increasing every year. For the present, they are the object of special political concern, and public support for more financial aid is surprisingly widespread even among the tax-paying middle-aged. How much of this enthusiasm is traceable to the unspoken thought that social security and medical systems relieve them of possibly more burdensome personal obligations is difficult to say. It seems not unlikely, however, that questions will ultimately be raised about the wisdom of taxing the healthy and contributory members of society to provide professional nursing care and an increasingly complex technology for merely keeping alive the ailing and noncontributory members.

It would be wrong, however, to overemphasize the financial burden the elderly will place on the young. True, the proportion of dependent elderly will continue to rise during this century toward a possible maximum approaching 20 percent, but this is far less than the nearly 50 percent of dependents under sixteen in some rapidly developing countries. It is true also that the elderly consume two or three times as much medical care as younger people do, but their educational costs are of course far less. Furthermore, there is hope in some quarters that the expensive diseases of the elderly will come under increasing control so that a century or so from now the elderly will lead reasonably comfortable, if somewhat less active, lives and then rather quickly and inexpensively disintegrate like the "wonderful one-hoss shay."

For some time to come, however, old age will be a period of increasing disability and suffering, both physical and mental. Decisions to terminate treatment or to intervene more actively will be undertaken principally to deal with situations clearly less tolerable than death, as judged by the patient, the doctor, and the patient's close relations. In too many cases, the situation is now allowed to deteriorate to the point that the patient has very little to say. This puts the burden of decision on others and raises the difficult legal and philosophical issues alluded to above. Whatever the merits or demerits of the more objective attitudes toward life-and-death judgments observed in other cultures so briefly reviewed above, it seems unlikely that we could make the appropriate readjustments on the scale necessary in the coming decades. On the contrary, it probably will continue to be difficult for doctors, relatives, and even judges to time the death of another person.

An alternative is to encourage the growing change in attitude toward the individual's right and capacity to select the time, place, and circumstance of one's own last thing. Most negative attitudes to suicide, its criminal or sinful connotations, have been greatly weakened. But we have yet to accept the positive steps necessary to make the taking of one's own life reasonably easy from either the psychological or the purely mechanical point of view. Thus many older people who might wish to take leave at the end of a life well lived fail to do so, partly because they fear that loved ones may regard it as a hostile act and partly because they might make a mess of it from lack of information.

Even more serious is the difficulty confronting those who wish to make sure that their lives are not unduly prolonged after they lose the ability to make decisions for themselves. The effort to provide for such contingencies by the device of letters to one's doctor or the drawing up of living wills has yet to gain full legal recognition. The failure to develop suitable arrangements of this kind is a source of sad concern to a number of people and an important factor in making them consider what might be called prophylactic suicide. Few command the strength of mind and sureness of decision that enabled the late and much respected Harvard professor and Nobel Laureate Percy Bridgman to terminate his own life on the last day he was sure of the power to do so.

The foregoing considerations are almost emergency matters demanding the immediate attention of men of goodwill. Presumably they will find workable solutions in a decade or two, or three. It will certainly take longer to develop a consensus about the less physical reasons for finding life no longer worth living, the sort brought forward in Osler's resurrection of Trollope's fanciful tale. Many people are likely to feel that the various achievements and contributions mentioned by Osler are not the sine qua nons of a life worth living and will simply turn back to another game of shuffleboard with other elderly persons. Those of us who were brought up during the Edwardian hangover of the days that nurtured the late Sir William with their unremitting emphasis on personal achievement and public progress may find it easier to understand his attitude than do those nurtured on more immediate gratifications.

However that may be, this is probably not the time to come forward, at least in the United States, with a specific program complete with suicide societies and how-to-do-it books or, worst of all, additional legislation. It does seem timely, however, to encourage an atmosphere of relaxed experimentation that can ultimately emerge with something better than we have now. Such matters are particularly hard to arrange in the United States of America which for all its Bill of Rights and constitutional amendments seems increasingly uptight, reactionary, and restrictive when it comes to allowing individual choice in matters of life and death. Most European nations have been clearly more relaxed about such matters as abortion, human experimentation, the introduction of new drugs, or the fertilization of eggs in petri dishes rather than fallopian tubes. It is my understanding that in Switzerland, scarcely a land of dangerous radicals, it is no longer a crime to provide technical help to someone who has rationally chosen suicide. Not long ago, the journal *Science* carried a brief notice of activities in England directed at clarifying and facilitating the right to suicide.[4] No doubt there will be more, especially from those northern European secular countries that have so long led the world in realizing the dreams of reason outlined by the French philosophes 200 years ago.

It is only fair to note that the *Science* article recounting the moves toward a right to suicide included a brief word from Cicely Saunders, whose resurrection of the hospice to restore some humanity to the twentieth-century "craft of dying" entitles her to respectful attention. Quite simply she stated her fear that establishing a right to suicide might carry with it an obligation. Of course she is right in citing the probability, but is it something to fear? As with all serious questions, the answer is ambiguous. All social pressures to sacrifice for the common good are assaults on individual rights and freedoms. Freud summarized a number of them, beginning with the incest taboo, "perhaps the most drastic mutilation which man's erotic life has in all time experienced."

More often allowed into consciousness is the need to control aggressive impulses in regard to members of one's family or a larger social group. Life itself is by no means excluded from the list of society's requirements; and few indeed are the tribes or nations which have not exacted the supreme sacrifice from their young males as a matter of course. We need free our thinking only very slightly from traditional shackles to marvel that a nation that found nothing unusual about sacrificing the flower of its youth at Passchendaele and Ypres should worry so much about implying (not requiring) that its elderly population give some thought to the possibility that enough is enough.

What reason is there, then, for thinking that enough is actually enough? In groping for an answer one thinks first perhaps of Elijah: "O Lord, take away my life, for I *am* not better than my fathers." Although some scholars argue that the idea of progress is of recent origin, others are not now so sure. Elijah was not the only prophet to look for better days or to suffer depression when sensing a personal failure to do better. Early in this chapter, we found secular reasons for believing that aging and death may actually have evolved so as to make room for a changed generation. Even though we were careful not to presuppose that every change would be for the better, it is clear that a species that attempts to stay the same in a constantly changing world is sure to become worse.

As already pointed out, it is probably a mistake to overemphasize the economic embarrassments of an increasingly aging population. These are plain enough in the burgeoning technical literature on social security systems, but we probably can afford them if it is only a matter of money. What is more worrisome, if more difficult to measure, is the long-term psychological or philosophical effect of devoting more and more of society's effort to a constantly increasing fraction of the population that has nowhere to go but downhill.

In closing it may be worth noting that our changing attitude to last days is part of a more general phenomenon. One of the keenly felt but less talked about aspects of an increasingly effective technology is the way it forces people to make decisions that used to be made by God (or an impersonal "nature"). We have already discussed how improvements in life-support mechanisms have changed the context of deathbed decisions. Similarly, more generalized progress in agriculture, housing, and public health has forced us to count our children and take precautions that the number not rise too fast. Developments in genetics raise difficult decisions regarding what kind of children we want and do not want. All of these specific, immediate quandaries are simply advance agents for more fundamental questions which used to be answered for us, or were kept decently shrouded in theological obscurity. Uneasiness over this new situation accounts in large part for the recent rise in interest in applied ethics and in philosophy as related to policy. So far, however, most of the efforts of professionals have been directed at finding ingenious ways of avoiding confrontation with the ultimate questions.

For example, progress in genetics makes it possible to avoid the birth of fetuses with certain kinds of identifiable defects. Further advances may expand the list, but soon we will encounter characteristics on which there is at present a lack of agreement. One of the earlier problems is likely to be concerned with aggression. Here is a personality trait which once had obvious survival value but is now less compatible with civilized life. What has been the response of philosophers and moralists to the possibility of identifying such traits? Have they been stimulated to reassess the problem of aggression with a view to determining how much we may still need and how much we might be better without? Not at all. Most of the effort has gone into denying that man is by nature aggressive, into asserting that, in any case, every individual has a right to the genetic pattern that has come down to him, or finally into trying to foreclose further research on the grounds that it is dangerous to know too much.

As we have already seen, the ancient question of what makes life worth living, though it can no longer be dismissed as simply another one of God's inscrutable mysteries, is never faced as such. Instead, the attempt is made to avoid it by redefining death, by resurrecting deontological notions of sanctity, or by reserving such decisions to "extraordinary" circumstances. Perhaps the most revealing of the "solutions" of the euthanasia problem is the doctrine that withdrawal of active treatment simply returns the life-or-death decision to God, who always had the decision before the doctor complicated things with his newfangled inventions. Thus does nostalgia seek to dull the pain of responsibility.

But the responsibility remains, and for the secular biologist such evasive action is unlikely to be convincing. Sooner or later, we will have to face our own version of the Day of Judgment. This may lack the grandeur of the Dies Irae with its Tuba Mirum, but the terror may well increase as the obligation to judge joins that of being judged.

NOTES

1. Lyn F. Lofland, The Craft of Dying: The Modern Face of Death (Beverly Hills, Calif.: Sage Publications, 1978).

2. Joseph Fletcher, Situation Ethics: The New Morality (Philadelphia: Westminster Press, 1966).

3. Harvey Cushing, The Life of Sir William Osler (London: Oxford University Press, 1940), pp. 666–67.

4. Cicely Saunders, "Hospices: for the dying, relief from pain and fear," Science 193:4250 (July 30, 1976), 389–91.

8

THE IMAGE OF "THE END OF THE WORLD": A PSYCHOHISTORICAL VIEW

Robert Jay Lifton

THE QUESTION OF END-OF-THE-WORLD IMAGERY TAKES us to the heart of contemporary threat, psychological theory, and man's ultimate role in his own and society's destiny. Conceptual and moral struggles merge here, as old models are found wanting and we grope for new ones.

I have chosen three sets of quotations—first, from Hiroshima survivors; second, from survivors of Buffalo Creek, a much smaller, little-known disaster; and third, from Daniel Paul Schreber, a famous psychiatric patient—because they say something about a continuum that I believe exists in relation to end-of-the-world imagery. At one end of the continuum, we find a more or less socially acceptable response to actual historical events involving extreme destructiveness. At the other end, we find what we consider a mental aberration or paranoid delusion. I emphasize the continuum in order to suggest that even at its extremes—Hiroshima and schizophrenia—there are important relationships and even similarities.

Christian millennial images can, at least at times, be included on the side of the continuum of the relatively acceptable interpretation. That is true as long as the theological structure of meaning, the eschatology involving something like Armageddon, is generally believed. Considering actual historical events, an apocalyptic interpretation is more acceptable in connection with the dropping of the first atomic weapon on Hiroshima in 1945 than the flooding of Buffalo Creek in 1972, simply because of scale. Yet when it is realized that Buffalo Creek, West Virginia, was completely destroyed as a small community—inundated with death, so to speak—imagery of world-ending associated with it becomes more understandable to an outside observer.

From this perspective, three levels of experience must be distinguished. There is first the external event, such as the Hiroshima bomb. We could also speak of the plagues of the Middle Ages as an external event, so much so that there were some notable similarities in the imagery used by plague survivors and survivors of Hiroshima.[1] Second, there is the shared theological imagery, or eschatology, that renders such imagery acceptable as a meaning structure. Finally, there is the internal derangement—the intrapsychic disintegration or personal Armageddon of psychosis found especially but not exclusively in certain schizophrenic syndromes. (These distinctions are necessary and even useful, but if maintained in an absolute sense, they become a barrier to our understanding of this kind of imagery. So I pose them in order to suggest their limitations, in order to move beyond their either/or categories.)

All three of the elements are present in each of the three experiences we are considering. If we take Hiroshima, for instance, there is an overwhelming external event and there is an internal experience, something like internal breakdown or overwhelming psychological trauma. There are, as well, immediate and lasting struggles with belief systems, which start from the moment of encounter with the external threat. The three elements are also present, although on a different scale, in the Buffalo Creek experience. And the same is even true in regard to schizophrenia. We generally think of schizophrenia as a strictly internal derangement, but it too is subject to external influences, and to the struggle for some kind of meaning structure. Hence the content, style, and impact upon others—the dialogue or nondialogue between schizophrenic people and society—vary enormously with historical time and place. Correspondingly, the end-of-the-world imagery of schizophrenia is strongly affected by historical and technological context.

HIROSHIMA, BUFFALO CREEK, AND DANIEL PAUL SCHREBER

When an atomic bomb was dropped over Hiroshima, the most striking psychological feature of survivors' response was the immediate and absolute shift from normal existence to an overwhelming encounter with death. A shopkeeper's assistant conveys this feeling rather characteristically, without explicit end-of-the-world imagery but in a tone consistent with that imagery:

> It came very suddenly. . . . I felt something like an electric short—a bluish sparkling light. . . . There was a noise, and I felt great heat—even inside the house. . . . I couldn't hear voices of my family. I didn't know how I could be rescued. I felt I was going to suffocate and then die, without knowing exactly what happened to me. This was the kind of expectation I had. . . .[2]

Survivors recalled initial feelings related to death and dying, such as "This is the end for me," or "My first feeling was, 'I think I will die.'" But beyond these feelings was the sense that the whole world was dying. That sense was expressed by a physicist who was covered with debris and temporarily blinded: "My body seemed all black, everything seemed dark, dark all over. . . . Then I thought, 'The world is ending.'"[3]

A Protestant minister, himself uninjured, but responding to the evidence of mutilation and destruction he saw everywhere around him, experienced his end-of-the-world imagery in an apocalyptic Christian idiom:

> The feeling I had was that everyone was dead. The whole city was destroyed. . . . I thought all of my family must be dead—it doesn't matter if I die. . . . I thought this was the end of Hiroshima—of Japan—of humankind. . . . This was God's judgment on man. . . .[4]

His memory is inseparable from his theology, in the sense that everyone's memory of such events is inseparable from fundamental interpretive principles.

A woman writer also remembered religious imagery, probably Buddhist:

> I just could not understand why our surroundings had changed so greatly in one instant. . . . I thought it might have been something which had nothing to do with the war, the collapse of the earth which it was said would take place at the end of the world, and which I had read about as a child. . . .[5]

This sense of world collapse could also be expressed symbolically, as in the immediate thought of a devoutly religious domestic worker: "There is no God, no Buddha."[6]

Some called forth humor, inevitably "gallows humor," as a way of mocking one's own helplessness before the total destruction. A professional cremator, for instance, though severely burned, managed to make his way back to his home (adjoining the crematorium) and said that he felt relieved because "I thought I would die soon, and it would be convenient to have the crematorium close by."[7]

Many recollections convey the dreamlike grotesqueness of the scene of the dead and the dying, and the aimless wandering of the living. All this was sensitively rendered by Dr. Michihiko Hachiya in his classic *Hiroshima Diary:*

> Those who were able walked silently toward the suburbs in the distant hills, their spirits broken, their initiative gone. When asked whence they had come, they pointed to the city and said "that way": and when asked where they were going, pointed away from the city and said "this way." They were so broken and confused that they moved and behaved like automatons.
>
> Their reactions had astonished outsiders who reported with amazement the spectacle of long files of people holding stolidly to a narrow rough path when close by was a smooth easy road going in the same direction. The

outsiders could not grasp the fact that they were witnessing the exodus of a people who walked in the realm of dreams.[8]

Above all, there was so great a sense of silence as to suggest the absence of all life. Again the woman writer:

> It was quiet around us . . . in fact there was a fearful silence which made one feel that all people and all trees and vegetation were dead. . . .[9]

In all this there was a profound disruption in the relationship between death and life, as conveyed by a grocer, himself severely burned:

> The appearance of people was . . . well, they all had skin blackened by burns. . . . They had no hair because their hair was burned, and at a glance you couldn't tell whether you were looking at them from in front or in back. . . . They held their arms bent [forward] like this [he proceeded to demonstrate their position] . . . and their skin—not only on their hands, but on their faces and bodies too—hung down. . . . If there had been only one or two such people perhaps I would not have had such a strong impression. But wherever I walked I met these people. . . . Many of them died along the road—I can still picture them in my mind—like walking ghosts. . . . They didn't look like people of this world. . . . They had a special way of walking—very slowly. . . . I myself was one of them.[10]

These Hiroshima memories, then, combine explicit end-of-the-world imagery with a grotesque dreamlike aura of a nonnatural situation, a form of existence in which life was so permeated by death as to become virtually indistinguishable from it.

The small disaster at Buffalo Creek, West Virginia (which I studied and consulted on),[11] was a flood which occurred in 1972 as a consequence of the dumping of coal waste in a mountain stream in a manner that created an artificial dam and increasingly dangerous water pressure behind it. After several days of rain, the "dam" gave way and a massive moving wall of "black water," more than thirty feet high, roared through the narrow creek hollow, killing 125 people and making nearly 500 homeless.

While interviewing survivors, I was struck by many resemblances to the patterns I had described in Hiroshima. There was not, of course, the Hiroshima aura of ultimate destruction and merging of death and life. But as a "total disaster" in the sense of the complete destruction of a finite area, it produced its own end-of-the-world imagery. Some memories of destruction become encompassing, with at least the momentary sense on the part of a number of survivors that "it was the end of time." In a way analogous to Hiroshima but much more limited, Buffalo Creek survivors described the contrast between the hopeful movement of life existing prior to the disaster and the hopeless stagnation after it. As expressed by an incapacitated miner:

It's a split decision. There's the life you lived before and the life you live after. Before the disaster it seemed like you got up and you looked forward; there was something I was going ahead to—the garden, the horses, the job. The garden is gone; there are trailers where the horses were; there's no job left.[12]

Memories of the disaster were still extremely vivid during interviews conducted thirty months after the flood. As one man interviewed in May 1974 put it: "Everything came to an end—just stopped. Everything was wiped out."

The third set of quotations I want to present are from a gifted man's account of his disturbed mental state. Daniel Paul Schreber, a distinguished German judge, would hardly have realized in 1903, when he published his *Memoirs of My Nervous Illness* of a decade or so before, that he was providing psychoanalytic psychiatry with what was to become the celebrated Schreber "case." From these memoirs Freud constructed a concept of schizophrenia that has informed, haunted, and confused psychiatric work on psychosis every since.

Schreber's own account of his psychosis is extraordinarily articulate, and it can be a source of considerable insight to anyone who studies it carefully. One of the smaller ironies of subsequent German history lies in the fact that the place in which Schreber had these experiences that were to contribute so much to human understanding, the asylum at Sonnenstein, was to become deeply implicated in the Nazi mass murder of mental patients under the euphemism of "euthanasia" just a few decades later.

Schreber was preoccupied with the idea of a "world catastrophe," which he thought at times necessary for the re-creation of the species, and for the possibility of his (Schreber's) giving birth to children in the manner of a woman. In one passage he describes some of this delusional and hallucinatory system in connection with observations on the stars and mysterious cosmic events:

When later I regularly visited the garden and again saw—my memory does not fully deceive me—two suns in the sky at the same time, one of which was our earthly sun. The other was said to be the Cassiopeian group of stars drawn together into a single sun. From the sum total of my recollections, my impression gained hold of me that the period in question, which according to human calculations stretched over three to four months, had covered an immensely long period. It was as if single nights had a duration of centuries. So that within that time the most profound alterations in the whole of mankind and the earth itself and the whole solar system might very well have taken place. It was repeatedly mentioned in visions that the work of the past 1,400 years had been lost. . . .[13]

When Schreber says "repeatedly mentioned" he refers to his "visions" or hallucinations. He attributes the figure of 1,400 years to be an indication of "the duration of time that the earth has been populated," and he remembers hearing another figure, about 200 or 212 years, for the time still "allotted to the earth."

> During the latter part of my stay in Flechsig's asylum [Prof. Flechsig was the director] I thought this period had already expired and therefore I was the last real human being left, and that the few human shapes I saw apart from myself—Professor Flechsig, some attendants, occasional more or less strange-looking patients—were only "fleeting-improvised men" created by miracle. I pondered over such possibilities as that the whole of Flechsig's asylum or perhaps the city of Leipzig with it had been "dug out" and moved to some other celestial body, all of them possibilities which questions asked by the voices who talked to me seemed to hint at, as for instance whether Leipzig was still standing, etc. I regarded the starry sky largely, if not wholly, extinguished.

Here the world "catastrophe" is accompanied by celestial re-creation, with Schreber himself at the center of it. Thus he goes on to speak of seeing "beyond the walls of the Asylum only a narrow strip of land" so strange and different that "at times one spoke of a holy landscape."

> I lived for years in doubt as to whether I was really still on earth or whether some other celestial body. . . . In the soul—language during [that] time . . . I was called "the seer of spirits," that is, a man who sees, and is in communication with, spirits or departed souls.[14]

These quotations from Schreber convey the kind of end-of-the-world imagery one encounters in acute and chronic forms of psychosis, usually paranoid schizophrenic psychosis. We will have more to say about schizophrenia and about Schreber, but here we may note that the psychotic dies *with* the world, in that his sense of inner disintegration includes his sense of self *and* world. But by rendering himself at the same time the only survivor, he expresses a characteristic struggle with vitality and pseudovitality.

SCHIZOPHRENIA AS THE KEY

To explore these psychological issues further, we must turn to the question of schizophrenia and its relationship to imagery of the end of the world.

Freud approached the Schreber case from the standpoint of his libido theory. He attributed its paranoid dimension to repressed homosexual wishes: to a strong "wave of libido" directed toward other men. But since this "single proposition: 'I (a man) *love him* (the man)' is completely unacceptable, it is reversed to 'I do not *love* him—I *hate* him'; and that second proposition in turn required, for justification, a third one: 'I do not *love* him—I *hate* him; because *he persecutes* me.'" Imagery of world catastrophe results from the withdrawing of virtually all libido from the external world: "His subjective world has come to an end since his withdrawal of his love from it."[15] Libido or sexual energy was instead directed at the self or more precisely the ego. This reversal of the path of libido Freud called "secondary narcissism." Freud believed that the megalomania of schizophrenia was due to this secondary narcissism, which was in turn "superimposed upon a primary narcissism," that is, the phase of early psychosexual development during which the child directs his libido toward himself. In schizophrenia one regresses to this infantile stage: the world ends because primary and secondary narcissism prevent love for, or involvement with, anyone or anything in it.

Reading Freud carefully, one finds that certain concepts assumed more closed or final form in connection with the ongoing ideological struggle. This turns out to be the case with his theory of schizophrenia. At the time Freud was evolving this theory, Jung was beginning to take issue with his ideas. Jung, his designated "son" and successor, had worked extensively with schizophrenic patients. While Freud's essay on the Schreber case preceded the break between the two men, Freud could not have been unaware of Jung's growing discomfort with Freud's way of applying libido theory to schizophrenia. Eventually Jung was to insist that imagery of the end of the world reflected the psychotic's withdrawal of all interests from the external world, not just his sexuality, and to argue for a more general (more than merely sexual) understanding of the entire concept of libido. Just after his break with Jung, Freud wrote two essays. In one, "On Narcissism," he stated that applying libido theory to schizophrenia created "a pressing motive for occupying ourselves with the conception of a primary and normal narcissism." He also, somewhat sarcastically, expressed what he took to be Jung's view that "the libido theory has already come to grief in the attempt to explain [schizophrenia]."[16] So we may say that Freud's views on imagery of the end of the world were in some measure a defense of—or at least a warding off of a beginning attack on—his own ideological world.

Similarly, Freud invoked the concept of narcissism in other conditions we might see today as characterized by actual or feared disintegration of the self, by the sense of "falling apart." I have in mind profound forms of depression or "melancholia" and the severe traumatic disorders related to World War I. Freud dealt with both of these syndromes by applying the concept of narcissism, thereby holding to a primacy of libido theory rather than probe death-related issues or "death equivalents." (There were always difficulties with Freud's view of schizophrenia. Even so loyal an explicator of psychoanalytic theory as Otto Fenichel raised questions about the theory of narcissism and reversal of libido, although he did not directly contradict the theory.[17])

Much recent writing questions this classical view, and moves in directions closer to my own work focusing on symbolization of life and death. A connecting principle, perhaps a form of continuity with Freud, is that of "deanimation"—the schizophrenic person's sense that his humanity has been taken away from him, that he has been turned into a thing, and that he can experience no actively functioning self. We know that the capacity to experience a vital self has to do with the health of the symbolizing function; one becomes a "thing" when impairment of that function results in extreme concretization and literalization.

Eugen Bleuler, who coined the word *schizophrenia*, gave considerable emphasis to literalizing tendencies, as have most subsequent writers. Burnham, for instance, speaks of the schizophrenic's "references to himself as a toy, puppet, or slave" and of a woman who "spoke of herself as a doll and even moved like a mechanical toy." Another patient told Burnham: "I have lost my soul." And another patient: "It's all a stage production. Everyone is acting and using stage names." And still another: "The people here are only pseudo-people, made of papier-mâché."[18] In a similar vein, I was told of a young woman who described herself as a machine and would hold out her arms and say: "Smell the plastic and the metal."

While these images may well reflect sensitive perception of actual hypocrisy and falsity in life experience, they undoubtedly also include long-standing feelings of unreality. They are a description of a "land of the dead," of a kind many schizophrenics feel themselves to inhabit: the world itself is dead and human history has ended. Again, the death imagery is directly related to desymbolization.

In my exploration of schizophrenia and other psychiatric syndromes, I have stressed three issues: death imagery and the simulation of death; the nature of the perceived threat; and the relationship to meaning. R. D. Laing's important early work explores precisely these areas in ways that are not always systematic but nonetheless illuminating.

In *The Divided Self,* Laing provided special insight into schizophrenia as a disorder of feeling—a special state of psychic numbing—emphasizing its relationship to psychic death. Put simply, the most extreme inner sense of deadness and unreality equals ultimate psychic numbing equals insanity:

A man says he is dead but he *is* alive. But his "truth" is that he is dead. . . .
When someone says he is an unreal man or that he is dead, in all seriousness, expressing in radical terms the stark truth of his existence as he experiences it, that is—insanity.[19]

For these patients, "To play possum, to feign death becomes a way of preserving one's aliveness." Thus what Laing calls the "false self" is in fact the dead self—the self that feels dead. This view is in keeping with Laing who, at another point, speaks of "the murder of the self" and of "becoming dead in order not to die."

The "death stance" in schizophrenia differs from the death stance in other psychiatric syndromes, such as depression, where it is also present. Schizophrenia is distinguished by a more profound level of disorder around death imagery, one that has to do with the fear of relationship or of vitality. The schizophrenic has a deep ambivalence toward relationships: they become infused with the threat of annihilation and are fraught with terror, even as he seeks them in his desperately lonely state. That is why the schizophrenic is so hard to help.

Concerning the nature of the threat in schizophrenia, Freud, as we have seen, focused on homoerotic impulses and the fear of homosexuality, particularly in paranoid schizophrenia. More recent work points instead to the threat to existence, to the fear of being annihilated, as central to schizophrenia. This does not mean that sexual confusion and fear of homosexuality are unimportant, but that they are an aspect of a more general category, rather than themselves the central threat perceived in schizophrenia.

Macalpine and Hunter, who produced the first full English translation of the Schreber *Memoirs,* also provided a valuable reinterpretation of that case. They questioned Freud's views, and stressed instead issues around death and life-continuity. They understood Schreber's psychosis as a "reactivation of unconscious, archaic procreation fantasies concerning life, death, immortality, rebirth, creation, including self-impregnation, and accompanied by absolute ambi-sexuality expressed in doubt and uncertainty about his sex." And they go on to say that "homosexual anxieties were secondary to the primary fantasy of having to be transformed into a woman to be able to procreate. Hence, Schreber's system centering on creation and the origin of life, whether by God or the sun, sexually or parthenogenetically."

They focused on Schreber's own experience of what he called "soul murder," a theme "of which Freud could make nothing," but one which may well have been "the center of [Schreber's] psychosis." Schreber's own elaboration of "soul murder" makes it clear that he was thinking along lines of death and life-continuity:

. . . The idea is widespread in the folklore and poetry of all people that it is somehow possible to take possession of another person's soul in order to prolong one's life at another soul's expense, or to secure some other advantages which outlast death.[20]

Macalpine and Hunter tell us that not only was the self being annihilated in soul murder, but so was all possibility of human connection. They saw this as an explanation for Schreber's end-of-the-world fantasy, as well as his delusion that he was immortal (". . . a person without a soul, i.e. life substance, cannot die"). That fantasy in turn could enable Schreber to imagine himself as "sole survivor to renew mankind." The perception of annihilation remains central.

Similarly, recent work by Harold Searles emphasizes the difficulty schizophrenic persons have in consistently experiencing themselves as "being *alive*." Many do not seem to fear death because "so long as one feels dead anyway . . . one has, subjectively, nothing to lose through death." Yet there can be an accompanying near-total inability to accept the finiteness of life (hence the grandiose delusions of omnipotence and immortality) because of the sense of never having really lived.[21] Behind both experiential deadness and literalized immortality is something close to Schreber's "soul murder," that is, the perpetual threat of annihilation.

The perceived threat of annihilation starts out early in life and may even have a significant hereditary component. This perception then becomes totalized, so that for many schizophrenics these early experiences become the whole of life experience. Thus there are profound questions of meaning, desymbolization, and deformation which must enter into a theory of schizophrenia.

The "soul murder" or inner disintegration of schizophrenia gives rise to extreme forms of numbing and deformation throughout the function of the self. At an immediate level, the schizophrenic feels himself flooded with death anxiety, which he both embraces and struggles against. At the ultimate level, his absence of connection beyond the self leaves him with the feeling that life is counterfeit, and that biological death is unacceptable and yet uneventful because psychic death is everywhere. This combination of radically impaired meaning and constant threat of annihilation is at the heart of the schizophrenic's imagery of the end of the world.[22]

DEATH AND THE CONTINUITY OF LIFE: PROXIMATE AND ULTIMATE LEVEL

To claim that schizophrenia has relevance for all end-of-the-world imagery requires the use of a psychological model or paradigm, which enables us to find common ground among the various end-of-the-world images I have mentioned. The paradigm presumes both a proximate or immediate level of experience, and an ultimate level close to what Tillich called "ultimate concern." That is, the schizophrenic not only fears annihilation but, as Searles and others point out, fears (and to some extent welcomes) being severed from the great stream of human existence.

Our paradigm, then, is that of death and the continuity of life—or, one may say, the symbolization of life and death. The proximate level involves the immediate, nitty-gritty experiences dealt with in most psychological work. The ultimate level involves the struggle for connection with those who have gone before, and those who will follow, our own limited life span; or what I call the symbolization of symbolic immortality.[23]

This sense of immortality is sought normatively in many ways: through living on in one's children, in one's works, in one's human influences, and in what most cultures symbolize as eternal nature. Continuity is also experienced in religious belief, whether or not it literally postulates a life after death, and, finally, in any direct experience of transcendence, in psychic states so intense that time and death disappear. This last case is the classic mode of the mystics, and is not unrelated to various experiences of world-ending. (There can be an element of ecstasy in the schizophrenic perception of the end of the world, along with its terror. The same has been found to be true for other aspects of schizophrenic experience.) Such experiential transcendence can be spiritual; it may be sexual; it can occur through athletic exertion or the contemplation of beauty. It is sometimes spoken of as "Dionysian," but it can take quiet forms as well.

Concern with connections beyond the self, the ultimate dimension in our paradigm, is often left to the theologians and philosophers. This is a mistake that those involved in psychological work should redress. What is involved here is an evolutionary triad. To become human one takes on simultaneously: first, the knowledge that one dies; second, the symbolizing function, the fundamental form of human mentation, requiring the internal re-creation of all that we perceive; and third, the creation of culture, which is by no means merely a vehicle for denying death (as many psychoanalytic thinkers, from Freud to Norman O. Brown, have claimed) but is integral to man as the cultural animal, and probably necessary for the development of the kind of brain he has come to possess. In struggles around the symbolization of immortality, then, man is struggling with these three elements, with the levels of psychic experience that define him as man.

The immediate or proximate level of experience involves three dialectics—connection versus separation, movement versus stasis, and integrity versus integration. Each of the three is familiar, having its beginning or prefiguring in various inchoate experiences from birth and perhaps even before. The negative end of each dialectic is what I call the death equivalent—imagery of separation, stasis, and disintegration. The sequence proceeds from the physiological (in terms of connection-separation, the newborn seeking out the breast, and later the mother) to the creation of images (the infant forming pictures of its mother and recognizing her) to symbolization (the eventual capacity for complex feelings of love and loyalty). Similarly, the newborn may cry when physically "separated" from its mother, and the developing infant, from early images of separation and loss, constructs a psychological substrate for the slightly later exposure to the idea of death. Thus, over the course of the life cycle, immediate involvements of connection and separation, movement and stasis, and integrity and disintegration become highly symbolized into elaborate ethical and psychological constellations.

MILLENNIAL IMAGERY AND CONTEMPORARY END-OF-THE-WORLD DILEMMAS

We can now ask: What do people who respond to millennial imagery experience at an ultimate level as well as a proximate level? In what way does millennial imagery, in its symbolization of immortality, connect or combine with these two levels? How is millennial imagery related to death equivalents such as separation, stasis, and disintegration? What further questions can one raise about the millennial imagery of clinical syndromes, including schizophrenia? What is the general relation of millennial imagery to death imagery and to the experience of inner deadness? How does millennial imagery relate to profound threat, individual or collective? And finally, is there more we can say about millennial imagery in terms of meaning and cosmology? To these difficult questions, a few general principles come to mind.

In schizophrenia and other clinical syndromes Freud understood symptoms to express attempts at what he called "restitution" of the disordered self to a healthier state. That principle has particular relevance to imagery of the end of the world, and in the Schreber case we saw how that imagery was bound up with the idea of the world being purified and reconstituted. In millennial imagery associated with religious thought, the element of revitalization and moral cleansing—the vision of a new and better existence—is even more prominent, and considerably more functional. Theological tradition can provide form, coherence, and shared spiritual experience, in contrast to the isolated delusional system of the individual schizophrenic person.

Ultimately we may say that millennial ideas of all kinds are associated with an even larger category of mythological imagery of death and rebirth. They can represent later theological (and sometimes political) invocations and refinements of earlier fundamental images. We miss the significance of millennial imagery if we see in it *only* the threat of deadness or the absence of meaning; but we also misunderstand it if we do not recognize in it precisely that threat and absence. In other words, millennial imagery always includes something on the order of death equivalents—of threatened annihilation—and, at the same time, in its various symbolizations, something on the order of renewal and revitalization.

In schizophrenia, that imagery of revitalization is radically literalized. The issue of literalization has general significance for schizophrenia, as an aspect of overall desymbolization. With desymbolization there is an inability to carry out the specific human task of constant creation and re-creation of images and forms, or what I call the formative-symbolizing function. What is called the "thought disorder" of schizophrenia involves a fundamental impairment to this function, the replacement of symbolic flow with static literalization.

An important question for religious millennial imagery is the extent to which it is experienced in literalized, as opposed to more formative or symbolized, ways. I had a conversation about Christian imagery of immortality with Paul Tillich toward the end of his life. Tillich's view was that the more literal promise of an "afterlife" was a corrupt form of theological expression, disseminated among the relatively poor and uneducated. In the more profound expressions of this imagery, Tillich held, the idea of immortality symbolized unending spiritual continuity. Many, to be sure, would argue with this view, and it is undoubtedly more true at certain moments of history than others. But it does help us to grasp distinctions among different expressions of millennial thought. And when a millennial vision becomes so literalized that it is associated with a prediction of the actual end of the world on a particular day on the basis of biblical images or mathematical calculation applied to such images or whatever, we become aware of a disquieting border area of theology and psychopathology.

The appearance of nuclear weapons in the mid-1940s evoked an image: that of man's extermination of himself as a species with his own technology. The image, of course, is not totally new. Versions of it have been constituted by visionaries—H. G. Wells is an outstanding example—at least from the time of the Industrial Revolution. But nuclear weapons gave substance to the image and disseminated it everywhere, making it the dubious psychic property of the common man.

Moreover, the element of self-determination must be differentiated from older religious images of Armageddon, "Judgment Day," or the "end of the world." Terrifying as these may be, they are part of a world view or cosmology—man is acted upon by a higher power who has his reasons, who destroys only for spiritual purposes (such as achieving the "Kingdom of God"). That is a far cry from man's destruction of himself with his own tools, and to no purpose.

There are several special features to this contemporary end-of-the-world imagery. There is, first, the suggestion of the end of our species, of something on the order of biological extinction. Second, it is related to specific external events of recent history (Hiroshima and Nagasaki, as well as the Nazi death camps). And third, unlike earlier imagery of world destruction—even that associated with such external events as the plagues of the Middle Ages—the danger comes from our own hand, from man and his technology. The source is not God or nature, but we ourselves. Our "end" is (in considerable measure) perceived as a form of self-destruction. We can therefore see in it little justification or significance. If some view nuclear holocaust as inevitable, they do so with resignation or hopelessness—as opposed to the meaningful inevitability of an eschatology or the submission to the awesome forces of nature.

This potential self-destruction has bearing on issues of widespread guilt as well as psychic numbing. The numbing—diminished feeling with denial—takes place not only in relationship to massive death, but also around the idea of human responsibility for that process. So there is numbing both toward the destruction itself and toward our guilt as potential perpetrators of that destruction. Traditionally, guilt is relatively contained within an eschatology: if man is guilty, he must be punished, he must be destroyed in order to be re-created in a purer form. Within our present context, however, one perceives a threat of a literal, absolute end without benefit of a belief system that gives form, acceptance, or solace to that idea.

This predicament takes us back to some of the questions mentioned earlier. Anticipating the possibility of nuclear holocaust, we experience profound doubts about our larger human connectedness (the ultimate dimension in our paradigm). For in a postnuclear world, one can hardly be certain of living on in one's children or their children; in one's creation or human influences; in some form of lasting spirituality (which may not be possible in an imagined world where there are virtually none among the biological living); or in eternal nature, which we know to be susceptible to our weapons and pollutions. The radical uncertainty of these four modes may indeed play a large part in our present hunger for direct experiences of transcendence—whether through drugs, meditation, or other altered states of consciousness. Similarly, there is a growing body of evidence relating perceptions of nuclear threat to different versions of what I have called death equivalents—imagery of separation, stasis, and disintegration. All of these, of course, become bound up with different forms of psychic numbing, or with something worse: with a pseudo-religion I call "nuclearism," involving the deification and worship of the very agents of our potential destruction, seeing in them a deity that cannot only destroy but also protect and create, even depending on them to keep us and the world going.[24]

Yet our exploration of end-of-the-world imagery suggests, in itself, a countering force. It is a precarious one, because it hovers on the anxious edge of ultimate destruction. Consider the two dimensions of the Dr. Strangelove image.[25] There is, on the one hand, the impulse to "press the button" and "get the thing over with," even the orgiastic excitement of the wild forces let loose—destroying everything in order to feel alive. But the other side of the Strangelove image, what I take to be its wisdom, is the insistence that we confront the radical absurdity or "madness" of the world destruction we are contemplating. It is similar to what Teilhard de Chardin had in mind, as an evolutionary theorist and mystic, in writing about the expansion of the "noosphere" or area of knowledge as the other side of our capacity to destroy ourselves. And it is what Erik Erikson means when he speaks about the relationship between our destructive capacity and our first glimpses of a form of human identity so inclusive that it embraces the entire species.

We must imagine something close to nuclear extinction in order to prevent it. We must extend our psychological and moral imaginations in order to hold off precisely what we begin to imagine.

Eugene Rabinowitz provides us with a very good example of just this possibility for renewal, when he writes about the circumstances in which he and other nuclear scientists drafted one of the earlier petitions against the use of a nuclear weapon:

> In the summer of 1945, some of us walked the streets of Chicago vividly imagining the sky suddenly lit up by a giant fireball, the steel skeleton of skyscrapers bending into grotesque shapes and their masonry raining into the streets below, until a great cloud of dust rose and settled over the crumbling city.[26]

This image of the "end of the world" inspired him to urge his colleagues to return quickly to their work on the "Franck Report" that he, Franck, Szilard, and a number of others in Chicago were instrumental in creating. To be sure, the Report's recommendation that the atomic weapon not be used on a human population without warning was not heeded. But it has become a central document in our contemporary struggle to imagine the end of the world in order to preserve the world.

NOTES

1. Robert Jay Lifton, *Death in Life: Survivors of Hiroshima* (1968; New York: Touchstone, 1976), pp. 367–95, 479–539, 525–39.
2. Ibid., p. 21.

3. Ibid., p. 22.
4. Idem.
5. Yōko Ōta, *Shikabane no Machi (Town of Corpses)* (Tokyo: Kawade Shobō, 1955), p. 63.
6. Lifton, *Death in Life*, p. 23.
7. Idem.
8. M. Hachiya, *Hiroshima Diary*, ed. and trans. Warner Wells (Chapel Hill: University of North Carolina Press, 1955), p. 54.
9. Ōta, *Shikabane no Machi*, p. 63.
10. Lifton, *Death in Life*, p. 27.
11. See Robert Jay Lifton and Eric Olson, "The Human Meaning of Total Disaster: The Buffalo Creek Experience," *Psychiatry* 39:1 (February 1976), 1–18. See also Kai T. Erikson, *Everything in Its Path* (New York: Simon & Schuster, 1976); and James L. Titchener and Frederic T. Kapp, "Family and Character Change in Buffalo Creek," *American Journal of Psychiatry* 133:3 (March 1976), 295–99.
12. Lifton and Olson, "The Human Meaning of Total Disaster."
13. Ida Macalpine and Richard A. Hunter, eds. and trans., Daniel Paul Schreber, *Memoirs of My Nervous Illness* (1903; London: William Dawson & Sons, 1955), pp. 84–85.
14. Ibid., pp. 85–88.
15. Sigmund Freud, "Psycho-Analytic Notes on an Autobiographical Account of a Case of Paranoia (Dementia Paranoides) [1911]," in James Strachey, ed., *The Standard Edition of the Complete Psychological Works of Sigmund Freud* (London: The Hogarth Press and The Institute of Psycho-Analysis, 1958), 12:63, 70; 14:75.
16. Freud, "On Narcissism: An Introduction," *Standard Edition*, 14:79. See also Sheldon T. Selesnick, "C. G. Jung's Contributions to Psychoanalysis," *American Journal of Psychiatry* 120:4 (April 1963), 350–56.
17. Otto Fenichel, *The Psychoanalytic Theory of Neurosis* (New York: W. W. Norton & Company, 1945), pp. 417–18, 424–25.
18. Donald L. Burnham, "Separation Anxiety," *Archives of General Psychiatry* 13:4 (1965), 346–58.
19. R. D. Laing, *The Divided Self* (Baltimore: Penguin [Pelican], 1965), pp. 37–38.
20. Macalpine and Hunter, eds. and trans., Daniel Paul Schreber, *Memoirs of My Nervous Illness*, p. 55.
21. Harold F. Searles, *Collected Papers on Schizophrenia and Related Subjects* (New York: International Universities Press, 1965), pp. 488–89, 495, 497.
22. Much American research in the last several decades has had to do with family transmission. Some of the work of Lyman Wynn, Margaret Thaler Singer, and Theodore Lidz emphasizes various forms of transmitted schism or irrationality which I would call desymbolization or deformation.
23. This emphasis on symbolization draws extensively on the work of Ernst Cassirer and Susanne Langer.
24. I discuss in much greater detail these and other issues raised throughout this chapter in my book *The Broken Connection: On Death and the Continuity of*

Life (New York: Simon and Schuster, 1979). See especially chapters 1, 2, 16, 22, 23, and appendixes A, C, and D.

25. *Dr. Strangelove; or, How I Learned to Stop Worrying and Love the Bomb,* 1963 movie with Peter Sellers.

26. Eugene Rabinowitch, "Five Years After," in Morton Grodzins and Eugene Rabinowitch, eds., *The Atomic Age: Scientists in National and World Affairs* (New York: Basic Books, 1963), p. 156.

PART III

9

THE END OF MAN IN TWENTIETH-CENTURY THOUGHT: REFLECTIONS ON A PHILOSOPHICAL METAPHOR

Matei Calinescu

THE DEATH OF MAN, THE DISSOLUTION OF MAN, THE DIS-
persion of man, the disappearance of man, and numerous other similar philosophical labels that became fashionable during the structuralist
1960s, first in France (where the new intellectual fashion explains the
extraordinary success of a book like Michel Foucault's *Les Mots et les
choses*),[1] then in other Western countries, confront the historian of contemporary culture with some remarkable and profoundly intriguing terminological questions. This chapter attempts to discuss these questions
and some of the larger philosophical issues that underlie them. But before
setting out to analyze the various kinds of meaning conveyed by the
language used to describe the end of man—which, as we shall see, covers
the whole semantic range that extends from the loosely metaphorical,
through the technical, to, occasionally, the literal—one can hardly help
being disturbed by the broad connotations of this language. It is particularly disturbing in a time like ours, marked by the memory of such unprecedented traumatic experiences as the two world wars, the Nazi
Holocaust, the Gulag in the Soviet Union, events in post-1945 Eastern
Europe and elsewhere, as well as by fears of a possible nuclear conflagration that might conceivably result in the extinction of civilization and the
human race itself.

This essay is based in part on a paper read at a symposium organized by the Centre
Européen de la Culture and the Institut Universitaire d'Etudes Européennes in Geneva in
June 1978, and published in *Cadmos*, 1:3 (Autumn 1978), 15–34.

The fact that apocalyptic expressions such as those mentioned above—
irrespective of whether they make claims to the status of neutral technical
terms—can become culturally fashionable, points to a larger modern syndrome, whose main characteristic is perhaps the constant, obsessive recurrence of the idea of the end. The end itself may be regarded as the
coming of the *eskhaton* (doomsday in a secular world without transcendence), or the achievement of the *telos* of history (its "final cause," its
goal), or a combination of the two in various degrees and proportions; it
may evoke anxiety or a paradoxical kind of joy; it may be colored by the
most somber pessimism or, again paradoxically, it may be considered with
a mixture of irony, self-irony, and even playfulness. Whatever the case,
the inescapable idea of the end remains fundamentally the same, unchanged by the great diversity of reactions, rationalizations, or emotions
that it brings about.[2]

This chapter will focus on the philosophical and aesthetic offshoots of
modern eschatological imagination during the twentieth century, but not
without reference to earlier thinkers whose influence on contemporary
culture is still pervasive. The end of man will be examined at once ter-
minologically and in its wider-ranging cultural implications, including the
problems raised by the emergence of secular humanism, the various
subsequent critiques of the idea of man, and the formation of "antihumanistic" doctrines—from Marx and Nietzsche to the structuralists. Some of
the aesthetic consequences of the latter theories—the "dehumanization"
of art and, more recently, the rise of an antihermeneutical poetics of the
death of the author and of playful inauthenticity, among them—will also
be taken into account. While it is impossible to ignore the sociohistorical
background of these developments in later modern thought, for reasons of
space as well as expository clarity, specific references to this background
will be kept to a minimum. The reader, it is hoped, will not fail to notice
independently the many striking analogies between the theoretical antihumanism promoted by the master thinkers of modernity (to use a phrase
borrowed from André Glucksmann)[3] and the examples of practical antihumanism in which the troubled history of our century is so rich.

The idea of the end is inscribed in the very concept of modernity insofar
as modernity is a radically secularized version of Judeo-Christian eschatology and of the particular consciousness of irreversible, ineluctably
ongoing time that results from the thought of the *eskhaton.* Both humanism and the various critiques that the concept of man has undergone
during the last two centuries are also the outcome of secularization, of the
shift from the traditional theocentric world view to the recognizably modern and increasingly ambivalent anthropocentric view. Modernity itself,
as I have argued elsewhere,[4] born from the sweeping movement of desac-
ralization, is a structurally polemical concept, intent on demystifying

everything, including itself. As such, it was bound to turn its sharply critical and self-critical attention to its own anthropocentric foundations. The critique of man is therefore by no means a recent development, although it acquired its more spectacular and dramatic dimensions during the last three or four decades.

The Renaissance and post-Renaissance prideful sense of man as an independently creative being and maker of his own history turned out to be no more than a rather short-lived illusion of early modernity. Once the spirit of modernity grew more mature and self-conscious, man became, during the eighteenth century of the philosophes, little more than a highly complex animal, determined in almost all respects by his natural, social, and cultural milieu. Ironically, it was at the same time that the universalist idea of man and the parallel idea that human rights were the only sacrosanct thing in the world attained their peak.

All the major elements of this paradox are interestingly blended in the concept of ideology, as elaborated by its inventor, Antoine Destutt de Tracy, and his followers. On the one hand, ideology or the science of ideas tells us quite unequivocally that all man's ideas are nothing but reflections of various natural and social determinisms and, moreover, that man's presumably highest values (of morality and justice, among others) are just fancies, meant to gratify and not to instruct. On the other hand, the same Destutt (whose *Éléments d'idéologie* were published between 1801 and 1815), makes quite clear that he himself speaks in the name of man and of the "best social order . . . that . . . corresponds to the permanent needs of man" (as George Lichtheim puts it), all this based on the patently unverifiable assumption " 'que la nature lie par une chaîne indissoluble la vérité, le bonheur et la vertu.' "[5]

The main elements of the critique of man, with all their strategic implications, were already there when, in the mid-1840s, Marx and Engels launched their first attacks against the universalist concept of man and against the very idea of a human nature or essence, speaking instead of concrete men, as producers and, to a much larger extent, *products* of their sociohistorical circumstances, of their "mode of production," and of the prevailing "relations of production." In *The German Ideology* (1845–46), in which the underlying meaning of the term *ideology* (as Engels was to explain later) already corresponds to the typically negative Marxist view of ideology as false consciousness, all the earlier philosophical promoters of the idea of man, including Hegel, come under harsh criticism for using the "trick of proving the hegemony of the spirit in history." After the "bourgeois" French Revolution and, generally, after the demise of the traditional forms of Christianity, man ("the rational human spirit," as Marx defines him in a marginal note) becomes nothing more than a means of playing rather effectively, that is, deceptively, the typical idealistic confidence trick. The authors write:

MATEI CALINESCU

Once the ruling ideas have been separated from the ruling individuals and, above all, from the relationships which result from a given stage of the mode of production . . . it is very easy to abstract from these various ideas "*the* idea," the notion, etc., as dominant force in history, and thus to understand all these separate ideas and concepts as "forms of self-determination" on the part of *the* concept developing in history. It follows then naturally, too, that all the relationships of men can be derived from the concept of man, man as conceived, the essence of man, *Man.* This has been done by the speculative philosophers. Hegel himself confesses at the end of the *Geschichtsphilosophie* that "he has considered the progress of the *concept* only" and has represented in history the "true *theodicy.*"[6]

This approach is more relevant to the contemporary, or at least part of the contemporary, philosophical discussion of the idea of man than we might suspect. Let us think, for instance, of the post–World War II quarrel (which became particularly intense during the years following Stalin's death in 1953) between the so-called humanist Marxists, whose arguments were mainly derived from the works of the early Hegelian Marx, and the theoretically antihumanist Marxists, ranging from the staunchly orthodox followers of the Marxist-Leninist Moscow line to such sophisticated and until not long ago quite fashionable thinkers as Louis Althusser (more about him later).

Whether Marx was at heart a humanist or a theoretical antihumanist is a moot question, and I do not intend to try to answer it here. The fact of the matter is that Marx was one of the first Europeans to become aware of the built-in philosophical weaknesses of the anthropocentric view of man, both in the ideology of eighteenth-century mechanical materialists and in the subsequent romantic-idealist reaction. On the other hand, though, while man appeared to him as a philosophically doomed concept, Marx never spoke apocalyptically, or even vaguely metaphorically, of anything close to the death of man. A prophet of sorts and the founder of a new "religion" (with its own version of theodicy),[7] Marx preferred to regard himself, in the fashion of his time, as a scientist, the creator of "scientific socialism," and as such fully entitled to scoff at the utopian dreams and grandiose humanistic pronouncements of his predecessors.

Insofar as the idea of man is concerned, by steadily criticizing it from the mid-1840s on, Marxism has managed to render what a number of twentieth-century philosophers persist in calling Marxist humanism—a notion as abstract and fundamentally unexplained as its opposite, the supposed theoretical antihumanism of Marx, of which Althusser speaks with a stubborn and obscure passion.[8] For Althusser (see, among other things, his polemical sortie against the British "humanist" Marxist, John Lewis), history is definitely a "subjectless process."[9] History is neither made by man nor for man. The dehumanizing effect of certain (capitalist) relations of production, denounced by Marx in *Das Kapital*, is for Althusser and his pupils the starting point of an enlarged and generalized theory of the dehumanization of history as a whole. That the "concrete men" of the happy communist future, to which occasional and rather perfunctory references are made, remain as a rule totally faceless should come as no surprise.

How, then, can we account for the enormous appeal that Marxism exerted until not long ago? The curious mixture between humanism and antihumanism is one of the possible explanations of this phenomenon. Marxism is both humanist and anti-humanist: depending on one's wishes or temporary ideological needs, one can plausibly emphasize either one of these tendencies: one can even hold both views at the same time, which is perfectly acceptable within the framework of George Orwell's theory of "doublethink" in *Nineteen Eighty-Four*. The notion of moral inversion, advanced by Michael Polanyi in his important book *Personal Knowledge: Towards a Post-Critical Philosophy* (1958) is also relevant here. Moral inversion is a process by which people can satisfy their fundamental moral passions through the sophisticated critical debunking of all the traditional moral values (goodness, compassion, humanism are mere ideological tools of manipulation in the hands of the bourgeoisie, aspects of the basic moral hypocrisy of capitalism). Polanyi writes:

> Why should so contradictory a doctrine [i.e., Marxism] carry such supreme convincing power? The answer is, I believe, that it enables the modern mind, tortured by moral self-doubt, to indulge its moral passions in terms which also satisfy its passion for ruthless objectivity. Marxism, through its philosophy of "dialectical materialism," conjures away the contradiction between the high moral dynamism of our age and our stern critical passion which demands that we see human affairs objectively. . . . These antinomies, which make the liberal mind stagger and fumble, are the joy and strength of Marxism: for the more inordinate our moral aspirations and the more completely amoral our objectivist outlook, the more powerful is a combination in which these contradictory principles mutually reinforce each other.[10]

"Humanism and Terror" (the title of a regrettable post–World War II polemical writing by the French phenomenologist Maurice Merleau-Ponty, at the time under the spell of a quasi-Stalinist version of Marxism) are, therefore, by no means as incompatible as they seem to be. On the contrary, with the blessing of dialectics, and challenging the more commonsensical mind, these concepts actually imply each other. Irrespective of how we explain its success, Marxism has clearly contributed to the erosion of the concept of man. Whether direct or indirect, and notwithstanding its contradictory aspects, this contribution is significant enough to deserve a major place in the overall history of the twilight of man in the philosophy of modernity.

Michel Foucault, though, prefers to disregard the Marxist critique of man, linking instead his *mort de l'homme* to the famous death of God announced a century ago by the mysterious madman in Nietzsche's *The Gay Science* (1882):

> The madman jumped into their midst and pierced them with his eyes. "Whither is God?" he cried; "I will tell you. We have killed him—you and I. All of us are his murderers. . . . God is dead. God remains dead. And we have killed him."[11]

"God is dead" is a statement that is quite obviously scandalous, and not exclusively in religious terms. From the point of view of our Western conception of linear and irreversible time, founded on the Judeo-Christian eschatological notion of history, one simply cannot speak of the death of God, for God is eternal (immortal) by definition. Within this frame of reference, to try to imagine God as mortal would be logically as absurd as trying to imagine, say, a third-sided square. If God exists, He can only be immortal, and if He does not exist, to speak of His death is to speak meaninglessly. But, as Octavio Paz has shown in his fine book on modernity in poetry, *Children of the Mire*, the death of God is not unthinkable in terms of the logic of myth and the cyclical concept of time.[12] Actually, the gods of archaic religions (so perceptively studied in the works of Mircea Eliade) are quite often direct participants in the cosmic drama of periodical death and resurrection.[13] And even in the modern tradition, the death of God can be conceived as a poetic paradox. Octavio Paz shows, for instance, that the theme of the death of God occurs long before Nietzsche: the early nineteenth-century romantic poets had already treated it, with a characteristic mixture of anxiety and irony.

If one reads the philosophical parable of Nietzsche's madman in relation to the content of Book Three of *The Gay Science*, there is little doubt that the God whose death is announced is the God of Christianity. Must we then say that the death of God is simply a metaphorical expression for a historical reality, namely, the collapse of Christian faith, assaulted by the innumerable philosophical suspicions of modernity? If we answered the question positively, we would impoverish the significance of Nietzsche's myth and would miss the transhistorical scope the philosopher clearly intended to give it. We also would be led to simplify Nietzsche's attitude toward Christianity itself, an attitude that is much more ambivalent than is usually thought. This ambivalence is more adequately expressed in the language of myth and metaphor than in the clear-cut language of historical discourse.

It is the atheists, Nietzsche suggests, who have killed God, but the influence of the most negative and poisonous elements of Christianity—

the religion of *"ressentiment,"* or repressed hatred, par excellence—continues to exert itself fully on them. The philosopher views atheism, at least the programmatic atheism adopted by such modern doctrines as socialism or anarchism, as nothing but a secularized version of Christianity, an empty Christianity in whose very emptiness the malodorous plants of *ressentiment* have better conditions of development than ever before. In this sense, the death of God is also a tragic event.

In *Thus Spake Zarathustra,* Nietzsche enlarges his philosophical myth of the death of God, relating it more specifically to the correlative themes of man and the "overman." We should observe that the term *man,* as used by Nietzsche, designates man not in the sense of a biological species, but primarily, if not exclusively, as a moral being. This meaning encompasses the concept of man both in the modern humanist tradition and in the older one of Christian humanism. It is Nietzsche's great originality to have seen a profound continuity where everybody else saw only appearances of discontinuity and rupture. For Nietzsche, secular humanism, as he stresses over and over again, is just an extension of theological humanism. Man is therefore a very old "invention," essentially untouched by modernity which, even in its most sweepingly antireligious manifestations, remains a continuation of the "Christian revolution."

Even when he speaks of man in general (that is, without using such epithets as "the last," or "the ugliest," or "the best"), Nietzsche refers to the same moral being, whose fundamental values are values of *ressentiment,* purely reactive, or—to employ an adjective he borrowed from the French and made into one of his significant technical terms—*décadentes.* And decadent values are in the first place hostile to life. Morality, Nietzsche writes in *Ecce Homo,* is only "the idiosyncrasy of decadents, with the ulterior motive of revenging oneself against life—successfully. I attach value to this definition."[14] If man is defined by his "will to decadence," we must note that his actual death is much less certain than the death of God (one should not forget that the advent of the superman is never spoken of as a certainty but only as a possibility, one that the killers of God might well prevent from coming true). Man, this wily and dangerous enemy of life, is seen by Nietzsche as having a really multiple existence, as illustrated in the philosopher's extraordinarily diverse typology of decadence. Clearly the end of God makes the end of man thinkable. But the author of *Zarathustra* remains strangely vague on this matter. How will man die? Is he going to die a natural death? Or, more likely, is he going to commit suicide? And if so, how, why, and when? One thing is sure: the hypothesis according to which the "superior men"—those who secretly prepare the possible flourishing of the superman—will murder the "ugliest man" should be discounted. Such a hypothesis simply goes against Nietzsche's style of thinking. The "last man" is protected by the very disgust he provokes—Who would be willing to define oneself by killing him?

Unlike Nietzsche, Foucault thinks that man is a recent invention. And, again unlike Nietzsche, he seems certain that this invention is nearing its end. So much so that "one can certainly wager that man would be erased, like a face drawn in sand at the edge of the sea." The question of man is specifically addressed in the last two chapters of *The Order of Things*, "Man and His Doubles" and "The Human Sciences." It is important to note that in his prophecy of the death of man, and also more generally, Foucault acknowledges Nietzsche as one of his great precursors. The German thinker, according to Foucault, sets up the major task that confronts the contemporary mind, "the radical reflection upon language," the realization that "language wells up in an enigmatic multiplicity that must be mastered." The great innovative undertaking of Nietzsche, he says, must be related to Mallarmé's contemporary and complementary one:

> For Nietzsche, it was not a matter of knowing what good or evil were in themselves, but of who was being designated, or rather *who was speaking* when one said *Agathos* to designate onself and *Deilos* to designate others. . . . To the Nietzschean question: "Who is speaking?", Mallarmé replies—and constantly reverts to that reply—by saying that what is speaking is, in its solitude, in its fragile vibration, in its nothingness, the word itself—not the meaning of the word, but its enigmatic and precarious being.[15]

The approach suggested by such quotations, which could easily be multiplied, is sufficient, I think, to prove not the influence of Nietzsche on Foucault but the opposite. Foucault is certainly attracted to Nietzsche, and particularly to Nietzsche's metaphorical style, but even while he uses certain Nietzschean phrases and formulas, it is finally Foucault who manages to exert a reverse influence on his great precursor. Such cases of reverse influence are always interesting insofar as they are instances of great originality of interpretation. The problem with Foucault is that his reading of Nietzsche is not only new or unexpected but, we feel, much too un-Nietzschean, to the point that some of the basic ideas of the German philosopher are either ignored or distorted beyond recognition. What cannot fail but strike one in this regard is the almost total abandonment by Foucault of the axiological dimension of Nietzsche's thought, a dimension indissolubly linked to the fundamental Nietzschean project of a "transvaluation of all values." Foucault's neglect of this essential element may be due, at least in part, to Nietzsche's own failure, after having so thoroughly "demystified" the old values, to define any really new ones. In any case, Nietzsche's whole critique of a man as a moral being, as a product of *ressentiment* and decadence, occupies an amazingly marginal place in the new image of his philosophy that we are offered. Clearly, the man of whom Nietzsche speaks and Foucault's man (that precarious recent invention) have very little in common.

Who, then, is the man whose demise Foucault is so obviously pleased to announce? Before answering this question, we should observe that in Foucault's language *man* is at the same time a technical term and the common word, semantically "overdetermined," of both ordinary and poetic language, a word which lends itself easily to a variety of metaphorical usages, a "fuzzy" notion whose rich connotations defy any attempt at a coherent definition. The "death of man" is therefore, in Foucault's work, constantly hovering between the status of a technical expression and a poetic phrase of apocalyptic intimations. The widespread appeal of Foucault's theory about the death of man is without doubt due to the latter aspect.

In the technical sense, Foucault's man is surely an outcome of modernity and, more specifically, of modern epistemology. Man, the author of *The Order of Things* tells us, this "strange empirico-transcendental doublet," came into existence toward the end of the eighteenth century, in a period marked by the "end of metaphysics" in Western thought, in a period when the "metaphysics of representation and of the infinite" was replaced by "an analytic of finitude and human existence." And Foucault adds: "For the threshold of our modernity is situated not by the attempt to apply objective methods to the study of man, but rather by the constitution of an empirico-transcendental doublet which we called *man.*" Again, man is nothing but one of the paradoxes of modern thought, "a mode of being . . . which extends from a part of himself not reflected in a *cogito* to the act of thought by which he apprehends that part; and which, in the inverse direction, extends from that pure apprehension to the empirical clutter, the chaotic accumulation of contents, the weight of experiences constantly eluding themselves, the whole silent horizon of what is posited in the sandy stretches of non-thought."[16]

It has become sufficiently clear, I hope, that for Foucault, "man" in the technical sense is just modern man as epistemological consciousness of himself—that modern man who, even though he has lost his essence or nature, no longer resists the dangerous temptation of anthropologism and ends up becoming the central fiction of the so-called human sciences. In short, for Foucault, there is no "man" except in modern culture. The classical *episteme*, as well as those that preceded it, were able "to speak of the mind and the body, of the human being, of how restricted a place he occupies in the universe, of all the limitations by which his knowledge or his freedom must be measured, but . . . not one of them was ever able to know man as he is posited in modern knowledge. Renaissance "humanism" and Classical "rationalism" were indeed able to allot human beings a privileged position in the order of the world, but they were not able to conceive of man.[17]

From this point of view, the man whose dissolution Foucault predicts (not without a trace of apocalyptic coquetry) turns out to be no more than a certain concept of man, a concept that the philosopher reconstructs from elements rather selectively taken from the *savoir* of a limited historical period. One can therefore legitimately ask oneself why, instead of qualifying the term *man* appropriately (as a more rigorous philosopher would have done), Foucault has preferred to use it as such, in all its ambiguous and quite often misleading generality. The reason I have proposed before, a reason that has to do primarily with the logic of success, must have played a significant role in this terminological decision. Fascinated with the prophetic Nietzschean formulation of the death of God and the possible advent of the superman, Foucault seems to have forgotten that Nietzsche's "last man" was the outcome of several thousand years, and that the would-be demise of this decadent being was likely to take at least as long. We also remark that, in establishing a close parallelism between the death of man and the death of God (a parallelism that is never directly suggested by Nietzsche), Foucault unwittingly draws our attention to one of the serious drawbacks of his conception of *savoir* (not knowledge as such but that which authorizes knowledge or gives it legitimacy as knowledge), a drawback that otherwise might have passed unnoticed.

True, in referring to the Nietzschean myth of the death of God, Foucault uses it mostly as if he were trying to give more depth to the idea that seems to interest him really: the announcement of the end of that recent and fragile being, man. But since he appropriates the statement "God is dead," one has the right to ask what is, in the philosopher's view, the more specific relationship between God and man, apart from the general assertion that the demise of the former implies the dissolution of the latter. For Nietzsche, one remembers, the notion of God denotes, quite unequivocally, a whole complex of moral and psychological functions: "God" is actually the counterconcept for "life," representing *ressentiment* against life and the "will to death"; moreover, the theme of the death of God in Nietzsche's thought is part of the larger context of a work rich in critical meditations on religion in general and on Christianity in particular. Nothing or next to nothing of the kind is to be found in Foucault. One is surprised to see how little attention the French thinker devotes to religious phenomena, even while he speaks so often of the death of God. As has in fact been observed (by, for instance, Michel de Certeau), in *The Order of Things* (and subsequently) Foucault simply ignores "the religious sciences, in spite of the fact that they have played an outstanding role, particularly in the elaboration of the *épistémè* of the classical age."[18] Is it that Foucault thinks, without ever saying it, that between his "epistemic structures" and religion (or theology) there are no specifiable relationships? But, then, why does he insist so heavily on the "death of God," seeming to attach such a great significance to this phrase? By taking Foucault's point of view, it is as if God had existed discreetly, having played no actual part in the elaboration of the codes of classical culture, having in no way limited the "conditions of possibility" of the epistemological field of classical thought, only to offer suddenly, toward the end of the nineteenth century, the rather melodramatic spectacle of his death at the hands of a frail newcomer, man, himself destined to be erased shortly.

If Michel Foucault has always objected to being labeled a structuralist, Claude Lévi-Strauss has not only accepted the label but, on various occasions, has spoken at length on behalf of the structural method and structuralism in general, opposing them in rather clear-cut terms to the major "unscientific" philosophies of our time and in particular to existentialism (once characterized as a "sort of shop-girl metaphysics"),[19] to phenomenology, and to all the "subjectivist" modern schools that, in his view, can only lead to the most irresponsible "verbiage with hermeneutical pretentions."[20] A practitioner of "structural" anthropology, Lévi-Strauss has been pushed by his dislike of contemporary philosophy to define himself, in the "Finale" of *L'Homme nu* (1971)—the last part of his "Wagnerian" tetralogy of *Mythologiques*—as almost an antiphilosopher, a man with only the most unavoidable, rudimentary, and "rustic" philosophical convictions. Leaving aside the fact that Lévi-Strauss was educated as a philosopher, a career that he subsequently abandoned, it is somehow surprising to see this supremely intelligent man failing to realize that his whole approach to the question of scientific knowledge involves a philosophical point of view certainly more sophisticated than the mere "rustic" beliefs that he is willing to declare.

In light of the foregoing remarks, it is clear that we should devote some attention to the idea of man expressed or only implied by one of the most prominent anthropologists of our time, less in his capacity as an anthropologist than in that as a *"philosophe malgré lui."* Furthermore, this reluctant philosopher has probably exerted a more powerful influence on contemporary thought (in the broad and "fuzzy" meaning of this phrase) than on the strictly specialized anthropologists to whom the largest part of his work has been explicitly addressed. One might even claim that Lévi-Strauss, wittingly or not, has done more than anyone else to restore to anthropology the philosophical dignity that has undergone a process of slow disintegration ever since the days of Jean Jacques Rousseau, whom Lévi-Strauss has always recognized as his most important precursor.

The man of whom Lévi-Strauss speaks is certainly different from Foucault's recent invention, but doomed nevertheless. If we were to seek for the most comprehensive definition of man given by this structuralist thinker haunted by the questions of non-knowledge and meaninglessness, it would be, apparently paradoxically, that man is a maker of signs, the animal that discovered "signification," *Homo significans*. And yet,

> The world began without man and will end without him. The institutions, morals and customs that I shall have spent my life noting down and trying to understand are the transient efflorescence of a creation in relation to which they have no meaning, except perhaps that of allowing mankind to play its part in creation. But far from this part according man an independent position, or his endeavours—even if doomed to failure—being opposed to universal decline, he himself appears as perhaps the most effective agent working towards the disintegration of the original order of things and hurrying on powerfully organized matter towards . . . an inertia which one day will be final.[21]

"Universal decline," "disintegration," and "inertia" that will be "final" can only be taken literally in this context. What Lévi-Strauss seems to imply in this gloomy reflection is that the end of man and the end of the world itself must be seen as the unavoidable result of the action of deep destructive forces that oppose "powerfully organized matter." The underlying metaphysical assumptions are those of an absolute, quasi-religious materialism, a sort of reverse Platonism. In view of the prehuman "original order of things," an order as perfect as that of the Platonic ideas (although in all other respects its symmetrical opposite), mankind's appearance marks an already advanced phase in the process of universal decay. The history of mankind itself is, taken independently, an illustration of the same movement toward entropy: primitive man was better and happier than civilized man; progress is in fact corruption; humanity attained the peak of its development in the neolithic age and has steadily declined ever since; the discovery of writing was a tragic and ominous event; and so on. As Mircea Eliade observes, Lévi-Strauss confronts us with "a kind of *mythology of matter* . . . a structuralist, algebraic type." Eliade goes on:

> The reasons for Lévi-Strauss's popularity are primarily to be found in his antiexistentialism and his neopositivism, in his indifference to history and his exaltation of material "things"—of matter. For him, "la science est déjà faite dans les choses": science is already effected in things, in material objects. Logic is already prefigured in nature. That is to say, man can be understood without taking *consciousness* into consideration. *Le Pensée*

sauvage presents us with a thinking without thinkers and a logic without logicians.[22]

The process of signification is ultimately nothing but a by-product of the movements of "powerfully organized matter." Furthermore, signification is itself subject to the corrosive action of randomness and inertia, whose forces relentlessly challenge the very principle of order and organization. No wonder then that Lévi-Strauss was literally right when he ironically characterized himself as a "vulgar materialist."

The cult of matter as embraced by Lévi-Strauss has a strong polemical dimension: his materialism is always self-consciously and aggressively anti-idealistic, to the point that the materialist creed may appear as primarily an ideological base for launching demystifying attacks against the most diverse cultural illusions and myths, including the individual, the self, and man himself. The individual, for instance, when considered more carefully, appears as a simple meaningless notion:

Yet I exist. Not, of course, as an individual, since in this respect, I am merely the stake—a stake perpetually at risk—in the struggle between another society, made up of several thousand million nerve cells lodged in the ant-hill of my skull, and my body, which serves as its robot. Neither psychology nor metaphysics nor art can provide me with a refuge. They are myths, now open to internal investigation by a new kind of sociology which will emerge one day and will deal no more gently with them than traditional sociology does. The self is not only hateful: there is no place between *us* and *nothing*. And if, in the last resort, I opt for *us*, even though it is no more than a semblance, the reason is that, unless I destroy myself—an act which would obliterate the conditions of the option—I have only one possible choice between this semblance and nothing. I only have to choose for the choice itself to signify my unreserved acceptance of the human condition; in thus freeing myself from an intellectual pride, the futility of which I can gauge by the futility of its object, I also agree to subordinate its claims to the objective demands of the emancipation of the many, to whom the possibility of such a choice is still denied.[23]

On the one hand, we have the irretrievably demystified self, on which nothing can be built anymore, and on the other, we have the *us*, which itself is seen as "no more than a semblance," but which appears as the only possible locus of hope, the only alternative to nothing. This sounds like a Marxist-humanist declaration, although its would-be Marxism is highly qualified, and the general tone in melancholy contrast to the message of acceptance of the human condition.

At this point it seems useful to call attention to Lévi-Strauss's acknowledged indebtedness, at least during his formative years, to Marxist thought. It is also noteworthy that he was not at all interested in the utopian or "futurological" aspect of Marxism ("Marx's quality has nothing to do with whether or not he accurately foresaw certain historical developments") but only in the "scientific" and inflexibly reductionist side of Marx's theory of society, which he does not hesitate to compare to physics. ("Marx established that social science is no more founded on the basis of events than physics is founded on sense data.")[24] And in respect to reductionism, Lévi-Strauss has been quite consistent: he has defended it throughout his work, among other places in the essay against Sartre's *Critique de la raison dialectique*, entitled "History and Dialectic," and included in *The Savage Mind* (*La Pensée sauvage*, 1962). Obviously, he was perfectly conscious of the destructive character of reductionism (knowledge proceeds in stages that lead to ultimate meaninglessness), and that is why, as a true "vulgar materialist," Lévi-Strauss thinks that the main task of the human sciences is precisely to dissolve man:

> I believe the ultimate goal of the human sciences to be not to constitute but to dissolve man. . . . Ethnographic analysis tries to arrive at invariants beyond the empirical diversity of human societies. . . . However, it would not be enough to reabsorb particular humanities into a general one. This first enterprise opens the way for others which Rousseau would not have been so ready to accept and which are incumbent on the exact natural sciences: the reintegration of culture into nature and finally of life within the whole of its physico-chemical conditions.[25]

The scientific project is for Lévi-Strauss (in keeping with the ideology of modernity in a broader sense) a strictly dehumanizing project. Leaving aside this unflinching belief in science and reductionism (a belief that he shares with many subtle and imaginative thinkers, although his personal exaggerations in this direction point to some deeper polemical obsessions and, more generally, to a surprisingly dogmatic frame of mind), Lévi-Strauss owes more directly to Marxism, not his idea of the dissolution of man into the physicochemical structure of matter, but his critique of humanism, of the philosophical humanism of Sartre and his followers (for Sartre, we recall, "Existentialism Is a Humanism"[26]) and of any conceivable philosophical humanism. But where does all this critique of humanism lead (in its resumption in the "Finale" of *l'Homme nu*) and what does all that sometimes passionate, sometimes simply grouchy antiphilosophical criticism uncover? Nothing but the obsessively renewed sense that humanity—not just the idea of man, not just the abstract phantom of humanism—is nearing its end. This time, however, the gloominess of the prophecy is mitigated by the involuntarily comic effect brought about by the narcissism of the author, who links the end of humanity to the conclusion of his major work:

Je comprends mieux qu'ayant moi aussi composé ma tétralogie, elle doive s'achever sur un crépuscule des dieux comme l'autre; ou, plus précisément, que terminée un siècle plus tard et dans des temps plus cruels, elle anticipe le crépuscule des hommes, après celui qui devait permettre l'avènement d'une humanité heureuse et libérée.[27]

(Now, after having composed my own tetralogy, I understand better that, like the other one [Wagner's], it must end with a twilight of the gods; or, more precisely, that my tetralogy, finished one century later and in crueler times, anticipates the twilight of man, even though the disappearance of the gods should have rendered the advent of a free and happy humanity possible.)

If the intellectual tradition that Lévi-Strauss must be situated in is that, as Susan Sontag puts it, of the "aggressively antiphilosophical systems of thought, taking the form of various 'positive' or 'descriptive' sciences of man" (Comte, Marx, Freud, as well as other pioneer figures of anthropology, sociology, and linguistics), the other response to the debacle of modernity "was a new kind of philosophizing: personal (even autobiographical), aphoristics, lyrical, antisystematic. Its foremost exemplars: Kierkegaard, Nietzsche, and Wittgenstein. Cioran is the most distinguished figure in this tradition writing today."[28] This general presentation of E. M. Cioran's philosophy is perfectly accurate and, moreover, shows a genuine admiration, confirmed by the occasional references to Cioran that occur in Sontag's subsequent writings. It is interesting to note that a writer usually associated with the New Left like Sontag was to introduce Cioran, a thinker sometimes seen as a representative of the right, to the English-speaking world.

Born and educated in Rumania, where he wrote several books, Cioran has lived in Paris and published exclusively in French ever since the end of World War II. Untouched by any of the postwar Parisian cultural fashions—from existentialism, to neo-Marxism, to psychoanalysis, to structuralism, and, now, poststructuralism—and essentially impervious to the temptation of any contemporary philosophical jargon, Cioran went on publishing his books, consisting of aphorisms and sometimes simple undated entries from a "philosophical journal": *Précis de décomposition* (1949), *Syllogismes de l'amertume* (1952), *La Tentation d'exister* (1956), *Histoire et utopie* (1960), *La Chute dans le temps* (1964), and others, until his latest, *Écartèlement* (1979).

Cioran's reflections revolve around a rather limited number of obsessive themes, the central one being without doubt decay, in all its forms and fashions: decadence, decline, fall, decomposition, deliquescence, dissolution, and so on. The origin of his thought is almost self-evidently in Nietzsche's critique of modernity and theory of decadence. One caveat is necessary here: Cioran has nothing to do with either the "French Nietzsche" or, more importantly, with the various German interpretations of Nietzsche, and more specifically—given the closeness of the theme— with German theoreticians of the decline of West such as Oswald Spengler. In respect to Spengler and to his once very influential work, *Der Untergang des Abendlandes* (1918), the similarity of some of his and of Cioran's conclusions should not detract our attention from the crucial differences between the two thinkers. Spengler is basically a philosopher of history in the German systematic tradition, influenced by Nietzsche but more ponderous than his master. The success of his "biological" theory of cultural cycles was due not so much to his sophisticated, often insightful descriptions of the major stylistic world views as to his somber prophecies. Not that Cioran is not a pessimist (and easily more so than Spengler); but he is a pessimist with a marvelous sense of humor, with an exquisite art of self-irony, and, above all, with that paradoxical saving grace of always "thinking against himself."

In a sense, for Cioran, man has always ended, to the point that, in man, being and ending are one and the same thing. With his inexhaustible passion for the end, Cioran's feelings about man are understandably ambivalent:

> I do not know if it is legitimate to speak of the end of man; but I am certain of the fall of all the fictions by which we have lived until today. Let us say that history is finally revealing its night side, and to remain in the realm of the unspecific, that a world is destroying itself. Well then, in the hypothesis that I alone can keep this from happening, I shall make no gesture, I shall not raise my little finger. Man attracts and appalls me, I love and I hate him with a vehemence which condemns me to passivity. I cannot imagine how to save him from his fatality. How naive we must be to blame or defend him! Lucky those who entertain toward him a clear and distinct sentiment: they will perish *saved*. To my shame, I confess that there was a time when I too belonged to that category of happy beings. Man's fate touched me to the quick. . . . A "humanist" in reverse, I supposed—in my still intact pride— that to become the enemy of the human race was the highest dignity to which one might aspire. . . . Since then, by dint of modulations, my illusions were to lose their virulence and creep modestly toward disgust, ambiguity, and bewilderment.[29]

Cioran's early "antihumanism" could already have been shared, as we saw, by both leftists and rightists, both of whom, during the 1920s and 1930s, claimed the title of revolutionaries. In time, however, with reflection and certainly exile, this youthful hatred of man, distilled from various major currents of modern thought, became more modulated, more ambiguous, and, perhaps, in its newly acquired "bewilderment" before man, somewhat resigned.

The continuity of Cioran's meditation on the disintegration of man is illustrated by the following quotation from his latest book, from the chapter "Après l'histoire," in which the author attempts to establish the cardinal points of what we might call (making use of his own term, *posthistoire*) the posthistorical consciousness.

> L'homme fait l'histoire: à son tour l'histoire le défait. . . . En la suscitant, en y investissant sa substance, l'homme s'est dépensé, amenuisé, affaibli. . . . La consommation du processus historique est désormais inexorable, sans qu'on puisse dire pour autant si elle sera traînante [as Nietzsche was inclined to think a century ago] ou fulgurante. . . . Il est en tout cas manifeste que l'homme a donné le meilleur de lui-même, et qui si même on devait assister à l'émergeance d'autres civilisations, elles ne vaudront sûrement pas les anciennes, ni même les modernes, sans compter qu'elles ne pourront pas se dérober à la contagion de la fin, devenue pour tous une manière d'obligation et de programme.[30]

> (Man makes history; in its turn history unmakes him. . . . In creating history, in investing it with his substance, man has expended himself and grown thin and weak. . . . The end of the historical process is henceforth inexorable, although one cannot yet say whether it will drag out slowly or take only a flash. . . . It is at any rate obvious that the best man could do is behind him, and that even if one were to witness the emergence of other civilizations, these would certainly be inferior to the ancient, and even to the modern ones, let alone that they would be unable to defend themselves from the infection of the end, when the end will have become for everybody a sort of duty and program.)

Even if man will continue to exist after all, his mind will be inescapably marked by the idea of the end, the end of himself and the end of everything, the end as a program and even as the content of a new eschatological categorical imperative.

The truth is that late modern thinkers have become accustomed not only to the idea of the end but to making of this idea a measure. It is according to this measure that many tend to discuss not only the concept of man but also such heterogeneous concepts as art, life in general, energy and resources (in economies), and the sacred (in theology or, more specifically, in its branch that is sometimes called theothanatology, from *theos* + *thanatos* + *logos* [god + death + science]). Thus it seems appropriate here to say a few words about the question of humanism in art, in modern art versus "postmodern" art. As the death of man is philosophically a many-sided issue, so is its aesthetic correspondent, which includes such problems, to be very brief, as the dehumanization of art, the death of the self in modern and even more so in postmodern literature and art, and, finally, the death of the author.

From the aesthetician's point of view, the latter problem is probably the more important. But before tackling it, let us start by dismissing right away the question of the death of the self, which I fear would take us too deep into the territory of literary criticism, and briefly considering the notion of dehumanization. It is a creation of the Spanish philosopher José Ortega y Gasset, who made it famous by his 1925 essay *La deshumanización del arte*. Opposed to romantic art, modern art displays all the signs of a profound aversion for the human person, and polemically turns its back on the whole humanist or romantic legacy of the nineteenth century. Dehumanization is, therefore, modern art's healthy reaction against that romantic humanism which is described by Ortega (rather confusingly) as a relatively short-lived "aberration in the history of taste." This means that the great artistic styles prior to romanticism (neoclassical, baroque, rococo, or whatever) also practiced what Ortega calls dehumanization. And that was precisely so, the philosopher reassures the reader, going on to broaden the definition of dehumanization to the point where it simply (that is, fuzzily) means no more than "will to style," stylization, or, just a little bit more clearly, deformation or distortion for stylistic purposes. Throughout the history of art, then, humanist romanticism is the only example of "styleless" or "amorphous" art. Modern art is finally not defined by dehumanization (which, under the conditions put forward by the philosopher himself, does not constitute a proper criterion, but by other traits, which Ortega discusses quite insightfully: unpopularity, anti-traditionalism, iconoclasm, humorism, and so forth.

In the meantime, the more closely the question of dehumanization is examined, the more it turns out to be a glaring pseudoquestion. Ortega is, all the same, very pleased with the term *dehumanization*, and so are, with very few exceptions (Renato Poggioli being one of them), many of his commentators, who have rendered this terminological choice famous (even though it is so misleading) while often failing to point out the truly incisive parts of Ortega's essay. And if we were to task ourselves why the word *dehumanization* appealed to so many intellectuals during the inter-war period and after, the answer would be simple: because of its definitely antihumanistic ring in a time when humanism (we have seen how) had come into such low repute and, moreover, seemed to be philosophically in a shambles.

Although he does not speak of either dehumanization or the death of the individual, Ortega raises precisely these questions in *La rebelión de las masas (The Revolt of the Masses, 1929)*, an important contribution to the theory of mass society. The very notion of "masses" (with its direct implications of loss of difference and the dissolution of the individual into the haunting, one might say entropic sameness of the mass), somehow evokes death, since life is by definition linked to such concepts as difference, individuality, improbability, or, more generally, remoteness from the points of equilibrium in the universe. Obviously, Ortega's "massmen" are a philosophical version of T. S. Eliot's "hollow men." But again, within the limits of this chapter, I can only suggest the relatedness of the question of the death of the individual to the broader problem of the end of man. I would add, though, that the real dehumanization of art—contrary to what Ortega thought—should be seen as a characteristic of mass society. Mass culture is in no way less dehumanized for being pseudohumanistically sentimental, escapist even at its most violent, aggressive even at its sweetest (Roland Barthes once noted the "aggressiveness of sugar"). In a word, dehumanized art is kitsch.[31]

As an aesthetic counterpart of the death of man, the so-called death of the author is probably more immediately relevant to our topic. Beyond the structuralist and poststructuralist technicalities, the problem poses itself, as I see it, within the larger context of modernity's critique of the idea of authority and of the effectiveness of that critique. Have we not witnessed, during the last two centuries or so, the steady erosion of the principle of authority, submitted by even serious philosophers to the grossest misinterpretations, to the most scathing and vituperative attacks, until the point was reached where the word *authority* itself underwent a complete and perhaps irreversible change, indeed a reversal, of its original meaning? Instead of conceiving authority as the very opposite of power (a view upheld in our century by only a handful of people, Bertrand de Jouvenel, and Hannah Arendt, among them), modernity has forced itself, following its particular logic of suspicion and demystification, to see authority exclusively as a manifestation of power. Thus an extraordinary semantic displacement has actually taken place, a displacement that goes all the way from the meaning of the Latin *auctoritas* (in which the idea of spontaneously recognized legitimacy is brought to the foreground) to the modern meaning of *authority*, which almost always denotes, and quite often connotes, domination, arbitrary exercise of power, oppression, tyranny, despotism, and even totalitarianism. The fundamental, although complex, relationship between authority and persuasion has been steadily denied by most of the modern (political) philosophers. We have reached a point where it would be interesting to study more systematically the negative semantic contamination of all the notions directly or indirectly linked to authority: such a study should cover the whole intellectual space that extends from the realm of aesthetics, in which the concept of author has all but disappeared, to the various philosophies of deconstruction, in which the rejection of authority usually takes the form of a critique of the idea of origin, an idea indissolubly connected with *auctoritas* (here the philosophy of Jacques Derrida would be the obvious example).

Among the many declarations concerning the death of the author that have been made over the last two or three decades, the following one, taken from Roland Barthes's little book *Le Plaisir du texte* (1973), seems to summarize best the views on this problem of one of the uncontested *maîtres à penser* of postexistentialist France:

> Comme institution, l'auteur est mort: sa personne civile, passionnelle, biographique, a disparu; dépossédée, elle n'exerce plus sur son oeuvre la formidable paternité dont l'histoire littéraire, l'enseignement, l'opinion avaient à charge d'établir et de renouveler le récit. . . .[32]

> (As institution, the author is dead; his civil, passional, biographical identity has disappeared; dispersed, it can no longer exert on his work the awesome paternity, whose story it was the task of literary history, education, or opinion to establish and continuously renew.)

It should be pointed out that Barthes, who managed to remain an original thinker throughout his career in spite of the fact that he was influenced by all the intellectual fashions of his time (from the neo-Marxism of his early writings, to structuralism, to psychoanalysis, especially in its Lacanian version, to poststructuralism), pushed his dislike of the notion of authority so far as to turn against even one of its farthest offshoots, namely, the idea of authenticity. There is, I believe, more to Barthes's attitude in this regard than a mere reaction against existentialism which, from Heidegger to Sartre, had made authenticity into one of the key concepts of philosophy. For Barthes, authenticity is nothing but another form of self-deception, and one of the worst at that; its real antonym (both theoretically and practically) is lucidity or self-consciousness. Barthes writes:

> Plus je suis "sincère," plus je suis interprétable, sous l'oeil d'autres instances que celles des anciens auteurs, qui croiaient n'avoir à se soumettre qu'à une seule loi: *l'authenticité*. Ces instances sont l'Histoire, l'Idéologie, l'Inconscient.[33]

> The more I am "sincere," the more I am interpretable, in light of other instances than those applying to the ancient authors, who believed that they had to obey only one law: *authenticity*. These other instances are History, Ideology, the Unconscious.

The death of the author leads almost inescapably to an aesthetics of self-conscious inauthenticity (inauthenticity has definitely become a value), in which the writer freely assumes diverse roles and shifts from one voice to another, always aware that he is the mere mouthpiece of the various instances that constitute his selves (history, ideology, desire, the unconscious, and so forth), but nevertheless a participant in the weaving of the great authorless text that we call literature. Furthermore, inauthenticity, according to Barthes and his numerous followers, renders possible a playfulness that old and serious authenticity could only have nipped in the bud. Indeed, it is mainly because it is one of the basic preconditions of this new kind of playful attitude that inauthenticity is given such a highly positive, and indeed honorific, meaning. In aesthetics, this is perhaps the latest stage reached by the older conflict between hermeneutics (which would have no sense without some version of authenticity) and poetics—a poetics that has now fully developed its implication of self-conscious, ludic inauthenticity.[34]

This chapter has discussed various critiques of the idea of man, including humanism and anthropologism—from Marx to Althusser, from Nietzsche to Foucault to Lévi-Strauss, from Nietzsche again to Cioran, from Ortega to Barthes, from left to right and from right to left, and beyond. Now I should like to return briefly to my introductory remarks and stress once again that, however it may function—scientifically or metaphorically, literally or figuratively, philosophically or aesthetically—the language of the end of man and of the end in general is typical of certain deeper trends of modernity itself, if we agree to see modernity as a secularized version of eschatology, constitutively polemical, antitraditional to the point of constantly turning against its own traditions, ruthlessly critical, radically skeptical. This radical skepticism has paved the way for the gloomiest futurologies as well as for the most poignantly (and dangerously) naive utopian fantasies. It has brought about anguished visions of the last man as well as simpleminded conceptions of a "new man"—the latter notion revealing its terrifying implications when related to such doctrines as Marxism or fascism, which drew their convincing power from the specifically modern phenomenon of moral inversion, as described by Polanyi.

There are signs, however, that modernity may have largely exhausted itself. The modern cult of doubt and crisis, once some of its chilling practical effects have become evident, seems to have lost much of its earlier appeal. The monistic-reductionist cast of mind encouraged by modernity (we have seen how Lévi-Strauss wanted to "dissolve man" and "reintegrate" life within the physicochemical structure of matter) is increasingly assailed by pluralistic approaches in philosophy, in the arts, in aesthetics, in political thought, and in the sciences themselves. The examples offered by current trends in the sciences are perhaps the most eloquent. If modern science had led to a "disenchantment of the world," as a result of which man came to regard himself as "alone in the indifferent immensity of the Universe, from which he emerged by chance" (French biologist Jacques Monod), the new science, as Ilya Prigogine and Isabelle Stengers point out in their fascinating book *La Nouvelle Alliance; Métamorphose de la science* (1979), is engaged in a vast project of "reenchantment of the world." This project presupposes, among other things, a reestablishment of the old alliance between man and nature that modernity had broken. Looked at from the perspective of this renewed alliance, the world appears as irreducibly diverse, inexhaustibly rich, and mysteriously inventive. Many of the phenomena that today's science tries to understand render necessary the utilization of terms that were completely foreign to the lexicon of modern science and of modernity in general, terms such as *life, destiny, freedom, spontaneity,* and *irreversibility.* Their common characteristic is that they are no longer removed from certain fundamental human experiences. That is why, the authors optimistically believe, the cultural dialogue, bringing together science, philosophy, and art, becomes possible again. The implicit pluralism of the whole argument of Prigogine and Stengers (the more technical details of which would be irrelevant in this context) is explicitly affirmed in the conclusion of the book. The new, rehumanized science rediscovers the sense of respect that the ancient Greek notion of *physis* (nature) had always implied. That the experimental dialogue will naturally extend itself not only to a cultural but also to an intercultural dialogue is the main philosophical message of the book:

> As we learn the "respect" that physical theory imposes on us in our relation to nature, we should also learn to respect other intellectual approaches, be they the traditional approaches of sailors and peasants, or the approaches created by the other sciences. We must learn no longer to patronizingly judge the population of knowledges and know-hows ("savoirs"), of the practices, and of the cultures produced by human societies but, on the contrary, how to combine them and how to establish among them new forms of communication which would increase our ability to cope with the unprecedented demands of our age.[35]

If today's science is in a process of rehumanizing itself, one must not be surprised that, after having brought to the foreground those who were ready to announce, joyously or somberly, the death of man, philosophy has seen itself obliged to conceive the possibility of man's resurrection—a word used, for instance, by Philippe Nemo in his book *L'Homme structural* (1975). Hardly had modernity managed to erase him, opposing to his old-fashioned defenders a "philosophical laughter" (Foucault[36]), than there he was back again, this stubborn man, resuscitated, rehumanized, and perhaps even "transhumanized" in our era which, for lack of a better term, some have called "postmodern."[37]

One might argue that such changes in the philosophical mood in no way alter the real problems of our age. The dangers that confront mankind in the nuclear era remain as great as ever, the future as uncertain, the totalitarian oppression in large parts of the world, and the totalitarian temptation in the democratic West, as strong. What then is the meaning of the return of man after the philosophical onslaught to which he was submitted throughout modernity? I am afraid such a question cannot be answered now. All we can say is that it would be as wrong to gainsay the significance of man's recent and as yet incomplete resurrection as it would be to blow it up. On a more modest plane, though, it seems in order to look at the banalization of the language of the end of man with a philosophical smile.

NOTES

1. Michel Foucault, *Les Mots et les choses* (Paris: Éditions Gallimard, 1966); trans. *The Order of Things* (New York: Pantheon Books, 1971; Vintage Books, 1973).

2. For a discussion of the philosophical antecedents of the French critique of humanism or anthropologism during the antiexistentialist and structuralist 1960s, see Jacques Derrida's "Les fins de l'homme," collected in his *Marges de la philosophie* (Paris: Éditions de Minuit, 1972).

3. See André Glucksmann, *Les Maîtres penseurs* (Paris: Grasset, 1977).

4. Matei Calinescu, *Faces of Modernity: Avant-Garde, Decadence, and Kitsch* (Bloomington: Indiana University Press, 1977).

5. George Lichtheim, *The Concept of Ideology and Other Essays* (New York: Vintage Books, 1967), p. 8.

6. Robert C. Tucker, ed., *The Marx-Engels Reader*, 2nd ed. (New York: W. W. Norton & Company, 1978), pp. 174–75.

7. See Alfred G. Meyer's 1970 Introduction to a new edition of his 1954 essay *Marxism: The Unity of Theory and Practice* (Cambridge, Mass.: Harvard University Press, 1970), pp. xiv–xv, which discusses the "religious kernel" of Marxism.

8. The less obscure "practical antihumanism" of Marxism, Stalinism, has been powerfully described in *The Gulag Archipelago* by Aleksandr I. Solzhenitsyn (1974; New York: Harper & Row, 1975).

9. For the "epistemological break" that separates the young Marx, still heavily indebted to Hegel, and the true or "scientific" Marx, see Louis Althusser's *Pour Marx* (Paris: François Maspero, 1965), *For Marx*, trans. Ben Brewster (London: Allen Lane, 1969), especially p. 229; and Louis Althusser and Étienne Balibar, *Lire le Capital*, 2 vols. (Paris: François Maspero, 1965), *Reading 'Capital,'* trans. Ben Brewster (London: NLB, 1970). For the notion of history as a "subjectless process," see Althusser's *Réponse à John Lewis* (Paris: François Maspero, 1973).

10. Michael Polanyi, *Personal Knowledge: Towards a Post-Critical Philosophy*, rev. ed. (Chicago: University of Chicago Press, 1962), p. 228.

11. Friedrich Nietzsche, *The Gay Science*, trans. Walter Kaufmann (New York: Vintage Books, 1974), p. 181.

12. Octavio Paz, *Children of the Mire*, trans. Rachel Phillips (Cambridge, Mass.: Harvard University Press, 1974).

13. Mircea Eliade has dealt with this problem most recently in the first volume of his magnum opus, *A History of Religious Ideas* (Chicago: University of Chicago Press, 1978). See also his *Myth and Reality*, trans. Willard R. Trask (New York: Harper & Row, 1963), p. 95.

14. Friedrich Nietzsche, *On the Genealogy of Morals* and *Ecce Homo*, ed. and trans. Walter Kaufmann (New York: Vintage Books, 1969), p. 333.

15. Foucault, *The Order of Things* p. 305.

16. Ibid., pp. 317, 319, and 322–23.

17. Ibid., p. 318. Foucault's ideology remains unchanged in his more recent and perhaps even more ambitious *L'Archéologie du Savoir* (Paris: Éditions Gallimard, 1969), *The Archaeology of Knowledge*, trans A. M. Sheridan Smith (New York: Pantheon Books, 1972). See, for example, pp. 332, 353.

18. Michel de Certeau, Review of *Les Mots et les Choses*, *Les Etudes*, 326 (March 1967), 360.

19. Claude Lévi-Strauss, *Tristes Tropiques* (Paris: Librarie Plon, 1955), *Tristes Tropiques*, trans. John and Doreen Weightman (New York: Atheneum, 1974), p. 58.

20. Claude Lévi-Strauss, *L'Homme nu* (Paris: Librarie Plon, 1971), p. 578.

21. Lévi-Strauss, *Tristes Tropiques*, p. 413.

22. Mircea Eliade, "Cultural Fashions and History of Religions," in his *Occultism, Witchcraft, and Cultural Fashions: Essays in Comparative Religions* (Chicago: University of Chicago Press, 1976), pp. 14–15.

23. Lévi-Strauss, *Tristes Tropiques*, p. 414.

24. Ibid., pp. 57–58.

25. Claude Lévi-Strauss, *The Savage Mind* (London: Weidenfeld and Nicolson, 1966), p. 247.

26. On existentialism and humanism, see Derrida, "Les fins de l'homme," especially pp. 136 and 147–61.

27. Lévi-Strauss, *L'Homme nu*, p. 620.

28. Susan Sontag, Introduction to *The Temptation to Exist* by E. M. Cioran, trans. Richard Howard (Chicago: Quadrangle Books, 1968), p. 11.

29. Cioran, *The Temptation to Exist*, pp. 123–24.

30. E. M. Cioran, *Écartèlement* (Paris: Éditions Gallimard, 1979), pp. 42–44.

31. For a discussion of the major definitions of kitsch and of the relationship between it and mass society, see my essay on "Kitsch," included in my *Faces of Modernity*, pp. 225–62.

32. Roland Barthes, *Le Plaisir du texte* (Paris: Éditions du Seuil, 1973), pp. 45–46.

33. Roland Barthes, *Roland Barthes par Roland Barthes* (Paris: Éditions du Seuil, 1975), p. 124. For a more detailed discussion of the importance of inau-

thenticity for Barthes, see Tzvetan Todorov's article "Reflections on Literature in Contemporary France," *New Literary History* 10:3 (Spring 1979), 523–31.

34. For a discussion of the previous stages of this conflict, see my article "Hermeneutics or Poetics," in *Journal of Religion* 59:1 (January 1979), 1–17.

35. Ilya Prigogine and Isabelle Stengers, *La Nouvelle Alliance: Metamorphose de la science* (Paris: Éditions Gallimard, 1979), pp. 294–95.

36. Foucault, *L'Archéologie du Savoir*, p. 353.

37. I borrow the word *transhumanization* from Ihab Hassan, who uses it in his *Paracriticisms* (Urbana: University of Illinois Press, 1975) and in *The Right Promethean Fire* (Urbana: University of Illinois Press, 1980).

10

MAN AS NOSTALGIA: THE IMAGE OF THE LAST MAN IN TWENTIETH-CENTURY POSTUTOPIAN FICTION

André Reszler

Qu'on me rende mon moi; j'y tiens.
—Michelet

BUT TELL ME PLEASE, WHY SUDDENLY . . . SUDDENLY, A soul?" mutters D-503 helplessly in Zamiatin's *We*," "There was none, yet suddenly. . . . Why is it that no one has it, yet I. . . ."[1] D-503 reacts with anxiety to his new awareness of his individuality. His feeling of isolation is exacerbated as he becomes progressively part of an "antisocial" network of personally oriented social relationships. He knows that the United State tō which he belongs needs only socially determined human beings; in the timeless world of utopian perfection there is no place for individuals. Is he therefore a sort of an anachronism, the lone survivor of an extinct individualist civilization? Or is he caught within the ambiguity of the myth of death and rebirth, the herald of a New Beginning? Is the "last" man of the utopian social order the "first" man of a new age of "imperfection"?

In *Nineteen Eighty-Four*, Orwell presents Winston Smith as another "last man." His very discovery of the self is a mortal threat to the fragile order of Eurasian perfection. It is for this reason that he is submitted to a carefully devised process of depersonalization. In the caves of the Thought Police, Winston Smith is progressively deprived of the individual traits of his personality. "What are you? A bag of filth. Now turn round and look into that mirror again. Do you see that thing facing you? That is the last man,"² yells O'Brien triumphantly, when Smith has finally been reduced to the purely social level of existence.

The figure of the last man in twentieth-century postutopian fiction opens a new chapter in the intellectual history of the modern individual. He is the distant heir to the Courtier, to the Renaissance man, and to the decadent late nineteenth-century *culte du moi*. In his defensive simplicity, however, he is closer to the "average man" of modern industrial society than to Emerson's "representative man" or to Gobineau's amateurish *fils de roi*.

In a way, Thomas More, Tommaso Campenalla, and the later line of eighteenth- and nineteenth-century authors of utopian fiction are the originators of the revolutionary/eschatological vision of a "new man,"³ of the application of the theory of probability to social and moral problems e.g., Adolphe Quételet and his *homme statistique*⁴, and, ultimately, of the contemporary structuralist ideology of the "death of man." Zamiatin, Huxley, Orwell, and Burgess belong to another European intellectual tradition: the one that takes as the essential values the individual, the principles of pluralism, multiplicity, and change, and uses them in its piecemeal approach to social engineering.

Utopia has been traditionally associated with the ideas of progress, social change, and rational city planning. However, if we examine the emergence of utopia in the historical perspective of the sixteenth and seventeenth centuries, we realize that it is essentially reactionary. In fact, it represents the first modern assault on the emergence of the modern individual—*l'uomo universale, l'uomo singolare*—and the changing view of the world which came with the Renaissance. Utopian fiction is against the open literary culture of the Courtier, the newly rediscovered Ciceronian principle of the *vita activa*, and the rehabilitation of wealth and worldliness. It prefers the austere simplicity and quasi-military discipline of Plato's *Republic*. It dreams about a new Middle Ages with its social stability and the clearly delimited horizons of a closed society.

The Renaissance man—Burckhardt's *grosse Individuum*—owes his autonomy to a fully developed individual consciousness. He makes his personality into a well-ordered universe which necessarily becomes the center of a fully developed network of social relationships. A man of multiple spiritual, cultural, and social allegiances, he is himself a multicentered human being: "unsatiable," "vagabond," and "versatile" (Montaigne). ("We are made up of bits, and so shapelessly and diversely put together, that every piece, at every moment, plays its own game. And there is as much difference between us and ourselves, as between us and others," says Montaigne.⁵) The diversity of the social order associated with the concept of the individual has its origins in the individual's own pluralistic psychic and intellectual makeup. "Openness" has thus both a personal and a social dimension.

As we shall see, in the closely knit framework of utopia's collectivist social order there is no room for man defined as an individual— "cultivated," nurtured, and cherished. In a way, the more flamboyant the triumphant individualism of the Renaissance city-state and court civilization, the more classical utopian literature insists on erasing the traces of individualism from its blueprint of social perfection.

The subordination of individual will to the "general interest" or "general will" was the fundamental principle of communal life in the utopian communities of the nineteenth-century United States. According to Charles Nordhoff, these communities laid "a total claim on their members"; the discipline they established was "more than military." "To abandon self, with all its desires, knowledge, and power" is one of the Rules for Daily Life adopted by the Inspirationists at Amana, Iowa.[6] Passions— desire, grief, friendship—are obstacles on the road to peace of mind and harmony.

CLASSICAL UTOPIA REVISITED

Before examining the reemergence of man as an individual in the utopias described by Zamiatin, Orwell, Huxley, Burgess, and others, let us turn briefly to some of permanent features of utopian imagination.

1. Utopian society is presented in both classical and "postutopian" works of fiction as historical phenomena of relatively recent origin. Thus, "Utopia was originally not an island but a peninsula," remarks Thomas More. Before its conquest by King Utopus, it was called Abraxa. It is this king who transformed its inhabitants—"a pack of ignorant savages"—into "what is now, perhaps, the most civilized nation in the world."[7] Similarly, the Republic of Icarie owes its name to a professional revolutionary, Icar, who, for the purposes of the story, put an end to the reign of Queen Cloramide in the year 1782, i.e., some forty-eight years before the publication of Etienne Cabet's Voyage en Icarie.[8] Winston Smith in Orwell's Nineteen Eighty-Four and the grandfather in Tibor Déry's Mr. G. A. in X[9] have spent their childhood during the last years of preutopian England and Hungary. Their memories are haunted; they are surrounded by objects that recall unmistakingly the "olden days" of imperfection.

2. For reasons that, to my knowledge, have not been clearly established up to now, no utopian writer has ever attributed the achievement of perfection to some radical change in human nature itself. Invariably, perfection comes from the superior nature of utopian social institutions. In his Histoire des Sévérambes, Denis Vairesse d'Allais makes it clear that

the Sévérambes are in no way different from other nations, nor lacking their passions. The origins of their happiness must rather be sought in the way they consider one particular aspect of man's nature—altruism—as the only solid basis of all social relationships. "La nature n'a rien fait de particulier pour les Sévérambes," writes Vairesse;

Ils sont nés avec le germe de tous les vices que nous apportons dans le monde; mais ce germe, étouffé dans sa naissance par la sage disposition des lois, ne peut prendre racine dans le coeur de ces peuples. C'est donc à la forme du gouvernement des Sévérambes qu'ils doivent leurs vertus; et l'auteur, qui est le législateur des peuples qu'il a créés, leur dicte des lois, dont l'effet est d'adoucir leurs moeurs, de diriger leurs passions, de manière à les contraindre à aimer la vertu, et à la pratiquer.[10]

(Nature has done nothing particular for the Sévérambes; they are born with the germs of all the depravity that we bring forth into the world; but these germs, stifled from the very beginning by wisely enacted laws, cannot strike roots in the hearts of these people. The Sévérambes owe their virtues to the form of their government; and the author, who is the legislator of the people he has created, imposes upon them laws that soften their manners and regulate their passions so that they are obliged to love virtue and to live according to it.)

In Cabet's Icaria, it is the state that "does everything." "Le bonheur ne vient que de la part de l'État." All the marvels that the visitors from France or England admire have their origin in the workings of "la République" and of "la communauté."[11] According to Bellamy, the Bostonians of the year 2000 have the same biological and psychological makeup as their great-grandfathers of 1887. It is not human nature that has changed in the meantime, but the basic "conditions of human life" and the "motives of human action" to which they give rise.[12]

3. "The account of every person, man, woman, and child . . . is always with the nation directly, and never through any intermediary," writes Bellamy.[13] In the utopian state, there is no division of power, no local autonomy, no carefully balanced multiplicity of schools, churches, or pressure groups. His motto might well be Mustapha Mond's statement according to which in the Brave New World "there's no such thing as a divided allegiance."[14]

Zamiatin's description of organized promenades in the United State is worth quoting here. It reads as a pastiche of the corresponding passage in Cabet's classical blueprint of utopian communality:

We were down in the street. The avenue was crowded. On days when the weather is so beautiful, the afternoon personal hour is usually the hour of supplementary walk. As always, the big Musical Tower was playing the March of the United State with all its pipes. The Numbers, hundreds,

thousands of Numbers in light blue unifs (probably a derivative of the
ancient uniform) with golden badges on the chest—the State number of
each one, male or female—the Numbers were walking slowly, four abreast,
exaltedly keeping step. I, we four, were but one of the innumerable waves
of a powerful torrent. . . ."[15]

4. Life in utopia is highly reminiscent of living conditions in army
barracks. On a visit to a factory workshop in Icaria, Lord Carisdale won-
ders if it is run by workmen or by the military. The female workers in
another atelier all wear the same "uniform dress." At ten o'clock, in
unison, they sing a hymn in praise of the "bon Icar." The militarization of
everyday life begins in infancy.[16]

All the citizens of twenty-first-century utopian Boston are members of
a vast "industrial army" in Bellamy's *Looking Backward.* "Under the national organization of labor, all industries are carried on by great bodies of
men, a hundred of (ordinary) farms or shops being combined as one. The
superintendent, with us, is like a colonel, or even a general, in one of the
(classical) armies."[17] Foremen have the rank of a captain, and so on. Bellamy's narrator remembers how he had conceived, on a rainy day, in late
nineteenth-century Boston, the need to introduce principles of military
organization into all the aspects of everyday life:

> A regiment was passing. It was the first sight in that dreary day which had
> inspired me with any other emotions rather than wondering pity and
> amazement. Here at last were order and reason, an exhibition of what
> intelligent cooperation can accomplish. The people who stood looking on
> with kindling faces, could it be that the sight had for them no more than a
> spectacular interest? Could they fail to see that it was their perfect concert
> of action, their organization under one control, which made these men the
> tremendous engine they were, able to vanquish a mob ten times as numer-
> ous? Seeing this so plainly, could they fail to compare the scientific manner
> in which the nation went to war with the unscientific manner in which it
> went to work? Would they not query since what time the killing of men had
> been a task so much more important than feeding and clothing them, that a
> trained army should be deemed alone adequate to the former, while the
> latter was left to be a mob?[18]

5. The utopian state recreates, by its reliance on reason, the natural
harmony of a long-ago Golden Age. When Etienne Cabet describes Icaria
as a "second Promised Land," an "Eden," an "Elysium," or a "new Earthly
Paradise," he integrates into his world view the powerful myth of the
Golden Age.[19] Bellamy's hero is introduced to the "millennium" of the
utopian perfection of twenty-first-century Boston by the "glorious daughter of a New Golden Age." The "new heaven and the new earth wherein
dwelleth righteousness" foretold by the prophet have become a reality.
"We are like a child which has just learned to stand upright and to walk."[20]

William Morris compares utopia to an "Earthly Paradise." Mankind is reborn and enters his "second childhood." In his *News from Nowhere*, Morris tries to recapture the essence of "that primitive Communism which preceded civilization" and the communal spirit of medieval England. "All I had seen hitherto seemed a mere part of a summer holiday," remarks his hero in the New London of the coming utopian century.[21]

"You see, it is the ancient legend of paradise. . . . That legend referred to us of today, did it not? Yes," writes Zamiatin ironically in *We*.[22] "They're well off. They're safe; they're never ill; they're not afraid of death; they're blissfully ignorant of passion and old age," declares Mustapha Mond about the happy residents of Huxley's *Brave New World*.[23]

6. Utopia's founder, King Utopus, has all the characteristics of a charismatic leader. It is he who lays down once and for all the constitution of the ideal city and draws up rules of everyday conduct, down to the minutest details. He is a great general—*dux* (as in Joachim of Fiore)—and as such, embodies the virtues of mankind's principal heroes, legislators, conquerors, and saviors. Cabet's "bon Icar" is a Christlike figure whose deeds form Icaria's foundation myth. Icarians owe all their passions—including their taste for vegetables and their love of music—to his exemplary teachings. ("The character of the leaders in Utopian communities . . . is of the greatest importance," remarks Nordhoff in his work on nineteenth-century America. "Vater" Rapp in New Harmony or John Humphrey Noyes in Oneida mold the habits "not only of daily life, but even of thought . . . just as the father forms the character of his children in a family."[24] Icar is beyond any doubt the literary archetype of the World Controller in *Brave New World* or of Big Brother in *Nineteen Eighty-Four*. Every utopian state has its "sun," its theocratic ruler who is the only citizen endowed with some of the basic characteristics of the individual: humor, irony, artistic sensibility, and intellectual discipline.

"La passion aveugle pour la liberté est une erreur, un vice, un mal grave, né de la haine violente et qu'excitent le despotisme et l'esclavage," writes Cabet.[25] (Man's blind passion for freedom is an error, a vice, an evil born out of violent hatred and nurtured by despotism and slavery.) Icar is during his lifetime the only free man in the Icarian Republic. But even his freedom is limited by the respect he owes to the institutions he has himself created; the principle of change is beyond his reach. He is, as are all his compatriots, a man without property, and as such, narrowly bound within the empty structure of his personality.

We shall now examine how these aspects of utopian imagination contribute to the socialization of man in the closed society of classical utopia. And we shall seek to understand why authors such as Zamiatin, Orwell, and Déry developed a new anticollectivist vision of the ideal city within the framework of the utopian novel.

A NEW UTOPIA?

"If we leave tomorrow for my home country, if we go abroad, we can still be happy," says G. A. to Elizabeth in Tibor Déry's *Mr. G.A. in X.*[26] The visitor from the "imperfect" world of pre-World War II Hungary feels no admiration for the cold messianism of X, a model city in which we recognize both the familiar landscape of classical utopia and the author's vision of socialist—"utopian"—Hungary.[27]

G. A. does not share Raphaël Hythlodaeus's uncritical enthusiasm for the social institutions of utopia. Nor does he believe that happiness can come from state control and social engineering, the twin sources of social harmony in utopian literature from More to the late nineteenth century. G. A.'s *eutopia* rather reminds us of the kitsch happiness of popular imagination: "We'll live there in a small garden full of real roses and tulips, near a forest on the shores of a stately river. We'll have a child and he'll laugh and weep from morning till night."[28] Elizabeth is no rebel to utopia's barren social order. In her mind, however, G. A.'s descriptions of birds and animals evoke, archetypal longings for an unknown "bourgeois" paradise. Her fragile love for the visitor from abroad is akin to her affection for her stubbornly eccentric grandfather, Déry's "last man" who personifies the creative power of remembrance.

Published in Hungary in 1964, Déry's novel belongs to the twentieth-century tradition of negative utopias. In fact, utopia as a literary genre came to an unannounced end in the last decades of the nineteenth century. With Bellamy's *Looking Backward* (1887) and Morris's *News from Nowhere* (1890), utopia—*l'esprit d'utopie*—loses the support of romance and relies on ideology in the form of political theory or journalistic literature for its survival.

Negative utopia is heavily dependent on classical utopia as far as its literary devices are concerned. Zamiatin's *We*, Huxley's *Brave New World*, Orwell's *Nineteen Eighty-Four*, Déry's *Mr. G.A. in X*, or Burgess's *1985*—all apply the constructivist approach of More, Campanella, or Cabet to the still fertile myth of the Golden Age.[29] However, to the essential themes of classical utopia—timelessness, stability, uniformity, and the like—they oppose themes which are clearly distinct from utopia's militant ideals: history, change, and the reemergence of the individual. Escape from the nightmare world of perfection, belief in the healing value of imagination (*l'inconnu*), rediscovery of love, suffering, and death, re-creation of the private sphere of personal relationships—all these establish the specific identity of this twentieth-century sequel to the modern history of utopia.

Postutopian fiction borrows from classical utopia the basic opposition of two irreconcilable worlds. In *Voyage en Icarie*, Cabet constantly enumerates the imperfections of "la malheureuse France" so that the reader can fully appreciate the achievements of "l'heureuse Icarie." In Déry's post-utopian fiction, the visitor from Hungary returns, finally, to his homeland. He does so because Hungary has ceased to be "unhappy" and appears as a center of true vitality, while the city of X has adopted the cult of death as its secular religion.

The kind of fiction we have just described as postutopian also reconsiders two issues that play a central role in utopian fiction: the disappearance of the individual and the willful suppression of time (and change). From Thomas More to Edward Bellamy, utopian writers have constantly devalued life as an individual experience; they have also tried to imprison change in the terror-struck immobility of an all-enduring present. From Zamiatin to Burgess, postutopian novelists rehabilitate the individual—represented as the last man—and the principle of change. They do this by discovering man as he existed in preutopian times, and by making use of the creative power of the past.

The Socialization of Man . . .

"Le moi n'est pas seulement haïssable: il n'y a pas de place entre un *nous* et un rien." (The self is not only hateful; there is no room for it between an "us" and a "nothing.") Claude Lévi-Strauss's classical statement about the "death of man" could well serve as a motto for the utopian fiction of Campanella, Restif de la Bretonne, Sébastien Mercier, and Cabet. The notion of death refers, in both cases, to the atrophy of the personal sphere of human existence. The new man who succeeds the "individual" has only a one-sided social existence. All his endeavors are socially oriented; his happiness is generated by the well-being of his environment.

An example from Cabet's *Voyage en Icarie* clearly illustrates the strength of social control over utopia's "dead" individual. Valmor, a young Icarian who introduces the admiring visitors from Britain and France to the workings of social perfection, is told by Dinara that she will break her engagement in order to marry another man. His lament shows that their relationship has been, in reality, a social one, with himself and his "loved one" as the mere representatives of two families. "Elle ne m'aime pas! . . . Depuis plus de dix ans, je concentre sur elle toutes mes espérances, toutes mes affections, tout le bonheur de mon avenir." But all of a sudden, the well-studied rhetoric of romantic love is shattered:

> Son frère et sa mère m'entretenaient dans une illusion qui me rendait heureux; et un mot a détruit à jamais pour moi tout bonheur! . . . O mon ami, que je suis malheureux de ma douleur, de celle de ma famille et de ma soeur! Car *tous nous* l'entourions de notre amour, et son refus *nous* accable *tous* de désolation. [Italics added.][30]

(She does not love me. For more than ten years, I have been concentrating on her all my hopes, all my fondness and all my future happiness. . . . . Her brother and her mother have entertained in me an illusion that made me happy; and one single word destroyed for ever my happiness. Oh, my friend, I am sick of my grief, of a grief fully shared by my family and by my sister. You must know that *we* have surrounded her with *our* love and that her refusal fills *all of us* with dismay.)

When Roland Barthes writes that "une sorte de 'ça' collectif se substitue à l'image que je croyais avoir de moi, et c'est moi, 'ça' (a kind of collective "id" is being substituted to the image I have had of myself, and this "id" is my real self.)[31] he shares Zamiatin's or Huxley's vision of the utopian experience. "Nobody is *one*, but *one of.* We are so much alike—" says the narrator in *We*.[32] "Ford, we are twelve; oh, make us one, / Like drops within the Social River; / Oh, make us now together run / As swiftly as thy shining Flivver," runs one of the Solidarity Hymns in *Brave New World*.[33]

In Zamiatin's *We*, the utopian community appears as a "powerful organism of millions of cells" organized along the lines of a "united church." No solitary voice ever violates the "magnificent unison" of its communal songs. "United into a single body with a million hands," the citizens or Numbers of the United State perform their daily duties as members of a well-organized army. Their very promenades graphically illustrate the Assyrian metaphor of social uniformity: "We were walking yesterday as usual, that is like warriors on the Assyrian monuments, a thousand heads and two composite, integrated legs and two singing, integrated arms."[34]

. . . and his Reindividualization

If, within the closely knit ranks of this semimilitary, semi-industrial army, an individual appears, his presence is felt to be a nuisance—a crime—an atavism. Hence, D-503, Zamiatin's last man, looks at his hands covered with long hair in horror. When, all of a sudden, he becomes conscious of his personality, he considers this process to be a "sickness," the reawakening of a long-suppressed dream, the reemergence of some long-forgotten, primitive history. In the God-dominated world of "plurals," it is the return of the solitary Devil: " 'We' is from 'God,' 'I,' from the devil."[35]

In Huxley's *Brave New World*, Bernard Marx feels that he is more than "just a cell in the social body." He shares with some of his friends the knowledge that he is, after all, an individual; the emergence of the perfectly socialized self, of unexpected and uncontrolled psychic energies: "Did you ever feel . . . as though you had something inside you that was only waiting for you to give it a chance to come out? Some sort of extra power that you aren't using—you know, like all the water that goes down the falls instead of through the turbines."[36] Like D-503, Bernard Marx is "sick," sick with individuality.

What endows postutopian fiction with its significance within utopian literature is not the underlying reevaluation of perspectives—the re-habilitation of history, change, and the corresponding escape from the nightmare world of "perfection"—but the reemergence of the individual. But has this latter altogether disappeared in the utopian novel from More to Zamiatin? Has not individual experience left its mark on utopian imagi-nation as an ineradicable, heretical, if minor characteristic within the all-too-well-integrated pattern of the model city?

In fact, the fight against unorthodoxy, against "heretics" who deviate from the narrow path of utopian perfection, dominates writings by More, Campanella, Andreae, and others on the following centuries. And invari-ably, utopian writers prescribe particularly harsh sanctions against "mad-men" and "criminals" who fail to respect the laws of King Utopus or of the "good" Icar. (Capital punishment and exclusion are utopia's answers to the individual's failure to conform. All crimes against perfection call for the maximum punishment.[37])

If no utopian writer portrays the individuals who show their individual-ity by revolting against the pervasive rules of utopian perfection, we know that they keep alive the European tradition of individual consciousness and the ideals of personalized human relationships. Zamiatin, Huxley, Orwell, and Déry bring to life More's or Campanella's stereotyped, ab-stract "heretics." Moreover, they give to these survivors of a postutopian/preutopian human condition a definitely prospective character. Utopia's "last man" appears thus as the precursor of a new, postutopian age.

THE VALUE OF THE PAST

"If you are a man, Winston, you are the last man. Your kind is extinct," ironically remarks O'Brien, Orwell's grand inquisitor in *Nineteen Eighty-Four*. In order to make clear that he is not referring to the disappearance of the human race, he adds: "We are the inheritors." The successor of man, the individual, is a new kind of socialized human being deprived of his aptitude for love, friendship, the joy of living, curiosity, courage or integrity, and whose loyalty goes ﬞ the Party. "We shall squeeze you empty, and then we shall fill you with ourselves."[38]

Winston Smith is in no way an "exceptional" man, a twentieth-century variant of Burckhardt's Renaissance man. He is, on the contrary, very much an ordinary man, a man of the street. He is distinguished from his fellow citizens only by a sudden emerging desire to live his life as an individual experience: to reconstitute his personality according to a new vision of man and of his social relationships.

His discovery of the self is intimately linked to another discovery: that of the past. In his quest for a new, "personalized" identity, he has to "re-learn," through precarious and dangerous experience, man's primitive emotions, by relying constantly on the guidance of objects, fading memories (and most importantly, the image of his mother), together with eyewitness accounts.

If there is nothing singular about Smith as a man, his situation is highly unusual. A particular section of his room remains outside the range of the telescreen from which all activities can usually be easily supervised. He starts to write a diary, a book which reminds us of life led as a personal adventure and of a literary genre intimately linked with the emergence of the individual. His odyssey is, at this point, perfectly self-centered. "He was a lonely ghost uttering a truth that nobody could ever hear." His message is addressed to no reader. It is but an "interminable restless monologue."[39]

However, if the diary confronts him primarily with his own limited experience, it immediately brings him into contact with the past. "It was a peculiarly beautiful book. Its smooth creamy paper, a little yellowed by age, was of a kind that had not been manufactured for at least forty years past. He could guess, however, that the book was much older than that."[40] The pen he uses is described as an "archaic instrument," an object which, by its very nature, suggests the existence of an irretrievably lost world.

The simultaneous discovery of life as a personal experience and of the past as an alternative to man's collective condition does not condemn Smith to isolation. The past is not a bittersweet form of nostalgia that definitively limits his horizon, but a source of creative action. The diary he keeps as a hopelessly isolated individual becomes a means of communication. "He was writing the diary for O'Brien—to O'Brien,"[41] writes Orwell, when Smith discovers that in utopia's anonymous human experience, there are many islands of personalized adventure governed by old-fashioned, private loyalties. "She had possessed a kind of nobility, a kind of purity, simply because the standards she obeyed were private ones. Her feelings were her own, and could not be altered from outside."[42] This is how the image of his mother appears in Smith's mind. And, on the basis of this image, he will develop his own private standards, his own personal relationships. All his actions are based on models which he painstakingly elaborates from the random materials of his quasi-archeological approach to the private world of remembrance.

Vive l'ancien régime might be Winston's motto. When he accepts O'Brien's invitation, they celebrate the revolutionary potential of the past in a vainglorious way:

[O'Brien] filled the glasses and raised his own glass by the stem. "What shall it be this time?" he said, still with the same faint suggestion of irony. "To the confusion of the Thought Police? To the death of Big Brother? To humanity? To the future?"

"To the past," said Winston.

"The past is more important," agreed O'Brien gravely.[43]

Anthony Burgess's ode to the past occurs in his book *1985*. Bev, Burgess's "personalist" hero, is on the point of being robbed by a baronial band of anticollectivist youths when he is saved by a phrase from Sophocles' *Oedipus at Colonus* which he quotes in the Greek original. Greek has become the overpowering symbol of antiperfectionist cultural heresy. "Give it me in Greek. Give it me real," Bev is asked by a member of the band in another passage of the novel, when he quotes Socrates' invocation to Kriton. "I want the past in front of me like it was all really there." "I can't remember the rest," says Bev, "sorry. You're right about the past. We owe no debt to the present or the future. Keep the past alive, pay the debt. Somebody has to do it."[44]

How does the past become the starting point of a new human experience? How does the "last man" in modern postutopian fiction become the precursor of a New Beginning? What are the values that Zamiatin, Huxley, Orwell, Déry, and Burgess associate with the solitary struggle of their respective heroes, each one representing tomorrow's triumphant *Herr Omnes*, or today's delinquent "last individual"?

VARIETIES OF THE PAST

Tell me about your life when you were a boy. What was it like in those days? Were things better than they are now, or were they worse?
—Orwell, *Nineteen Eighty-Four*

"Oranges and lemons, say the bells of St Clement's. You owe me three farthings, say the bells of St Martin's!" The fragmented lines of a popular rhyme appear in Winston Smith's mind as the epitome of the preutopian past of Oceania. Although he has never heard church bells ringing, he has the illusion of actually hearing the bells of a lost London as if they still "existed somewhere," thanks to the disheveled memory of an old man whose decadent memory is nothing but a "rubbish-heap" of disconnected, insignificant details. A question like "Was life better before the Revolution that it is now?" has become once and for all unanswerable.[45]

As I have said in an earlier section of this chapter, for the "negative" hero of postutopian fiction, the past is never truly distant. He carries its fragments as part of an inalienable heritage. All of Smith's memories connected with the image of his mother evoke a time when "there was still privacy, love, and friendship, and when the members of a family stood by one another without needing to know the reason."[46]

When he comes upon a glass paperweight in Mr. Charrington's antique shop, he is immediately struck by its apparent uselessness. "What appealed to him about it was not so much its beauty as the air it seemed to possess of belonging to an age quite different from the present one."[47] It is already part of the personal world which he is trying to organize in order to reconquer the past that has been ravished from him. He will establish private loyalties and create personal norms of everyday behavior.

The room he rents, finally, above the antique shop—the metaphor is truly telling—is not only a secure hiding place where he can meet Julia, but also a "world, a pocket of the past where extinct animals could walk." The "sort of ancestral memory" that is aroused in him whenever he enters the room is reminiscent not only of the past, but of the future he would like to enter.[48] In postutopian fiction, nostalgia has an obvious anticipatory function.

In Zamiatin's We, when I-330 wants to awaken D-503 to a new, anticollectivist existence, she naturally takes him to the Ancient House. This structure, covered by a glass shell, is near the wall from which the visitor can catch a glimpse of the landscape on the other side of the frontier that separates the United State from the ancient territories of history. It is inhabited by an ageless old woman. Inside the house—a fragment of preutopian civilization—D-503 has the feeling that his very existence is in danger. He sees "the same strange 'royal' musical instrument and a wild, unorganized, crazy loudness of colors and forms like their ancient music. A white plane above, dark blue walls, red, green, orange buildings of ancient books, yellow bronze candelabra, a statue of Buddha, furniture with lines distorted by epilepsy, impossible to reduce to any clear equation." I-330 disguises herself as a *femme du monde* from the early twentieth century. D-503 feels as if he were "trapped in a strange cage": "I felt that I was caught in the wild hurricane of ancient life."[49]

The Past as Utopia

"The past was erased, the erasure was forgotten, the lie became truth," writes Orwell in *Nineteen Eighty-Four.*[50] In the terror-stricken world of utopia, the closed structure of the present casts its shadow on the past. Life as it has actually been lived in the "old days" has been replaced by a set of prefabricated clichés. As all the museums have been closed, all historical monuments blown up, books published before the foundation of the model city burned or rewritten, some other approaches to the past have to be devised if it is to serve as a link between the present and the future.[51]

The decadent world of the "proles" in *Nineteen Eighty-Four* and the Indian Reservation in Huxley's *Brave New World* project well into the present/ancient ways of feeling, thinking, and acting. Those who have no access to their treasures have to rely on the testimony of "archaic" objects or on the power of irresistible psychic urges or archetypes. The past lives in everybody's mind, but its presence is similar to the dry riverbed which all of a sudden fills with water after a long period of drought.

Forbidden or forgotten worlds also offer a key to the marvels of the past. Although the exact meaning of words such as *parents, mother, father, brother, sister, husband, wife, lover,* or *home* is highly problematical for most people, their empty shells testify to the rich experience of multiple human relationships.[52]

In Déry's *Mr. G. A. in X,* Elizabeth is familiar with the names of birds, animals, trees, or seasons. She is, however, unable to establish any precise relationship between the "latent" section of her vocabulary and reality. Did her grandfather really have, in his childhood, a parrot in the cage hanging in his room under the roof? She tends to consider lions purely imaginary animals. "The lion is the emblem of what does not exist." She does not share G. A.'s longing for animals. ("I would give ten years of my life for the barking of a dog," cries the visitor from Hungary in a moment of deprivation.) Yet when G.A. evokes the "shadow" of a blackbird, she is suddenly convinced of the reality of "empty" words. One day, in fact. G.A. draws in black pebbles the silhouette of a bird:

"What kind of bird is this?" she asked. "An eagle?"
"It's not a bird," said G.A., "only the shadow of a bird."
"Which bird's shadow?"
"Of a blackbird," said G.A.
The girl gave a deep sigh. "Where is the blackbird?" she asked.
"In my head," said G.A. "That's where the shadow comes from."
"Can it whistle?"
"Dioo-fioo-fioo," whistled G.A.
The girl sprang to her feet and ran to G.A., stretching her around his shoulders. "Dear G.A.," she begged him, "let it go free. Let me hold it for a moment."
"You mustn't touch it," said G.A., "or else it will turn into ashes."
They were alone in the garden, the tenants were still asleep. The girl took G.A.'s head into her hands and inhaled his breath deeply.
"I sense the smell of the blackbird," she said with joy and sorrow. "Dear G.A., let the blackbird fly from your mouth into mine."[53]

Déry's Last Man

In Déry's model city a peculiar death cult takes the place of state ideology.[54] The whistling of a bird, the barking of a dog represent, therefore, love of life or, in other words, love of the past.

210   ANDRÉ RESZLER

"Those who love life cannot be virtuous," runs a well-known proverb in
X. The inhabitants, who can no longer resist the irrepressible call of
death, take part in a mass parade clearly modeled on the May Day cele-
brations in East European socialist countries. Elizabeth's grandfather is
the only citizen of X who does not share this collective passion for "passing
away." In order to protect himself against the mounting pressures of
society, he withdraws into his room—a room which reminds us of the
room in Orwell's *Nineteen Eighty-Four* above the antique shop which
Smith rents in order to recreate an island of exclusiveness, or the apart-
ment in the Ancient House in Zamiatin's *We* where D-503 and I-330
meet. "On the wall, above the wash-stand, there was a mirror, the first
mirror G.A. had seen in the city. And in the corner of the mirror, tucked
under the frame, there was a yellowed photograph showing the faded
image of a woman."[55]

Although the old man's life has no clear social significance, his very
survival is a matter of the greatest importance. He is the last representative of a generation with a firsthand knowledge of X's preutopian past. He
is the only one who knows what life was like during the last years of the
ancien régime. "I must preserve myself as a vivid protest against the state
of unconsciousness that covers a growing portion of this planet, and which
might obliterate the memory of an age when men truly lived, suffered or
were happy." He adds: "I want to be the last guardian of a cemetery that is
aimlessly revolving in space." His suffering tells him that life is inseparable from the very characteristics of imperfection. Utopia is the realm of
quietude, harmony, and the void. "If I pass away, there'll be nobody to
protest against the state of unconsciousness that is on the point of overwhelming the planet."[56]

Elizabeth shares her grandfather's love of life. She refuses, however, to
accompany G.A. when he decided to return to his home country. G.A.'s
attempt to find companions who might reject the utopian way of life in X
and opt consciously for the imperfect world of Hungary (the Hungary of
Horthy) finds resonance in other circles. "I will gladly suffer all possible
disappointments, I will gladly face the pains of a new beginning, the
shortcomings of imperfection, if by . . . [my departure] I might establish
my claim to a new experience of aimless joy or suffering," proclaims one of
the dissidents who respond to his proselytizing.[57] The acceptance of the
human condition, the historical world of imperfection, is Déry's answer to
socialist utopianism. It is, as we shall see, the answer of the twentieth-
century postutopian novel.

What are, in fact, the values that Zamiatin, Orwell, Huxley, and Déry
oppose to the utopian ideal of Community, Identity, and Stability?

FROM NEGATIVE UTOPIA TO "POSITIVE" HISTORY

I want to learn to lie and to suffer.
—Déry, *Mr. G.A. in X.*

Classical utopia established its central values in opposition to the humanistic ideals of Renaissance culture. Postutopian fiction rediscovers these values and rehabilitates the individual. (It should be noted here that both classical utopia and postutopian fiction fail in their attempts to reconcile the contrasting or dichotomous principles of man and society, stability and change. Their philosophy is necessarily one-sided, and unable to establish a higher synthesis of human and social dialectics.)

Postutopian fiction rejects the abstract notion of man as it has been put forward by classical utopia. It encourages the rebirth of the individual. In doing so, it adopts a kind of populist attitude to the philosophy of renewal. For Orwell, it is the proletariat—the "proles"—on the margins of utopian society who have maintained the archetype of a purely "human" human being. "They were governed by private loyalties which they did not question. What mattered were individual relationships, and a completely helpless gesture, an embrace, a tear, a word spoken to a dying man, could have value in itself."[58] Compared to a prole, Julia is only a fragmented individual. All she can do is to disentangle a part of her self from the totalitarian social organization into which it has been integrated; to re-create the psychological foundations of a self-centered universe by letting "corruption" undermine the barren edifice of "purity," "goodness," and perfection.

Huxley's atypical heroes are intensely aware of their personal gifts. They value life to the extent to which it has a clearly established "individual significance and importance." Almost without realizing it, they undermine the effects of the biological and psychological conditioning that have been applied to them.

"There are two forces in the world, entropy and energy," explains Zamiatin's rebellious last woman in *We.* Entropy leads to quietude and equilibrium, whereas energy tends to destroy established ways of acting, thinking, and feeling. She worships the principle of "perpetual motion," the Mephistophelian religion of freedom and rebellion.[59] The revolution that had brought about the creation of the United State—utopia—might well be presented by official propaganda as the last revolution. The number of revolutions is infinite. "Don't you . . . know," I-330 asks D-503, "that only differences—in temperature, only thermic contrasts make for life? And if all over the world there are evenly warm or evenly cold bodies, they must be pushed off! . . . in order to get flame, explosions! And we shall push!"[60]

It is the Savage who, in Huxley's *Brave New World,* gives the most powerful wording to the individual's antiutopian revolt: "I don't want comfort, I want God, I want poetry, I want real danger, I want freedom, I want goodness, I want sin." In short, he is claiming the "right to be unhappy": the right to hunger, to anxiety, "the right to be tortured by unspeakable pains of every kind."[61] Similarly, the old man in Déry's *Mr. G.A. in X* clearly equates life—and love of life—with suffering: "In a distant corner of my conscience I am telling myself pleasure: I am feeling pain . . . I am feeling pain . . . I am alive."[62]

Beyond the abortive revolts of postutopian fiction, the negative aspects of utopianism, of social messianism, of the secularized political religions of the twentieth century, appears the image of man "as he has always been" as well as the familiar landscape of history.

And yet the fact that the last man has the unlimited power of the state and of public opinion against him might make him lose faith in his ideals. How can he affirm his right to exclusiveness—difference—his nostalgia for the forbidden realm of the past, from a position of total isolation?

In spite of the overwhelming pressures of a hostile majority, Winston Smith knows that "they" are wrong and that he is right. "Being in a minority, even a minority of one, did not make you mad. There was truth and there was untruth, and if you clung to the truth even against the whole world, you were not mad."[63] Sanity is not, after all, statistical. In spite of his isolation, he is not entirely alone. He discovers, from time to time, the existence of isolated individuals at odds with utopia's strict conventionality. At the end of *Brave New World,* Helmholtz and Marx join a host of "dissident" intellectuals on a faraway island. In *We,* when D-503 is told that a soul has formed within him, he also learns that individual soul formation has spread like an epidemic. Around the figure of the last man, whole islands of individual resistance are constituted. And on these islands, conspiracy prevails.

In the closing scene of Ionesco's *Rhinocéros,* when Bérenger realizes that he is the last representative of the human species, he endeavors to turn himself into a rhinoceros. It is only when he fails in his attempt to do so that he reassumes his humanity. His determination to defend, at whatever cost, his personality is enhanced by the fact that he is the last man. "Contre tout le monde, je me défendrai, contre tout le monde, je me défendrai! Je suis le dernier homme, je le resterai jusqu'au bout! Je ne capitule pas!"[64] (I'll defend myself against the entire world, I'll defend myself against the entire world! I am the last man and I'll resist up to the very end. I won't surrender.)

"We admitted no private sphere, not even inside man's skull," writes Rubashov in his prison cell awaiting his execution. "The definition of the individual was: A multitude of one million divided by one million." What Arthur Koestler describes in his novel *Darkness at Noon* is nothing but the end of utopian communism in Soviet Russia, the rediscovery, by a onetime revolutionary, of the self, the "accursed inner voice." It is from an old peasant fellow prisoner that he learns about the beauty of life during the last years of the ancien régime. "Mother of God, what merriment it was. . . ."[65]

In Solzhenitsyn's *The First Circle,* the young diplomat Innokenty Volodin leads the life of a utopian "hollow" man. One day, however, he comes upon a collection of old photograph albums, theater programs, and art magazines that had belonged to his mother. All of a sudden he experiences the revelation of a lost world of artistic refinement, personal culture, the beginning, in the 1910s, of a new pluralistic social experience. He feels that he has found something which he lacked: love, friendship, solidarity. "The essence of life will never be captured by even the greatest formulas."[66] He rejects utopianism, social constructivism, ideology, in order to fashion his life according to the vital values of the past.

We cannot tell whether postutopian fiction's last man is the last individual, or a vital link between the past and some future time of a new beginning. We know, however, that classical utopia has been the forerunner of the collectivist intellectual tradition of the nineteenth and twentieth centuries. Negative utopias may well be the harbingers of a new age of individualist humanism, thus announcing the renaissance of pluralism and anarchist-conservative pragmatism.

NOTES

1. Eugene Zamiatin, *We,* trans. Gregory Zilboorg (New York: E. P. Dutton, 1952), p. 85.

2. George Orwell, *Nineteen Eighty-Four* (London: Penguin Books, 1979), p. 219.

3. See my essay on *Mythes politiques modernes* (Paris: Presses Universitaires de France, 1981), pp. 158–70.

4. Adolphe Quételet, *Sur l'homme et le développement de ses facultés, ou Essai de physique sociale,* 2 vols (Paris, 1835).

5. *The Complete Essays of Montaigne,* trans. Donald M. Frame (Stanford, Calif.: Stanford University Press, 1965), p. 321.

6. Charles Nordhoff, *The Communistic Societies of the United States* (1875; New York: Schocken Books, 1965), p. 50.

7. Thomas More, *Utopia,* trans. Paul Turner (1516; London: Penguin Books, 1978), pp. 69–70.

8. Etienne Cabet, *Voyage en Icarie* (Paris: Au Bureau populaire, 1848). All
translations from this work are mine.

9. Tibor Déry, *G.A. ur X.-ben* (Budapest: Szépirodalmi Kiado, 1964). Published in 1964, Déry's novel was actually written in prison in the late 1950s. All
translations from this work are mine.

10. Denis Vairesse d'Allais, *Histoire des Sévérambes* (Amsterdam, 1787),
pp. vii–viii.

11. Cabet, *Voyage en Icarie*, p. 143.

12. Edward Bellamy, *Looking Backward: 2000–1887* (Boston: Houghton Mifflin, 1890), p. 84.

13. Ibid., p. 367.

14. Aldous Huxley, *Brave New World* (New York: Harper & Row, 1965),
p. 182.

15. Zamiatin, *We*, pp. 6–7.

16. Cabet, *Voyage en Icarie*, pp. 60, 137, and 89.

17. Bellamy, *Looking Backward*, p. 177.

18. Ibid., p. 456.

19. Cabet, *Voyage en Icarie*, p. 3.

20. Bellamy, *Looking Backward*, p. 409.

21. William Morris, *News from Nowhere*, ed. James Redmond (London: Routledge & Kegan Paul, 1970), p. xiii.

22. Zamiatin, *We*, p. 59.

23. Huxley, *Brave New World*, p. 169.

24. Nordhoff, *Communistic Societies of the United States*, p. 396.

25. Cabet, *Voyage en Icarie*, p. 404.

26. Déry, *G.A. ur X*, p. 308.

27. As far as the utopian character of contemporary East European socialism is
concerned, see a brilliant essay by Constantin Dumitresco, *La Cité totale* (Paris:
Éditions du Seuil, 1980).

28. Déry, *G.A. ur X*, p. 308.

29. Anthony Burgess, *1985* (London: Arrow Books, 1980). For the relationship
between the myth of the Golden Age and utopia, see my essay on "Mythe et
utopie" in *Revue européenne des sciences sociales et Cahiers Vilfredo Pareto* 18:53
(1980), 75–84.

30. Cabet, *Voyage en Icarie*, p. 144.

31. Roland Barthes, *Roland Barthes par Roland Barthes* (Paris: Éditions du
Seuil, 1979), p. 89.

32. Zamiatin, *We*, p. 8.

33. Huxley, *Brave New World*, p. 95.

34. Zamiatin, *We*, pp. 129, 13, 118.

35. Ibid., p. 121.

36. Huxley, *Brave New World*, pp. 69, 53–54.

37. Concerning the totalitarian aspects of utopia, see my essay on "Utopie et
terreur" in *Cadmos*, 3 (spring 1980), 129–38.

38. Orwell, *Nineteen Eighty-Four*, p. 206.

39. Ibid., p. 10.

40. Ibid., pp. 8–9.

41. Ibid., p. 69.
42. Ibid., pp. 134–35.
43. Ibid., p. 144.
44. Burgess, *1985*, p. 139.
45. Orwell, *Nineteen Eighty-Four*, pp. 84, 79.
46. Ibid., p. 80.
47. Ibid., p. 81.
48. Ibid., p. 123.
49. Zamiatin, *We*, pp. 26, 27.
50. Orwell, *Nineteen Eighty-Four*, p. 63.
51. See Huxley, *Brave New World*, p. 39; also Cabet, *Voyage en Icarie*.
52. Déry, *Mr. G.A. in X*, p. 319.
53. Ibid.
54. Déry's fundamental ideas are particularly close to Igor Chafarévitch's statements about socialism as a variant of the death wish. See *Le phénomène socialiste* (Paris: Éditions du Seuil, 1977), pp. 325–40.
55. Déry, *Mr. G.A. in X*, p. 228.
56. Ibid., p. 236.
57. Ibid., p. 436.
58. Orwell, *Nineteen Eighty-Four*, pp. 59, 134–35.
59. Zamiatin, *We*, pp. 153–54. In *God and the State* (1882), Russian revolutionary and militant anarchist Mikhail Bakunin gave a specifically anarchist coloration to this romantic Satanic myth.
60. Zamiatin, *We*, p. 163.
61. Huxley, *Brave New World*, p. 184.
62. Déry, *Mr. G.A. in X*, p. 237.
63. Orwell, *Nineteen Eighty-Four*, p. 173.
64. Eugène Ionesco, *Rhinocéros* (Paris: Editions Gallimard, 1959), p. 199.
65. Arthur Koestler, *Darkness at Noon* (New York: Bantam, 1968), pp. 80, 208, 188.
66. Aleksandr I. Solzhenitsyn, *The First Circle*, trans. Thomas P. Whitney (New York: Harper & Row, 1968), p. 344.

11

WRITING OFF THE SELF

Richard Poirier

S INCE THE BEGINNINGS OF LITERATURE IN THE WEST, HU-
man beings have wanted to re-present themselves, but they have
also wanted to do something nearly the reverse. They have wanted to
reduce or even eradicate the human self. Examples can be found in
writers so diverse as Vergil and Dante; Spenser, Bacon, and Milton;
Racine, Mallarmé, and T. S. Eliot; Artaud, Stevens, Beckett, and Pyn-
chon. Whatever such writers have in common, they are of course mark-
edly dissimilar, and to account for the dissimilarities I would propose that
there are three quite different ways in which some of them, and a few
others, have suggested that the human self should be dissolved, or de-
created, or dispersed, or dismissed. Necessarily, then, I am concerned
with variations on this topic or idea, and, more specifically, with the
problems in writing and in reading created by passages which recom-
mend that human beings might just as well erase or exterminate themselves. The problem is that the human self very likely finds it intolerable
to remain in a state of impoverishment or incipient extermination even
while that self is able to imagine that the very idea of the human is
perhaps not an inevitable or preferred alternative. There is no way any
writer, no matter how extreme his views on the subject, can be indifferent
to this problem, because to write at all is to salvage, however reluctantly,
some part of the existent humanity, the formulas and codes that belong to
a shared human inheritance, even if your writing is an invitation to reject
and disperse it.

Of the three central modes of self-eradication in literature, the first
need only be mentioned to be readily understood, which is but one
indication of its centrality to Western thinking and of its generally uncritical acceptance as a "good way to go." You wish to bring an end to the self,
even at the peril of your physical being, in the expectation of some better
life; you surrender the self and the will in order to save the soul, as in
Dante, Spenser, Milton, T. S. Eliot, and aspects of D. H. Lawrence. But
there is always in such instances a recreative countermovement to self-

216

disposal; it is as if self-erasure were a prelude to a redemptive act. As a result, there is also, always, a presumption of narrative, an expectation that human reality evolves in and through narrative movement. Christ in his death and resurrection is the central example, and it provides an indispensable paradigm for the Western conception of narrative.

This traditional mode will be discussed here only when it helps clarify two other more recent and, to my mind, more exciting ones—exciting, that is, in the kinds of writing stimulated by them. One, which can be called European, will be represented by Foucault and Nietzsche; the other, the American, by Emerson, William James, and Stevens. Neither the European nor the American contingent assumes a creative counter-movement to human dissolution, and there is little or no expressed concern in either for the human soul as the projection of the self into an afterlife. Both are implicitly critical of the concept of narrative development, the mythos of narrative. But these two traditions, if they can be called that, exhibit marked and important differences on the issue of voice and of the possible inferences from voice of human presence.

Assume, for instance, that we are listening to a voice—and not all critics bother to listen, even when they are able to hear it—a voice that invites us to do away with ourselves. What can be its possible attractions? On what measure of time, in what measure of space, does this voice ask to exist, when in the same breath it asks that the traditional self be deprived of time and space? Which self, you or I—or the writer? Living in time and space as we read and listen, where and who can we imagine ourselves to be if we assent to the proposition that we should not be at all, that a happier future would be one in which humans like ourselves, and all they have done toward the invention of the self, are assured of irrelevancy? These may seem like primitive or vulgar questions, proper not to literary critics but only to the lost humans of Theodor Adorno, men and women who could not ask them anyway since, in the mass, they have ceased to exist as individuals. For them the question of self-eradication has already been answered. Do the questions even matter, then, except to those, ever fewer in number, who are capable of thinking about them?

Perhaps that is the real, the only question. It is not possible confidently to assume that a "voice" allows the inference of a person, a presence, a self behind it. This is not a matter simply of the loss of individual identity to stereotype, to cant. Recent theory, for which Jacques Derrida provides an impetus, has more basically challenged the relative primacy of speech as against writing and, with that, the logocentricism that implies a metaphysics of presence on which claims for the priority of speech, of voice, and of the creative Word are founded. The self who speaks, the self who listens are, in that sense, not real enough even to be obliterated. However, while some English and American readers have a theoretical interest in the nonexistence of the self, few of them can get as genuinely agitated about it as do the French; and for the reason that in the Anglo-American, but especially in the American-Emersonian tradition, there is no one, so far as I know, who has chosen to treat voice as if it were an issue of metaphysical importance or who has given to it such historical reverberation as it gets from being linked to a term like *logocentrism*. Deconstruction has been taken for granted in the great line of American literature from Emerson to Henry Adams to Stevens, where the identity of the human self is nearly always problematic. It is a literature which from the outset has already rescinded the authority of the social, ecclesiastical, and political institutions that in European literature are strong enough flexibly to define the self and measure its compliant or resistant movements. Where such institutions are recognized in American literature they often exist as Force, "the interpolation of the perverted mind and heart of man," as Hawthorne puts it at the beginning of "The New Adam and Eve." Inklings, fragments of a "true" self are discovered intermittently only in acts of recession from the systems that would define it, in acts of retreat into monologue or landscape or silence. From the "eloquence" of Emerson to the "sound of sense" in Frost, voice is imagined as a species of dramatic extemporization; the self behind voice is contrived for a particular and transient circumstance which, as likely as not, is also in the process of receding—a myth to be explored for its local or immediate utility, a social demand to be negotiated.

I find it impossible to ignore the sound of the human voice in writing or out of it, but voice seldom refers me to a self that, to begin with, is ever quite sure of its identity. How could it be? Unless it comes from mad Tamburlaine or Lear or Ahab, the voices heard in Anglo-American literature are not allowed even to pretend that they master the materials, the language, on which their very claim to existence depends. Nor is the English language itself assumed to be stabilized or pure, subject to the rulings of an Academy. In the literature of England and America, voice has always struggled with a language which, meanwhile, is often in contention with itself. Hence, the energetic wonder called forth by Shakespeare's language—and by Melville's or Mark Twain's. For a critic like myself, immersed in this literature, voice is therefore not distinguishable from the human will. Writing is a struggle to impose voice or will on the intractable and fluid material of language, language which irresistibly refers to historical, social, and mythological implications that remain very much alive in it. Especially of American literature it can be said that if it confronts the possibilities of self-eradication without a sense of nostalgia for the humanistic and religious traditions being dislodged, it is also without the evident anger or dismissiveness, which is a perverse form of nostalgia, found in the European figures I am about to discuss. American literature is, supremely, the literature that *knows* the distinction between voice and writing, and the problematic relation between voice and presence. It plays with these distinctions not for moral but for mortal stakes— the salvation of voice is nothing less than the salvation of the will. It has altogether less to do with the salvation of the soul.

Despite chronology, I begin with Foucault and Nietzsche because to understand the extreme form of self-eradication which they sometimes articulate is to be in a better position to recognize that the radicalism in the Anglo-American examples I will be citing is perhaps more daring and certainly more mysterious. The voice we hear in the more eloquent passages in Foucault is often narcissistically determined that it be admired for the operatic extremity of the cultural role proposed for its author. Take as an example the passage frequently quoted from the end of *The Order of Things*, the title in 1970 of the English translation of *Les Mots et les choses* of 1966. I quote in English because while keeping in mind an admonition from Frost—that poetry is all that is lost in translation—I am satisfied that what I say about the passage, and about a subsequent one from Nietzsche, could be said also of the original:

> If those arrangements [of knowledge] were to disappear as they appeared, if some event of which we can at the moment do no more than sense the possibility—without knowing either what its form will be or what it promises—were to cause them to crumble, as the ground of Classical thought did, at the end of the eighteenth century, then one can certainly wager that man would be erased, like a face drawn in sand at the edge of the sea.[1]

These are the accents of someone who feels that he has already exposed and categorized the forces of civilization with extraordinarily tactical prowess. In the text that precedes this passage he has discovered the "arrangements of knowledge" by which man of the present dispensation was brought into being, so that he can now predict—or "sense"—how the arrangements might disappear, and he can confidently "wager" on the apocalyptic results of this disappearance. There is in all this an audible, a Nietzschean excitement. But there is also something from Marx, which, if it delimits the vision of human dissolution, also thereby substantiates, as we will see, the polemical zeal with which Foucault proposes it. Arrangements or structures reveal themselves, as Marx would have it, principally at the moment and in the act of breakdown. Thus the *episteme* of the Classical period—those rules of discursive formation that would govern what can be said even by parties in dispute—became recognizable as such only when, by breaking apart, they revealed how they had been unnaturally put together. According to Foucault's calendar, this began to happen to the Classical period around 1790–1810, when it was to be replaced by our present order of things. That new epistemic order is now in its turn, and for the first time, becoming visible to us as it, too, begins to collapse, to expose its design through its fractures.

Though these quite crude periodizations were to be blurred by Foucault's later work, they nonetheless provide here and throughout his writing a license for the rhetorical flourish with which he customarily wrote about the disappearance of man, of modern man. Foucault's voice urgently wishes to waste him, to hurry him off the stage, and that he intends the polemical note as a calculated necessity is obvious from some remarks made in 1967 in an interview a year after *Les Mots et les choses* appeared:

> When one is dealing with the Classical period, one has only to describe it. When it comes to the modern period, however, which began about 1790–1810 and lasted until 1950, the problem is to free oneself from it. The apparently polemical character [in his writing about the modern period] derives from the fact that one has to dig out a whole mass of discourse that has accumulated under one's feet. One may uncover with gentle movements the latent configurations of earlier periods; but when it is a matter of determining the system of discourse on which we are still living, when we have to question the words that are still echoing in our ears, which become confused with those we are trying to formulate, the archeologist, like the Nietzschean philosopher, is forced to take a hammer to it.[2]

It was not until "L'ordre du discours," the 1977 Appendix to the American edition of *The Archaeology of Knowledge,* that Foucault fully conceived of "event" as the emergence into visibility of subterranean and circuitous discursive formations. But he never, even in *The Order of Things,* chose to think of "event" as simply or as conventionally as his rhetorical use of the word might allow us to infer from the passage at the end of this early book. Which is to say that whether we are reading early or later Foucault, "arrangements of knowledge" emerge only from astonishingly complex and devious movements and never from what is normally thought of as an event. Since nowhere in Foucault do "arrangements" appear as the result of an event, a reportable happening, they cannot, except rhetorically, disappear as the consequence of one. The word "event" at the conclusion of *The Order of Things* is knowingly provocative, a come-on. So is the melodramatic suspense induced by a phrase like "at the moment," as if the reader were tensely holding onto the book in expectation of a happening. We are to be rhetorically persuaded that history unfolds with a kind of conventional narrativity, even though he has at this early stage intimated what will be insisted upon in "L'ordre du discours" and thereafter: that narrativity is designed to repress the recognition of those movements of force that do not fit into what we are allowed to recognize as narrative. Narrative is a form of repression—and it is also a form necessary to Foucault's polemics.

My intention, again, is not to argue against Foucault's ideas. Rather it is to investigate the status of the writing at a point where he has chosen to excite the reader and himself with the prospect that human beings are about to lose the power to recognize themselves as human. It is important to note the oddity and instability of such moments as measured not merely against our ordinary disposition, but even more against the writer's customary procedures. The oddity here is highlighted by the specific trope with which the passage—and the book—is brought to a close: the comparison of a man to a face drawn in the sand. The voice stretches this comparison, doubles it in an accent of lurid gravity, so that the face is not only drawn in sand but at the edge of the sea. Because of certain inescapable connotations, passed on to us by writing, the image is close to hackneyed. Is this the sand of Matthew Arnold's Dover Beach,' allowing for the pebbles? Not likely, but the possibility is there, at least for English readers. Is this the edge of the sea out of which we are supposed to have crawled in an evolutionary movement that is going to reverse itself? Another unlikely possibility, since Foucault is not here, or anywhere else, suggesting the end of man as a physical species. He calls only for the end of human vanity and of the particular organizations of knowledge that are both its creation and its support. But there is some Darwinian echo nonetheless and it may be stronger, rhetorically, than the more delicate and intended suggestion: what will be destroyed will be a drawing of man, a self-representation. The drawing, when one thinks of it, is yet another evidence of human vanity.

This is a voice that exults in its own daring; it asks us to celebrate its flamboyance. What is important for our purposes is that, at the same time, its maneuvers with language are outrageously deferential to the "human," to traditional human tastes, including a taste for theatricality. The passage indulges itself in the human vanities it purports to dismiss. A face of man drawn in the sand is of necessity drawn simply, perhaps even childishly. It is far less encumbered with the trappings of human exultation than is the face of man that emanates from Foucault's sentences, from the presence, the voice, the will that can be heard in them. If the face drawn by Foucault's words were "erased," then with it would go any justification for writing as grandiose as his on this occasion. Indeed, the very scene of erasure, which is made so spectacular for writer and reader, would not, such is the logic of the whole book, ever occur in history, in the sands of time. It could occur only in writing, in some change of discourse.

What is to be said of this? Perhaps we can get closer to the phenomenon by looking at a passage in Nietzsche that clearly anticipates Foucault, though without his calendar. The passage is taken from a posthumously published fragment, "On Truth and Lie in an Extra-Moral Sense":

In some remote corner of the universe, poured out and glittering in innumerable solar systems, there once was a star on which clever animals invented knowledge. That was the haughtiest and most mendacious minute of "world history"—yet only a minute. After nature had drawn a few breaths the star grew cold, and the clever animals had to die.

One might invent such a fable and still not have illustrated sufficiently how wretched, how shadowy and flighty, how aimless and arbitrary, the human intellect appears in nature. There have been eternities when it did not exist; and when it is done for again, nothing will have happened. For this intellect has no further mission that would lead beyond human life. It is human, rather, and only its owner and producer gives it such importance, as if the world pivoted around it. But if we would communicate with the mosquito, then we would learn that it floats through the air with the same self-importance, feeling within itself the flying center of the world. There is nothing in nature so despicable or insignificant that it cannot immediately be blown up like a bag by a slight breath of this power of knowledge; and just as every porter wants an admirer, the proudest human being, the philosopher, thinks he sees the eyes of the universe telescopically focused from all sides on his actions and thoughts.[3]

Spatial images, images of miniaturization, expansion, telescoping, abound here. What they suggest is obvious enough: that man, especially what Nietzsche calls the intellect of man, is no more significant, in relation to the cosmos, than is a mosquito in relation to the air in which it floats. Each is solipsistically assured that it is the center of a flying world. It might be said of both man and mosquito that they are "wretched . . . shadowy . . . flighty . . . aimless . . . arbitrary"—and doomed. But anyone should be embarrassed to offer commentary on matters already made abundantly obvious. Images so reiterated and redundant call for translation only by someone so dull-witted as to be beyond reading the passage to begin with. Instead, the images refer us backward to their source, to the imperious will and energy of the author. We are free to decide either that this voice is haughtily contemptuous of its auditors, or that it assumes auditors who, like itself, do not need to be persuaded of human insignificance; they want merely to join in exuberant ranting about it. The energy of the voice owes nothing to possible dissent. It does not propose even to anticipate it. So that the spatial images, far from communicating anything important about the ratio of man to universe, refer us instead to a speaker who, in imagining the end of man, is expansively enthusiastic, above and beyond mosquito-man. Rhetorically, he is in a position much like Foucault's, for while it might be argued that Nietzsche is far more sweepingly dismissive and that Foucault addresses himself only to the latest in a series of epistemic dispositions, the fact is that neither of them proposes that there is waiting for the species any other form of self-representation. Foucault is no more nostalgic than Nietzsche, and if he sounds more expectant, then his expectations are wholly unspecified.

It is necessary to move carefully at this point. We have been listening to voices that invite us to join in the drama of apocalypse, and as Frank Kermode has shown, in *The Sense of an Ending*, human beings seem always to have found this a thrilling opportunity for advancement.[4] The reasons for finding it so in these instances are especially peculiar, however. That is, with Nietzsche and Foucault we get excited by the drama of self-obliteration as we might with any other writer. But there is something else at work here, a kind of cultural and social snobbery. Surely some measure of our excitement comes from the fact that the voice seems to assume that we who listen, like those who speak, are somehow *more* than human. We are being offered some exclusive and exonerating privilege, an inducement to the kind of pride that, on the other side of extermination, would in earlier times have made us ineligible for sainthood. Though the words we hear condemn mankind, the sound of them, the mode of address, clearly exempts the speaker and his auditors. These are not the voices of ordinary mortals speaking to other ordinary mortals.

The phrase "ordinary mortals" or "ordinary man" means no more now by itself than it ever did, and I would explain it by saying that these voices of Foucault and Nietzsche do not, as do the voices we recognize as, say, "George Eliot" or "William James," suggest that we are listening to ordinary mortals who can express themselves at a level of extraordinary articulation and who do so for the good of their fellows. No. These are the voices of genius uninhibited by fellow feeling or even the pretense to fellow feeling. More important still, there is no trace of the peculiar fear often exhibited by genius—especially in English and American writing— the fear that the price to be paid for it is a barren alienation from ordinary life. Rather, this is genius whose language does not suppose, within the discursive formations of the "modern" period, any specific audience at all. At most, it expects to be overheard by acolytes or aspirants to genius. Ordinary people are not conjured up by this language as its likely audience. Yet, even the grandest of us have a few "spots of commonness," as George Eliot might say, and even aspiring Foucaults and Nietzsches are to be included, during their necessarily more humdrum moments, with those who on a given morning or an afternoon are not thinking of the people around them, possibly including their children, as even theoretically expendable, no matter how strongly on other occasions it seems advisable to assert that it would be better if they did not exist in the form bequeathed them. What of ordinary listeners, then, or extraordinary listeners in their ordinary moods? How, to repeat, are we to take these passages?

When writing—or any reading of it—arrives at a point of such intransigence, it becomes impossible, even at the risk of digression, to ignore a collateral issue. I am referring to anxiety, especially strong in Anglo-American cultural and literary criticism, about the dangers of modernist or radical or uncompromising rhetoric. Are we now, is not civility, is not civilization itself imperiled by this rhetoric? To expedite matters, let me say that, were I voting on this question, I would vote no—and for the reason, in part, that writing, and the reading of it, should be regarded as no more than one kind of experience among many. It has to be said, of course, that it differs from most other kinds of experience because of the extraordinary degree to which, when it is done with any semblance of genius, it calls for examination and for reexamination, the degree, that is, of its calculated solicitation. For that very reason, however, writing on a page reminds us that it is *not* life on either side of it—before we look at it and when we stop looking at it. Writing exists in a mutually modifying but very confused, accidental, and varying relation to other, altogether less calculated, usually less examined, and comparatively messy experiences of life. Even while all critics now pay lip service to the fact that literature is not to be taken literally, the vast majority of them have ingenious ways of ignoring obvious facts about the relation of writing and reading to the passage of time. They confuse the passage of time with the passage of history, with time conceived as an already defined pattern of significance or an imagined pattern of events, and they want the materials and activities of their profession, namely, writing and reading, to be related to history in an ideal, direct, glamorous, and even potentially perilous transaction. Critics like to worry about what literature will do to "other people," and it seems all the more powerful to those who, despite professional credentials, do not seem to know how writing is written and how writing is read.

Under these circumstances, what to some must seem especially disturbing is that Foucault's or Nietzsche's sort of writing exhibits here a willful indifference to *any* sort of life that might exist in a tangential relationship to it. The mode of address is oblivious to the claims of ordinary, muddled, time-ridden existence. It is equally oblivious to the values of historical inheritance or perpetuation—values nonetheless recognized, usually with a kind of anguish of constraint, elsewhere in Foucault and very beautifully in Nietzsche's "On the Use and Misuse of History for Life."[5] Both Foucault and Nietzsche exhibit a European, as distinct from any comparable American, enthusiasm for self-eradication. The difference, speaking very crudely, is that on the European side there is a tendency to express this enthusiasm in terms of historical apocalypse while, as we will presently see, the American tendency is usually more private, witty, more drifting, so that instead of the prospect of historical apocalypse, the reader is offered something like quotidian self-erasure.

One reason for this difference goes back precisely to an Anglo-American distrust of genius, genius that is not organic with life. And this is in turn related to a complicated distrust of literature itself. As twentieth-century examples, T. S. Eliot, F. R. Leavis, and Lionel Trilling, each in a very different way, sound at times as if literature might indeed imperil civilized life,[6] a view which could only result from some prior idealization of litera- ture and of literary tradition, as if these were uniquely the carriers of life ordered and transmitted to us as a potential creative force. It might be objected that a European like Herbert Marcuse[7] is no less an instance of this feeling than is Leavis, its greatest critical proponent in English, but the very similarity would then point to a characteristic difference. Mar- cuse offers an exorbitant idealization of literature as a sphere of social negation, while Leavis insists that the values of literature ultimately find their source in what he imagines was once the language of a historical organic community of real English people, who find articulation in such a figure as John Bunyan.

In the extreme and more pessimistic versions of this Anglo-American mythology, literature can betray its sacred trust nearly to the degree that it becomes prophetic, visionary, apocalyptic—separated or alienated from the daily. Think, for example, of Trilling's classroom drama "On the Teach- ing of Modern Literature": "I asked them to look into the Abyss, and, both dutifully and gladly, they have looked into the Abyss, and the Abyss has greeted them with the grave courtesy of all objects of serious study. . . ."[8] Or of Susan Sontag's resentment of the social and prejudicial power of metaphor, a resentment which, however admirable in anyone then in the grip of illness likely to be fatal, proves in retrospect not only unpersuasive but historically misleading.[9] In any event, I obviously can- not share such concerns for the pernicious power of literature and, at the same time, insist on demonstrating the thwarting problematics of literary or any other kind of expression. The concern is further objectionable for its implicit aspersions on the wit, resourcefulness, and common sense of the "other" people such critics claim to be worried about. Critics some- times like to flatter themselves that they are handling explosive materials far more capably than can the average person. In fact, most people who read do so with an instinctive awareness that it is reading that they are doing, that it is an activity quite different from other activities, and that it is not easily translated into "life," whether of love or crime or what Trilling would call "modernism in the streets." The point of an earlier book of mine, *A World Elsewhere*,[10] as the source of its title in Shakespeare's

Coriolanus ought to have suggested, is that literature by its very nature is prevented from creating such a world except in certain rare moments and only *while* it is being read. Constraint is implicit in writing and in the very act of reading.

Thus it is that Foucault and Nietzsche offer, in my view, an occasion for participating in the only momentarily exhilarating and cleansing imagination of self-eradication. Indeed, the excess of rhetorical power and the lack of caution which makes it so enlivening, on occasion, to read Foucault, and especially Nietzsche, is at the same time the most telling evidence that each is aware of the resistance in language itself to any persuasive argument for self-obliteration. It is in the nature of writing that whatever Foucault and Nietzsche say will be taken as metaphor and subjected to its constraints. They know this. They also know that, under attack, almost any adherent will retreat to the position that what they have written, what anyone writes, is to some degree a fiction. And so it is. But that is why they try *not* to be taken metaphorically or fictionally. They ask to be taken literally, and that, of course, is most difficult to do. A paradox comes into existence in these cases because something needed to be said nearly beyond language, and even while noting its tribulations in language, it is still that something with which we should try to be concerned. It is paradoxical that a writer should call for the obliteration of man as we know him even while exhibiting the need for his approval and approbation, and it is paradoxical that a reader should agree to the necessities of self-obliteration using as his guide the mental faculties and educated feelings that are not only objects to be done away with but the provocation for their destruction. But paradox does not neutralize or cancel out any of the possibilities.

What I am intimating is that the effort to talk about the end of human beings should be taken as a clue to one of their astonishing attributes—the capacity to accept, if only for a moment, the argument that their own kind is an impertinence. The effort is a testament to the power of our nonhuman will, and explains in part why Nietzsche is a compelling and necessary figure. When he says that with the end of man "nothing will have happened," the "nothing" will include his having said so, his testimony that this is true, his writing. At last, he is really talking, as is Foucault in his sand image, about erasing his own rhetorical discourse. In that sense the writing is, to look forward to Stevens, "nothing that is not there and the nothing that is."

If we will only elude the inexorable paradox, if we will only literalize, believe what is being said, and take responsibility for the belief—then it becomes possible to recognize what is in fact more significant than the paradox: to recognize the affirmation of human feeling that is *un*sanctified and *un*sponsored. Those who want merely to stop at the paradox would also want, perhaps without even knowing it, to claim that all feeling about the end of the human should reinvest itself in the enterprise of preserving and enhancing traditional ideas of the self, like the Christian enterprise of salvation. Getting excited by the prospects of the end of man—the extinction, again, not of a genetic, biological species but of our invention of the human—is no less noble or ignoble than getting excited by projects for the continuation of man in his present form, enhanced or spiritualized. It could be argued that of the two possibilities, the desire for self-obliteration—with no preconceived image ready to receive whatever is left—reveals a more invigorating impatience with the repressive consequences that attend the work of redemption. We are asked, then, to get excited about a future which will be brought about by our own extinction; we are enjoined by a rhetoric of persuasion the power, even the vestiges of which are also to become extinct. ("There have been eternities when it [the human intellect] did not exist," according to Nietzsche, "and when it is done for again, nothing will have happened.") Those animals which have before called themselves human will in some new form have become immune to this style of persuasion, immune to style itself, deaf to any language shaped by the pressures of a reality which will by then have been discarded.

This is heady stuff, and it could be contemptible to the extent that the expressed desire for human dissolution is programmatic or ideological, a creation precisely of elements said to be expendable. But of course it is the tendency of ideological thinking that it should be ungrateful to its source. If it is agreed that human beings are a consequence of the "arrangements of knowledge," and not the other way around, what then is to be said of the evidence that human beings have the capacity to wish themselves radically other than what they are? To wish themselves evacuated from those "arrangements of knowledge"? And to do so without the comforts of religion? Is that capacity also to be erased? The very source of the longing to be nonhuman? To ask these questions is not to deprive Nietzsche or Foucault (who harbors a profound admiration for the flexibility of human power) of the assent anyone wants to give them. Rather, it is to encourage a degree of consent that can be transferred to those other writers who, without violating the contract with the human invention of life—and also without religious or humanistic pieties—express the desire for entrance into a life alien to what we now call human. If we are willing, that is, to entertain the extremities of Nietzsche and Foucault, we become immediately enabled to appreciate sporadically similar aspects of Emerson or Thoreau, Pater or Ruskin, Lawrence or Stevens, aspects which have been ignored or suppressed in the interest of accommodating whatever they say to the overall humanistic tendencies exhibited in their work and, even more, in the work of their interpreters.

Take as one instance a remarkable sentence in a letter written from London in 1889 by William James to his wife Alice, the more remarkable because James, like his father before him, had good reason, in a curiously similar experience of visitation, to be terrified by the loss of self.[11] "The best thing by far which I saw in Brighton," he wrote, "and a thing the impression of which will perhaps outlast everything else on this trip, was four cuttlefish (octopus) in the Aquarium. I wish we had one of them for a child—such flexible intensity of life in a form inaccessible to our sympathy."[12] We are asked by this voice not to separate the evocation of the nonhuman from the human, or the appreciation of "intensity" from the assurances of "our sympathy"—not, so to speak, to exclude the cuttlefish from the human family. In the tone is a loving complicity, so that the wish to have a guppy for a child does not need to be explained, needs scarcely to be remarked on, when coming from a husband to a wife whose four children probably called for a sometimes exasperating expenditure of human sympathy. The sentence is appealing because the wishes it expresses are quite strong ("a thing the impression of which will perhaps outlast everything else on this trip") while being in no way grandstanding or provocative. There is an expressed desire for an extraordinary, nonhuman child, but it is expressed by a man firmly committed to the humanly domestic. What is said here depends casually and thus fully on the understanding of the person who shares the speaker's thoughts, as well as his offspring, his life, his writing. It is as if the dazzling image of a nonhuman "flexible intensity of life" was actually prompted by the assured existence of an equally flexible intensity of domestic and family feeling.

In this small and charming instance James is making contact with nonhuman options in a way found also in certain passages of Emerson, Thoreau, Whitman, and Stevens. It may not be an exclusively American way, but it seems more unabashed and austere in the American instances. There are passages in which they look, indeed stare at the possibility of self-dissolution, at the stripping away of human attributes. They do this with an impressive indifference to consequences, without apologies or extenuations, without bribes offered to the shocked or disturbed reader, none of those reassurances that Wordsworth feels compelled to give to himself and to us. No matter how wonderfully strange the given moment in *The Prelude*, Wordsworth tends tiresomely to intrude the cautionary note, as if all the power in the writing were for the utilitarian purpose of building up one acceptable human faculty or another. The American instances are different. American writing is full of compulsive and also inadvertent imitation, of artificiality—Cooper being the exemplification—which exerts a pressure of accommodation on visionary moments. So that passages of the kind I am discussing do indeed carry the sounds and signs of the writer's commitment to human forms already shaped by earlier literature. But it is also the case that those evidences of compliance are, in the Thomistic sense, mere accidents, part of the necessity of writing under the aegis of unavoidable tradition. Or, as in Melville, Hawthorne, Twain, they are a necessity that excites the most sophisticated kind of counterliterary play. These acts of audacity, like the play of vernacular and obscenity against refinement of diction, are gestures that dispel the Wordsworthian fear of genius, of separation, of losing touch with ordinary humanity.

The most obvious example of this American audacity—the famous passage in Emerson's *Nature* where he claims to be transformed into a transparent eyeball—will for my purposes also be the best, because having been made so familiar by literary commentary, it needs to be brought back to its strangeness:

> Standing on the bare ground,—my head bathed by the blithe air and uplifted into infinite space,—all mean egotism vanishes. I become a transparent eyeball; I am nothing; I see all; the currents of the Universal Being circulate through me; I am part or parcel of God. The name of the nearest friend sounds then foreign and accidental; to be brothers, to be acquaintances,—master or servant, is then a trifle and a disturbance. I am the lover of uncontained and immortal beauty.[13]

Emerson being who he was and writing when he did, the passage is surrounded by language weighted with the sounds of countervailing social contract. Humans may count as a "disturbance," but the human reader is being socially courted nonetheless. Even so, the passage is uncorrupted by any promise that the experience it describes will be good or useful to the conduct of social arrangements or even to daily life. No wonder Emerson in this mood has resisted all attempts at translation or utility. Some people ice-skate, or their children do, and without much trouble at least a few of them can expect to share with the boy in Wordsworth's *The Prelude* the whirling out of the self into the world of mysterious sounds and visions. But who expects to repeat the Emersonian experience, or even to imagine the experience, while standing on a plot of bare ground? The passage does not call even for emulation: no metaphoric coordinates are proposed within which this "eye" or "transparent eyeball" could be negotiated into some more familiar or usable shape. Emerson insists that man and not-man are simultaneous states, like the "occult relation between man and vegetable" mentioned a little further on in *Nature*, or like the vision in the later, and shorter, essay called "Nature":

> We talk of deviations from natural life, as if artificial life were not also natural. The smoothest curled courtier in the boudoirs of a palace has an

animal nature, rude and aboriginal as a white bear, omnipotent to its own
ends, and is directly related, there amid essences and billets-doux, to Him-
maleh mountain chains and the axis of the globe.[14]

To repeat, this is an inquiry into those passages where human beings are
eradicated or temporarily displaced or transformed into shapes not recognizably human; and, more significantly, it is an inquiry into what human
readers can make of such passages. So far, I have been concerned with the
degree to which writing can register these extraordinary occurrences
either with ideological exhilaration, as in Foucault and Nietzsche, or, as in
William James and Emerson, with an exhilaration that exists in a kind of
gap or interlude within the ordinary, nonideological movement of life, of
life imagined, that is, as if it were not less but, because extemporized,
immeasurably more than the result merely of some "arrangements of
knowledge." Emerson and Nietzsche are therefore different from one
another, but neither—and this is the important point—will participate in
the tradition by which self-eradication is a mere prelude to the reentry of
an enhanced self into already existing "arrangements of knowledge."
Whether it be Emerson or Nietzsche, a nonideological process or an
ideological one, it is presumably possible to experience such an interlude
without calling for any of the religious and humanistic sanctions at work in
the life around it and without contributing to these sanctions. It is possible to confer value on moments of transformation or dissolution without
looking ahead toward a narrative of fulfillment. Instead, the moment is
endowed with something as vague as wonder or beauty, cleansed of the
desire to translate these into knowledge already arranged or even in
prospect of being so.

   Why is it important that this aspect in literature be isolated and described? Not, as far as I am concerned, so that anyone may be persuaded
one way or another about the desirability of exterminating the inherited
self. The issue, rather, is the way in which the human voice, the human
presence affirms itself in literature even in the act of imagining the end of
it. Literary criticism operates under a still nearly universal assumption
that the human presence is a humanistic one. The possibility of being a
human while at the same time not being one, of looking on a landscape
from which the human presence has been banished, and of enjoying all
this without even characterizing the enjoyment by such a word as deprivation—this is something criticism has never sufficiently recognized in
any direct or assertive way. Trained to read books and film and the
dance—before the advent of Balanchine and the final acceptance of his
unique choreographic genius—as if the question of human presence,
humanistically and therefore narrativistically enacting itself, was not

really a question at all, most critics then respond to the absence of that human presence as something lamentable, or insist, often against the evidence in the writing, that in fact it has to be "there." Though the acquirements of selfhood may be treated with exuberant hostility, as in the novels and poetry of Lawrence, it is nearly always assumed, except by a critic as resourceful as Leo Bersani in *A Future for Astyanax*,[15] that the difficulties this entails for the reader are resolved by translating them into programs for human improvement. And where, as in Wallace Stevens, there is an acknowledged reduction to the so-called First or primary or reduced Idea, there has been a reluctance to believe that some of his best poems enact a drama in which the human will remains unactivated by this reduction.

Very often in Stevens the human will feels so little menace in reduction that it does not even exhibit that self-regarding fear which, in Schopenhauer, needs to be overcome if one is to experience the sublime. (In the process of that experience, as Schopenhauer describes it, a human being becomes conscious of objects hostile to the expression of the will. But "through a free and conscious transcendence of the will and the knowledge relating to it," he is then able to contemplate these objects passively and without fear, "raised above himself, his willing and all willing."[16]) Stevens's earliest volume, *Harmonium*, only implies the notion and process of the reduction to some elemental reality, and he did not then call it, after Charles Peirce,[17] the First Idea. It was not until 1942 that he gave explicit license to the term in a letter about *Notes toward a Supreme Fiction:* "If you take the varnish and dirt of generations off a picture, you see it in its first idea. If you think about the world without its varnish and dirt, you are a thinker of the first idea."[18] Obviously, this is a careless and tired definition, and for something better we should turn to *Notes* itself, the section entitled "It Must Be Abstract":

How clean the sun when seen in its idea,
Washed in the remotest cleanliness of a heaven
That has expelled us and our images . . .

The death of one god is the death of all.
Let purple Phoebus lie in umber harvest,
Let Phoebus slumber and die in autumn umber,

Phoebus is dead, ephebe. But Phoebus was
A name for something that never could be named.
There was a project for the sun and is.

There is a project for the sun. The sun
Must bear no name, gold flourisher, but be
In the difficulty of what it is to be.[19]

The sonorities of "purple . . . umber . . . slumber . . . autumn . . . umber" are playfully repetitive in their ridicule, a ridicule that moves beyond Phoebus to include those who need to be told to "let" him die. The funereal rotundities that announce the death of a god are in themselves so much junk left over from the project of the sun that "was"—hence their jocular treatment. We would expect, logically, a deference toward what he calls "a project for the sun" that "is." But it, too, is given a share of trouble. "The sun," we ephebes are instructed, "must bear no name." And yet the poet, himself an ephebe once, a poet in early manhood, immediately ignores his own edict: he calls the sun "gold flourisher." The nearly offhand suggestion is that the genesis of gods is an irresistible consequence of the way we use language. The "difficulty of what it is to be" comes from all of us, especially from poets, who cannot leave anything alone; to re-present things is the inescapable result of using or even thinking in words.

Stevens can be stoical and grim in his contemplations of imaginative impoverishments, of winter landscapes in the mind. But even when most powerfully eloquent, he can also be playful about the "difficulty" of things as they pass from the authority of one conceptual frame into another. Though he can assert that the "thing" is free of "rotted names" ("The Man With the Blue Guitar"), the movement of his verse shows that the freed thing is often merely on its way to another subjugation under another name, which is also destined for rot. To reduce anything to a First Idea is not to arrive at "nothing"; it is to arrive, rather, at another fabrication and to the fiction of firstness. Beyond this is still the unsatisfied aspiration, the impossible possibility—which is to see something without having to think about it, without having to meet it with words, without having to recreate it, to see it as a transparent eyeball would see it, with no sense of its dependence upon us.

That there should be an intercourse with things more "real" or cleaner than any offered by language, an intercourse truer and more honest than language will allow—this is on the face of it a peculiar ambition for a poet, though it is at work in some of the greatest of them. It is an intensely private, cold, astringent desire. It exists like a joke to one's self on everyone else and on the perceived world. Frost is capable of these jokes to an almost retaliatory degree against readers who trust to his folksiness. It is an ambition that looks beyond audience both because it is too precious and disturbing to be shown and because it is continually betrayed and undermined by any effort to talk about it, to go public, as it were.

We cannot know when a great poet feels betrayed even as he flaunts his mastery and love of language to the world. The flaunting, along with an admission that the mastery may count for nothing, shows especially in late Stevens but hovers everywhere in his work. His tactics are all to the fore, as if to say that if you do get any comfort or pleasure from his work, it is thanks entirely to his calculation or, as in "The Rock," by the emergence of forces mysteriously inherent in nothingness itself, the "metier" of nothingness. He is stoical and luxuriating, embattled and utterly relaxed by turns, and the rather mechanical, the carefully managed and modulated shifts in his poetry from one mood to another are evidence, it would seem, of his casualness about his moods, of the fact that they are not often inwardly compelled. As I read his poetry, it does not finally show the anxieties about the human presence or the necessity for assertions of the human will that are central in Harold Bloom's account of it. I bring Bloom into the argument not primarily to question his readings of Stevens, but because he is a brilliant example of how the idea of the human is more powerfully assertive even in highly sophisticated interpretations of literature than in literature itself. Criticism, with its emphasis on structures that must develop rather than recede, apparently finds it nearly impossible to recognize the quite casual way in which literature calls us sometimes to witness the disappearance of the human. Precisely because Bloom is regarded as an avant-garde critic, he is an especially instructive illustration of the persistence into contemporary theory of the critical problem I have been addressing. His reputation for being difficult, innovative, and courageous obscures the evidence that he is also deeply conservative.

In fact, Bloom's exploratory willingness, the avidity in locating points of extreme self-doubt or dissolution in poetry, recoils on itself in the direction of his humanistic, sometimes sentimentally humanistic convictions. So that while he does refer to a stoicism and to a remarkable degree of psychic repression in Stevens,[20] he nonetheless always assumes that, failing the intercession of the human will, the process of reduction will lead inevitably to what he calls "the reductive fallacy": that "the ultimate truth about us is, by definition, the very worst that can be said about us," that we arrive at a place of "destruction," "ruin," the "worst."[21] Since this is humanly intolerable, reductiveness is instead imagined as a sort of spring which, pushed down to a point where it touches the root nerve of the will, then recoils, projecting us into a creative upward movement which reconstitutes the self and the world. Most people like to think in this way about literature and about life. It is apparently a necessary way to think, and it unquestionably saves us from despair to be assured that the worst returns to laughter. However, reduction need not be thought of as loss or deprivation but as exploration and gain, and in any case moral suasion has nothing to do with the kind of reduction that promises a world prior to human presence and subsequent to it, a world in which the issue even of dependence so important in Schopenhauer—Are we dependent on it? Is it dependent on us?—is temporarily annulled.

We catch glimpses of such a world, for example, in Emerson's "Fate" where he observes that "we cannot trifle with this reality, this cropping out in our planted gardens, of the core of the world,"[22] or in the *Journals* for 1847 where he says that "we wish to get the highest skill of finish, an engraver's educated finger, determination to an aim,—and then—to let in mania, ether, to take off the *individual's interference* and let him fly as with thunderbolt [my italics]."[23] Nor can a process of reduction when inexorably linked to some form of redemption as both cause and justification embrace the daring of writers more equivocating than is Emerson, like Ruskin, with his sporadic desire to see the universe un-peopled and himself invisible. Disputing a letter addressed by Carlyle to Emerson, Ruskin wrote:

> In the beginning of the Carlyle-Emerson correspondence, edited with too little comment by my dear friend Charles Norton, I find at page 18 this—to me entirely disputable, and to my thought, so far as undisputed, much blameable and pitiable, exclamation of my master's: "Not till we can think that here and there one is thinking of us, one is loving us, does this waste earth become a peopled garden." My training, as the reader has perhaps enough perceived, produced in me the precisely opposite sentiment. *My* times of happiness have always been when *nobody* was thinking of me. . . . My entire delight was in observing without being myself noticed,—if I could have been invisible, all the better.[24]

The tradition Harold Bloom describes, and in which Emerson or, say, Ruskin would be uncomfortable, belongs a good deal more to quite other writers than those he favors, writers ranging from Dante to T. S. Eliot who validate the processes of reduction by resort to terms derived from religious exercises for the salvation of the soul. Obviously Bloom does not subscribe to this tradition, but his vocabulary and his procedures implicate him in it. His critical method is to some extent a trope of the processes of descent-ascent, and it necessariy prefers poems and interpretations that reveal a crisis in the spiritual, the psychic, and poetic career of the writer. The poetic drama of reduction or dissolution to "firstness" becomes thereby an indication of such a crisis and not, as it easily might be, an expression—momentary in its effect, exploratory in its aim, possibly enlivening—of how it is for certain human beings to envision human disappearance. Bloom is always and everywhere a literary critic dedicated to the energies at work in language, and if he is also a humanist it is to ask that humanism in poetry be confirmed in the movements of language. When he finds in the language evidences of humanistic crises, he then, inevitably, also expects to find evidences of what he calls a crossing. "A crossing within a crisis-poem, like a poetic crisis, is a process of disjunction, a leaping of the gap between one kind of figurative thinking and another."[25]

In its adduced psychological or aesthetic consequences, however, a "crossing," with all its Freudian implications, is little different from what in an older, religious vocabulary would be described as the struggle for wholeness, for salvation, for the reconstitution of the self. And if this is not found in the particular poem, then the poem is placed by Bloom in the gravitational pull of other poems where it can be found. Such an account of poetic processes is essentially what could be extrapolated from that religious poetry in which, having descended "Into the world of perpetual solitude, / World not world, but that which is not world"—to quote Eliot in one of his more tiresome puns, about movement and abstention from movement in a world that whirls—it is imagined that one ascends into a new form potentially salvageable and more worthy. This sequence goes back from Eliot through Milton to Spenser of Book II of *The Faerie Queene,* to Dante, and the Bible, and it has sexual analogues, again out of Dante, in the treatment of buggery in Lawrence and, both more wittily and superficially, in Mailer. This latter mode could be called, to quote Eliot on Baudelaire, "an attempt to get into Christinanity by the back door."[27]

Bloom has his reasons for not admiring Eliot, and I link the two only to dramatize how his "crises" and "crossings" commit him to a reading of poetry which, on crucial occasions, is marred by his insistence on a restitutive process little different, in the dogmatic urgency of its phrasing, from what could be expected in the poetry of Christian redemption. This dogmatism emerges most clearly when a poem cannot convincingly be shown to dramatize within itself a "crossing" or an assertion, such as is given in Stevens's "An Ordinary Evening in New Haven," of the poetic will in response to deprivation. Take, as a conveniently brief example, "The Death of a Soldier" by Stevens:

> Life contracts and death is expected,
> As in a season of autumn.
> The soldier falls.
>
> He does not become a three-days personage,
> Imposing his separation,
> Calling for pomp.
>
> Death is absolute and without memorial,
> As in a season of autumn,
> When the wind stops,

When the wind stops and, over the heavens,
The clouds go, nevertheless,
In their direction.[28]

Bloom offers a paraphrase of the poem which adheres strictly to the notion of the First Idea, or rather to his particular version of it:

But what has the First Idea, or an idea of Firstness, to do with the poem *The Death of a Soldier*? Stevens seeks what is not possible, in a tradition that goes back to Homer yet never has gone beyond Homer. He seeks to see earliest what the death of a soldier is. His reduction is fourfold:

1) The soldier falls expectedly, in and by seasonal contraction; this is primal *ethos*, the soldier's character as it is autumn's, and so a limitation of meaning.

2) The soldier is not and has no part in Christ; he will not rise, after three days, separated from the common fate and requiring celebration.

3) Any death, by synecdoche, is as final in itself and beyond language as is an autumnal moment of stasis.

4) That is, any death is also without consequence, in the context of natural sublimity; for us, below the heavens, there is stasis, but the movement of a larger intentionality always goes on above the heavens.[29]

To begin with, this account proposes a clarity of movement that the poem itself does not exhibit. Instead, the voice drifts away, soliciting us as it does so, from the narrative and argumentative assertiveness of the first two stanzas. Beginning in line 8, the poem passes into something like reverie, and though the speaker retains some of his exacting economy, as in his careful "nevertheless," it is by now at the service of developments that cannot be talked about with the finality of such earlier phrasing as "Death is absolute and without memorial." Consider what happens to the phrase "As in a season of autumn." At first it sounds like a clarifying illustration of the inevitable contraction of the seasons, of human life, and especially of the life of a soldier. But then the phrase is repeated, and with a qualification that releases it from its initial relatively inert metaphoric function. What was a clarification turns out to have been only a partial glimpse of something; "As in a season of autumn" becomes "As in a season of autumn, / When the wind stops," and then becomes something still more attenuated, "As in a season of autumn, / When the wind stops, / When the wind stops and, over the heavens, / The clouds go, never-theless, / In their direction." As if by introspective meandering behind the ostensible forward movement, and prompted by repetition of earlier phrasing, what was a metaphor for the contraction of human life comes gradually to include, really to induce its opposite—a movement in the heavens that has a life of its own. By that peculiar process of reiteration so characteristic of Stevens's poetry, what was a signifier, the season of autumn, becomes the signified of the poem. We thus are encouraged to forget any story of human death as, imperceptibly, we find ourselves within a movement that has no story; we are forgiven time in a prospect of space.

The reader is brought to a change and shift of attention here by the maneuverings of line and by echoings that lull rather than alert attention. If the results can be called powerful, it is a power of restraint on any human urge to *figure* in the scene. Stevens has phased the poem into a mood wherein the human will, instead of registering its supposedly inherent resistence to self-dispersion, simply relaxes into it. Any willful assertion in the second half of the poem would sound merely obtuse and impertinent; so would any reminder that we have been reprieved from willfulness. Instead, we experience a stasis on the ground, as the wind stops, and simultaneously the aspect of clouds moving "nevertheless," oblivious to our local sense of things. Bloom objects always to the loss of human will, and where the loss does occur, as here, where the human recedes in the presence of powers independent of it, he tends, as do nearly all critics, to correct the balance by exerting his own will in and on the poem. This often takes the form of engineered readings of particular words. In this case he does odd things with the phrase "over the heavens." It is taken to mean "above the heavens," surely so forced a reading that a larger motive or need impels it. By placing the moving clouds "above the heavens"—whatever that could mean—he is able to ascribe to them what he calls a "larger intentionality" and, more important, to make it inaccessible to the poet and the reader. But it is only a "larger" intentionality for those who want to assume that the human will should somehow have been activated by it and competed with it. If the human will really is in recession then, so far as Bloom is concerned, it may participate in the peculiar effects on the ground but not in anything going on "above" the heavens. This may sound like a small distinction, but it is in fact a central and major one. If the human will is not to assert itself in the poem, then for Bloom it thereby deprives itself, in a "reduced" world, of contact with the sublime. But why cannot the sublime be experienced precisely by the relaxed indifference of the will? That is what the poem, like many others by Stevens, aspires to: a represented and enhanced experience wherein everything on the ground and "over"—that is, across—the heavens is occurring all at once, an experience wherein this simultaneity is rendered in a manner beautifully placid, cleansed of contradiction and friction. The clouds need have nothing to do with "the movement of a larger intentionality" but rather with the marvelous absence both of larger intentionality and of any dependence on the smaller intentionality of the human will. They move "nevertheless," and it is their freedom from having to mean anything that awes and pleases us. Meanwhile, the human presence, asserted earlier in a phrase like "three-days personage," is, by implication, dissolved into the scene, like the dead soldier.

The poem eschews those anticipatory connotations implicit in all humanistic conceptions of reductiveness—the conviction that it is preliminary to the will's effort at reconstitution. Structurally the poem is identical to "The Snow Man" and the many other poems by Stevens in which, as James Guetti points out, "the exhaustion of the more rational imaginative powers seems always . . . an exercise of mind that readies us to participate in a different sort of perception and energy."[30] In Bloom's account there is a kind of desperation to locate "crossings," evidence of will in the form of rhetorical shifts—to the point, indeed, where he sounds as if he is ready to give up on the poem entirely, though not before hearing an "undersong" which I cannot be alone in finding inaudible. Commenting on his paraphrase, Bloom remarks that it

> omits what matters about the poem, which is rhetorical gesture, tonal *askesis*, dignity of a minimal *pathos*, excluding lament. Yet what it most omits is the poem's undersong, which is its *logos* or crossing. Rhetorically, the poem intimates that any such earliest seeing of the soldier's death is dehumanizing, intolerable, not to be sustained. This brief poem is almost all *ethos*, all contraction; the human in us demands more of a poem, for us, and where *pathos* is so excluded a death-in-life comes which is more that of the poem's shaper, speaker, reader than it could have been of the fictive soldier before he fell.[31]

From so disciplined a critic, this is a remarkable break in decorum. The soldier is called fictive, but he is nonetheless suddenly endowed with a real historical life. And why? So that he might testify against the validity of the poem and its author. This is not so much a reading as a plea "for us," on behalf of "the human in us," in the soldier, and in Bloom. His prose answers the plea denied by the poem; it supplies the pathos or will to power over fate to which the poem refuses to rise. In fact, it is to concede too much to say even that the pathos is absent; it is absent only if it is assumed that it ought to be there. Instead, the poem asks us to countenance a refusal of grief; it refuses to grieve for a dead soldier and, more significantly, it refuses to grieve for our lost selves. We become transparent to the world, Emerson's great eyeball.

Stevens, it need hardly be said, is not finding some benign way to carry out the project of Nietzsche or Foucault. Rather, with Emerson, he shows that freedom is one of the characteristics of Fate. The poem itself is the visible and audible evidence of that freedom. The performance of the poem is a signature of human will and power that affirms its presence in the very act of absenting itself. For him, as for his American predecessors, deconstruction is a given; if it is sometimes preliminary to a reconstitution of the self, it is at other times a necessary stage of a process in which the self is a passive observer of its own alternately crescive and transparent possibilities.

"I am a victim of neurasthenia and of the sense of the hollowness and unreality that goes with it,"[32] William James wrote to his friend G. H. Howison, a professor of philosophy at the University of California, and it could be said that some version of this, as an enhancement of experience and of thinking, however painful and terrifying, is to be found in the other American writers I have mentioned. James's "will to believe" proceeds from the necessity not for affirmed selfhood and most assuredly not, from the author of *A Pluralistic Universe*, for unity. It comes instead from the more basic desire simply to stay alive, facing into the "pit of insecurity beneath the surface of life."[3] Against the doubt of existence, one does not posture a "self" but only a "belief," and not even a belief in the self so much as in the will to believe in life. "Believe that life *is* worth living," he advised, "and your belief will help create the fact."[34] So far as any human self goes, it may be willed into and willed out of existence without loss of consciousness or loss of subjective life, and any act of belief, in the self or in its dissolution, is no more than a modification in the stream of thought. Quoting from Benjamin Paul Blood, an American philosopher, poet, and mystic who in 1874 wrote *The Anaesthetic Revelation and the Gist of Philosophy*—a book expressing a belief in pluralism based on the use of anaesthetics—James allowed into his own text an eloquence rhapsodic even for him:

> Reason is but one item in the mystery; and behind the proudest consciousness that ever reigned, reason and wonder blushed face to face. The inevitable stales, while doubt and hope are sisters. Not unfortunately the universe is wild,—game-flavored as a hawk's wing. Nature is miracle all; the same returns not save to bring the different. The slow round of the engraver's lathe gains but the breadth of a hair, but the difference is distributed back over the whole curve, never an instant true,—ever not quite.[35]

It is fitting that as James came to the end of his life one of his last essays, "A Pluralistic Mystic," was a tribute to his friend Blood, at the conclusion of which he writes: "Let *my* last word, then, speaking in the name of intellectual philosophy, be *his* word:—'There is no conclusion. What has concluded, that we might conclude in regard to it? There are no fortunes to be told, and there is no advice to be given.—Farewell!' "[36] If this is an echo of Emerson in "The Poet" or "Nature" or "Experience," it is an echo that reaches toward the last poem of Wallace Stevens, a poem called "Of Mere Being," where he celebrates "The poem at the end of the mind, / Beyond the last thought."

NOTES

1. Michel Foucault, *The Order of Things* (New York: Pantheon Books, 1971), 387. Originally published in France as *Les Mots et les choses* (Paris: Éditions Gallimard, 1966).
2. The interview can most conveniently be found in Raymond Bellour, *Les Livres des autres* (Paris: l'Herne, 1971), pp. 23–32.
3. Walter Kaufmann, ed. and trans., *The Portable Nietzsche* (New York: Viking Press, 1954), pp. 42–43.
4. Frank Kermode, *The Sense of an Ending* (New York: Oxford University Press, 1967).
5. Friedrich Nietzsche, *The Complete Works of Friedrich Nietzsche*, 18 vols., ed. Oscar Levy (New York: Macmillan, 1909–1911; New York: Russell & Russell, 1964), vol. 5, pt. 2, pp. 6–106. In this volume the English title is "The Use and Abuse of History," though the title in German is "Von Nutzen und Nachteil der Historie für das Leben." See also the discussion in Paul de Man, *Blindness and Insight: Essays in the Rhetoric of Contemporary Criticism* (New York: Oxford University Press, 1971), p. 145.
6. See, as a notorious example, T. S. Eliot, *After Strange Gods* (New York: Harcourt Brace, 1934); a central text for F. R. Leavis on this score is the greatly underestimated *The Living Principle: English as a Discipline of Thought* (New York: Oxford University Press, 1975); for Lionel Trilling, best see *Beyond Culture: Essays on Literature and Learning* (New York: Viking Press, 1965).
7. Herbert Marcuse, *One Dimensional Man* (Boston: Beacon Press, 1964).
8. Trilling, *Beyond Culture*, p. 27.
9. See Susan Sontag, *Illness as Metaphor* (New York: Farrar, Straus & Giroux, 1978).
10. Richard Poirier, *A World Elsewhere: The Place of Style in American Literature* (New York: Oxford University Press, 1966).
11. There is the trauma, for example, ascribed in *The Varieties of Religious Experience* (1902) in the chapter "The Sick Soul" to an anonymous Frenchman but which, according to William James's son Henry, was experienced by James himself in the spring of 1879. See F. O. Matthiessen, *The James Family* (New York: Alfred A. Knopf, 1947), pp. 217–18. In 1844, when William was two years old, his father Henry, living in the neighborhood of Windsor, England, had a roughly similar experience: see ibid., pp. 160–68.
12. Henry James, ed., *The Letters of William James*, 2 vols. (Boston: Little, Brown, & Co., 1926), 1:287.
13. Edward Waldo Emerson, ed., *The Complete Works of Ralph Waldo Emerson* (Boston: Houghton, Mifflin and Company, 1904), vol. 1, p. 36.
14. Emerson, "Nature," in *Complete Works*, vol. 3, p. 182.
15. Leo Bersani, *A Future for Astyanax: Character and Desire in Literature* (Boston: Little, Brown & Co., 1976), pp. 156–85.
16. R. B. Haldane and J. Kemp, eds., *The Works of Schopenhauer* (London: Routledge & Kegan Paul, 1883) vol. 1, p. 261.
17. For the idea of "firstness" in the American philosopher Charles Peirce, see

Justin Buchler, ed., *Philosophical Writings of Peirce* (New York: Dover Press, 1980), especially chap. 6.

18. Holly Stevens, ed., *Letters of Wallace Stevens* (New York: Alfred A. Knopf, 1966), pp. 426–27.

19. Holly Stevens, ed., *Wallace Stevens: The Palm at the End of the Mind, Selected Poems and a Play* (New York: Vintage Books, 1972), pp. 207–208. © 1942 by Wallace Stevens. Reprinted from *The Collected Poems of Wallace Stevens* by permission of Alfred A. Knopf, Inc.

20. See particularly Harold Bloom, *Poetry and Repression: Revisionism from Blake to Stevens* (New Haven, Conn.: Yale University Press, 1976), pp. 292–93.

21. Harold Bloom, *Wallace Stevens: The Poems of Our Climate* (Ithaca, N.Y.: Cornell University Press, 1977), pp. 53–54.

22. Emerson, "Fate," in *Complete Works*, vol. 6, p. 143.

23. Merton M. Sealts, Jr., ed., *The Journals and Miscellaneous Notebooks of Ralph Waldo Emerson*, vol. 10, *1847–1848* (Cambridge, Mass.: Harvard University Press, 1973), pp. 53–54.

24. E. T. Cook and Alexander Wedderburn, eds., *The Works of John Ruskin* (London: Library Edition, 1903–1912), 35:165–66. See also the discussion of this aspect of Ruskin in Jay Fellows, *The Failing Distance* (Baltimore, Md.: Johns Hopkins University Press, 1976), pp. 158–87.

25. Bloom, *Wallace Stevens*, p. 2.

26. T. S. Eliot, "Burnt Norton," in T. S. Eliot, *The Complete Poems and Plays: 1909–1950* (New York: Harcourt, Brace & World, 1952), p. 120.

27. T. S. Eliot, *Selected Essays* (New York: Harcourt Brace, 1932), p. 337.

28. Holly Stevens, ed., *Wallace Stevens: The Palm at the End of the Mind*, p. 33. © 1923, renewed 1951, by Wallace Stevens. Reprinted from *The Collected Poems of Wallace Stevens* by permission of Alfred A. Knopf, Inc.

29. Bloom, *Wallace Stevens*, p. 49–50.

30. James L. Guetti, *Word-Music: The Aesthetic Aspect of Narrative Fiction* (New Brunswick, N.J.: Rutgers University Press, 1980), p. 45.

31. Bloom, *Wallace Stevens*, p. 50.

32. *Letters of William James*, 2:22–23.

33. William James, *The Varieties of Religious Experience* (New York: Longmans, Green, 1902; Garden City, N.Y.: Doubleday Image Books, 1978), p. 168.

34. William James, *The Will to Believe* (New York: Longmans, Green, 1897), p. 62.

35. Ibid., pp. vii–xii. The passage quoted by James is from B. P. Blood, *The Flaw in Supremacy*, published by the author (Amsterdam, N.Y., 1893). See also Matthiessen, *The James Family*, pp. 227–28.

36. William James, *Essays in Philosophy*, ed. Frederick H. Burkhardt, Fredson Bowers, and Ignas K. Skrupskelis (Cambridge, Mass.: Harvard University Press, 1978), p. 190.

PART IV

12

THE ACTUARY OF OUR SPECIES: THE END OF HUMANITY, REGARDED FROM THE VIEWPOINT OF SCIENCE

Philip Morrison

THE CHAPTERS IN THIS BOOK AMOUNT TO AN EFFORT TO
evoke and analyze various aspects of the mind, ideas which some
might choose to call psychological, some mythical, others cultural. Surely
there lies the core of the whole enterprise. But it is impossible to get
along in our day without concern for the external, the merely factual.
Since the Enlightenment our era has been more and more dominated by
scientific considerations. Nor should one doubt that some more detached,
later analyst of our science would be able to perceive that within this
explicitly factual material was packed much of the same mythical, self-
searching quality as the rest. I shall therefore claim no special detachment
for this discussion, except that it is committed to the difficult enterprise of
trying to look at the real world as it is given to us. Admittedly we look
mainly through social and personal glasses, necessarily lenses not of the
eye alone but of the mind. We cannot transcend their particular resolu-
tion. But we can try.

Thus I hit upon the slightly quizzical title "The Actuary of Our Species"
on the grounds that it was indeed the job of the actuary to look with a cold
eye upon life, upon death, and try to strike fair odds. It is perfectly plain
that we are in a special position here, because the genuine actuary derives
this credibility from plentiful statistics, from the fact that while no human
life is predictable, human lives, as a class, satisfy the weak law of large
numbers. They can somehow be predicted; people make money on mortality in the life-insurance trade. If we are, as we now think, the only
species of our self-aware kind, then actuarial possibilities do not even

come into question. With that slight apology for my statistical metaphor, I want first to outline the central point: science has been able to make a broadly reliable judgment of the place of human beings in space and time, a grand assessment of just where and when we are.

HOMO SAPIENS IN SPACE AND TIME

It follows from that assessment that we can offer roughly persuasive predictions and assertions about events we have never seen, never experienced, at least in comparable degree. First of all, consider our place in space. Barring a small fringe of true believers, that is nowadays a subject met with considerable objectivity in the public view. Nobody cares much about it. And what we have to say is commonplace. But it was not always so. We are told that the philosopher Anaxagoras was exiled from Athens because he taught that the sun was a fiery sphere and as big as the Pelopennesus. Since the sun was ascribed immortal properties, his claim was regarded as impious. Perhaps he had political enemies as well, so out he went. We now know his views to be sound, if rather understated, and nobody now seems to be excited about that very much. By the time of Newton it was clear what our position was in space. We then understood what I still think to be one of the priceless jewels of scientific knowledge: namely, the clear fact, which we can demonstrate, that the sun is a star and all the stars are suns. That class is one class which nevertheless contains both the hot disk that we see every day, the source of human life, of all life on earth, and also that collection of bright points, twinkling in the night sky, their utility at best for prognostication or navigation, but not for anything else. The fact that these two are the same, and that they differ solely because of our relative position of view, is a remarkable truth. It is the kind of truth which is inescapably present in many (but not all) results of contemporary science, not arguable, but permanent, hardly subject to the general critique of the ebb and flow of thought. The historians and philosophers do not often talk about that. They prefer to discuss more theoretical matters, abstract, even mathematical issues, so complex as to partake of more subjectivity. But I doubt very much that the time will come when reasoning people will think other than this. Huygens was one of the first to publish these arguments, but the view was widespread in the seventeenth century. It was not unknown before then; there were hints and predecessors ever since Copernicus, perhaps since Nicholas of Cusa in the fifteenth century, but it does not much matter. By the time of the speculative philosophy of the eighteenth century, based firmly on the huge success of Newton, Halley, Euler—say, Kant—it was already conjectural that the little patches of light that the few astronomers had seen in their telescopes which were not stars, elliptical in form in the feeble telescopes of the days before photography, were galaxies like the Milky Way galaxy. Therefore we lived in an island universe, where Milky Way after Milky Way was scattered through space, each an archipelago of suns. This was still conjectural. It was hotly debated over 200 years, to be settled only in the first half of this century. Now we know it to be so; almost no one doubts that the extent of space we have to deal with is measured at least in the billions of light-years. That is a truism of our day, which every child knows from television.

So much is only a static backdrop. It says nothing about change. One point does remain, a very important point. But it really requires some physical theory to appreciate it before I draw the next conclusion. Judging from space alone you would not think that time was involved. But we know that through the velocity of light, an inescapable and absolute limit of velocity in which we have high confidence, if not absolute certainty, any extension in space implies extension in time, through the connection made by light. If we can see things that we argue are billions of light years away, then (unless an extraordinary special creation was made with the light set halfway in space, which opens a way of altogether getting around any philosophical arguments about the past) you could not admit time could be shorter than the transit time of light across space. These two views connect to give rise to a truly profound gulf in space which has been occupied by human thought only quite recently. Newton did not know that light had any special role in velocity. He conceived of possible infinite velocities; all scientists really did until the turn of this century and Einstein. Newton was quite prepared to accept, and indeed worked systematically and quite well, on building a historical chronology of his own, to patch up the Bible by using the documents of other Middle Eastern cultures and of antiquity to give us a firmer chronology. He published a formidable book, in which he established a chronology, tolerably in agreement with other theologians of the day, the famous 4004 B.C. Day of Creation. (That date is not to be taken as a dogmatic final result, but just as one result by some particular scholars with a lot of influence on King James's Bible committee, and so included in the Book.) It was much debated, just as geological dates are debated still. Newton himself believed approximately the same thing: our earth was created some 10,000 years ago, give or take a few thousand years. This time scale did not change during the Enlightenment. Even the Enlightenment scholars first saw no way of getting at it and mostly they let it go. Of course, as science grew there came a succession of thinkers on geological time. A conspicuous and early one was Halley himself, Newton's friend and collaborator, who computed from the salting of the sea that geologic time had to be measured in hundreds of millions of years. It could by no means be 10,000 years. Generally, unbelievers and the Enlightenment understood something was very wrong, but they were unable to present any secure physical age to substitute for the learned historical one.

With the growth of systematic geology at the outset of the nineteenth century, the whole situation began to change. Still, time was not marked well in geology. As Mark Twain made deliciously clear, the geological calculations, especially in those days, had to proceed by naive linear extrapolation. You found that the sea bottom near Dover, say, would go up a fraction of an inch in a century or whatever it was, and then you said, "Well, since it's up a thousand feet and you can multiply linearly, anybody can exhibit wonderful depths of time." But of course this is an extremely imprecise argument; it gave rise to much ridicule. Twain's is one of the best. He points out that the Mississippi River can be shown to shorten its course by washing out oxbows, cutting across them at the rate of a mile and a half a year. You can show that a certain time ago it must have been sticking out above the Gulf of Mexico 50,000 miles! It is clear that linear extrapolations of this kind are not very happy. One can be more serious than that, too. For when Darwin came on the scene in the middle of the nineteenth century it was the great time, the Victorian equivalent of the Enlightenment, when the geologists had become the implicit champions of the secular. Darwin took on the same role when he said there was no special creation even for living things. (But the geologers had already had their opprobrium and their triumphs, for example, at Cornell University. It was founded as a nonsectarian school, much criticized by its neighbors for its godlessness, lack of compulsory chapel, and the rest. The library of the geology department at Cornell is the only decorated chamber within the frugal original foundation, the only lovingly funded portion, where the architect was allowed a little license to spend a few thousand dollars to decorate, to make something handsome and grand. Around the geology library are cast-iron reliefs of the then new paleontological reconstructions; I look at them to realize that here is the spirit we see in the proud Roman design of the Massachusetts Institute of Technology, or the elegant design of many nuclear laboratories of the 1950s. A certain air of importance is imputed to the scientist by his surroundings.) But the Victorians did not have a good time estimate. They knew it had to be pretty long. All the biologists kept saying was that geological time is infinite. That was the best Darwin could do. (He was poor in arithmetic and either did not quite grasp the formal meaning of the word *infinite* or at least did not care to be precise about it.)

A struggle began between the physicists and the evolutionists of the day over the question of time scale. Lord Kelvin, a prodigious worthy, a grandee of science, the inventor of the laws of thermodynamics, more or less, a man with no small sense of the pronunciamento, insisted from good thermal calculations that the sun and hence the earth could not be above a few tens of millions of years old. And indeed within his lights he was right. It was only at the turn of this century that physicists had the scope to understand that indeed the geologists and Darwin were right all the time: geologic time was a hundred times longer than Kelvin said, which was all they meant by "infinite." They wanted some billions of years, and that is just what they got.

Lord Rutherford has a superb reminiscence over the point. As a young and enterprising physicist from the colonies, teaching at McGill University, he was invited to London to give a distinguished lecture on his new work on radioactivity. He was very proud that he could carry about in his pocket a rock, in those days one of half a dozen rocks on the face of the earth about which one could say: we know the age of this stone. He knew that the old Kelvin was in the audience. He was very worried about what he would say because he had shown that Kelvin was manifestly wrong. Kelvin had calculated the age of the sun from the maximum energy release possible under the use of gravitational forces. Of course, no chemical fuel will do; if you tried to burn a mass of coal or gasoline the size of the sun—imagine the oxygen is magically supplied—it will only last, at the sun's rate, for a few hundred thousand years. The nature of the sun is not that it puts out so much energy, it is not that it is so bright. It is bright only because it is so big. In fact, the metabolism of the sun is a good deal slower than your metabolism or mine. Per unit mass the sun develops only one part in a few thousand as much heat as the metabolism of a human being; the sun is not much more active metabolically than a piece of cold granite. The trick about the sun is that its output endures over a very long time without an external supply of fuel: not much power per unit mass, but sustained for a long, long time, the indispensable condition for our slow evolutionary rise. Kelvin before 1900 had no idea of that at all. Ernest Rutherford had to explain that Kelvin had been ignorant of radioactivity. He feared flatly to contradict the old boy, who would sit up front, perhaps to pound his stick on the floor when a misstatement was made. But Rutherford happily hit on just what to say. Nothing is more important, he said, than the great work of Lord Kelvin, who had given an absolute limit to the lifetime of the sun under the assumption that no new energy source was available. Now we had found radioactivity, just as this remarkable prediction had implied. The old man nodded cheerfully off to sleep.

In fact geological time is limited, the sun's age too is limited; now we know even more remarkably that the galaxy's age is limited as well. All these points show us that there was some kind of cosmic birthdate. That need not, to be sure, mark the birthdate of all that is, which is what theorists now like to think. They are probably wrong now, as they were before. And I will not join them in that. But the existence of the starry universe in which we now live is definitely finite. The galaxies all had a birth; we know that date crudely; I do not think we will ever change our view. We might somewhat modify the estimate. The age of all the discrete objects the astronomers see, all the stars and galaxies to the limits of the telescope, is in the order of 10 billion years, a couple of times the age of sun, moon, the meteorites, and the earth's fabric itself.

THE TREE OF LIFE

The geologic record is plain: there has been life on earth, in an unbroken genealogy, one biochemical kinship, for more than 3.5 billion years. Most of that time—say about 2.5 billion years or more—all life was a proliferating, complex low mat of colonial blue-green and green algae, and the associated microorganisms. Life never left the extreme lowlands; life was a phenomenon of the shallow waters, whether salt, brackish, or fresh. It spread over the tidal flats and the stream banks, bogs, and marshes of the forming continents. Never did it become actively mobile; but steadily its biochemical powers grew. Very likely it began to change the entire chemical environment, modifying the atmosphere itself to enrich it in time with oxygen to near-modern value. It hoarded iron, calcium, and phosporous, which once were mere dilute traces in the weathered rocks and the volcanic gases. But life endured everywhere in the shallow wet world.

Of course there were ecological catastrophes in plenty: floods, volcanoes, tidal waves, even prodigious meteorite impacts. Yet life spread. Finally it pushed beyond the shallow waters, first for the shelves and then the depths; it left the water margin itself in time, beginning some half billion years ago to carry its essential internal fluids onto dry land. A couple of hundred million years before that land invasion, out in the shallow seas and the coastal waters, mobile life had begun, the first animals with structures strong enough to allow easy locomotion. Plants too gained the strong polymer framework which would allow tall stems, sun seeking beyond the edge of the lapping waters. Life now covers the earth's surface from near-pole to near-pole, and from the darkness of the depths to bright Alpine snows. In all this time, though species have come and gone in their billions, the fabric of life has remained continuous and enduring, by virtue of its diversity and steady reproduction, not by a mere rock-like toughness. Rocks, all rocks, erode.

What is striking is that the system of life has plainly withstood every environmental change during a couple of dozen orbits around the galaxy. Not the cosmic environment, not internal changes in our sun, not even the more intimate complex unfolding of earth, both of gradual and of catastrophic change, have ever brought an end to life. The extinctions which are so tantalizing a feature of the record of the past—What happened to the dinosaurs?—have never been general. The population as a whole, the overall biomass, may well have changed drastically; any given species, and many whole orders, even whole phyla of living forms, have come to an end. But the living fabric, which has been raveled, worn, even ripped, has never been wholly severed. The tree flourishes though the leaves fall.

Spectacular changes, earthquakes, tidal waves, huge meteorite collisions must have been more or less local in time and place, at least limited in their effect. The more widespread changes, changes in the solar photon, in the ambient temperature, or in the chemistry of air and sea, have mostly been so slow and so much within the range of adaptability of life forms that they have not brought life to an end over all that time. There is plainly a powerful feedback loop at work. When the air lacked oxygen, anaerobic cells flourished. As toxic oxygen grew in abundance, the cells found what had been a dire poison to be the very stuff of opportunity of increased vigor. That is the context in which human life, the life of a few species—but most novel ones—is to be seen. Our distribution is certainly wide, from pole to pole, by land and sea; our response grows rapidly, once we see danger ahead. It seems probable that we have, or will soon have, cut our ties with natural selection, with slow-driving forces of organic evolution. For better or worse, we have taken our long-range future under some sort of control.

So much everyone believes. We need to look at the endings which remain possible, in the domain of the environment, and in the biology of our species itself. Above all, we need to ask what the powerful culture which has given us some freedom from the old laws of change ironically entails as a source of novel danger to the longevity of the species.

MOTHER EARTH AND FATHER SUN

The long past has evidently witnessed cataclysms on a scale beyond our historical or even human experience. The modern eruption of Krakatoa is just about the largest volcanic explosion we have ever read about. In late August of 1883 that island volcano in the straits between Java and Sumatra blew up fearfully. It flung out overnight about twenty cubic kilometers of rock as dust and larger chunks, leaving a caldera three or four miles across. Its tidal waves inundated the nearby coastal towns with a wave 100 feet high, drowning 35,000 people. Its high-altitude dust spread around the earth, yielding blue moons and red sunsets for a couple of years, during which the world temperature declined. But the long-dead volcano whose cold caldera is now the wide green pasture called Valle Grande near Los Alamos, New Mexico, spewed out in its time ten times more ash and pumice, leaving a collapsed opening much larger than that of

Krakatoa. We cannot say that it happened all at once, though that is quite probable; the event took place about 1.5 million years ago.

The point is clear, all the same: catastrophic eruptions, earthquakes, hurricanes, even tidal waves are all localized in effect, even allowing for the great variation possible over geologic time. There is no sign of internal energy sources which could be mustered to modify the earth as a whole. A city, a nation, even a whole oceanic culture could be ruined by such disasters. But the species can hardly be at risk. A tidal wave might damage the coasts of a whole ocean, with London, New York, Cape Town, and Rio all heavily inundated. But Madras would hardly know of the event without its tide gauges and barographs. The people of the high plateaus in Colorado or Kenya would remain largely unmoved. Life, and the life of humankind, is too widespread to fear such an end.

Consider the Universal Deluge, the Noachian Flood of Scripture. It is not likely that the waters were in fact available for a worldwide flood. The Book is building myth out of limited experience in the ancient lands between the rivers. That story is compelling in imaginative force, but the geologists have found hard evidence of real events almost as striking, almost as far beyond mere recorded experience. (This story is in fact yet not quite sure, but it is based on strong new evidence.) It appears that the whole Mediterranean Sea itself, Mare Nostrum of Rome, was at no great time in the past not a sea at all but a low desert, a huge arid salt-covered basin like the Mojave Desert, though much larger. This was only six or eight million years back, a time before our hominid kind evolved, but certainly witnessed by our forerunners, the apes. After a long persistence of this desolate barrier between Europe and Africa, one fine day a high barrier at Gibraltar finally gave way. Over that huge lip, over high cliffs, the green Atlantic Ocean poured into the dry low Mediterranean basin, as the Colorado River poured into the Salton Sea in California on a merely local scale before World War I. The flow was prodigious; the falls of Gibraltar were scores of miles wide and a mile high. In a hundred thousand years the sea was filled. A couple of hundred million years farther back, the Atlantic itself was only a narrow rift, like the Gulf of California.

The earth indeed changes, but the changes, dramatic to the point of hyperbole, are nevertheless coherently within the domain of our science. We need not adopt a narrow methodology, like the uniformitarianism which could characterize a less mature geology. Flood and fire are not to be excluded; all we need is evidence for them, the linked circumstances of a coherent view, and the familiar laws of matter in motion yield extraordinary novelties. But life is more persistent than mountain or sea.

Take the kimberlite pipes, where diamonds are mined. They appear to be a sort of cold volcano, suddenly arising without warning, anywhere, even far from the rings of fire which include most volcanoes and earth-quake epicenters. But they do not threaten our species. It seems possible that one fine day a square mile or two of rock could erupt to fly high into the air, the fierce jet from the deep hot mantle of earth spalling the rocks above, to fall back down over a ravaged countryside. It has happened a thousand times or so before, over all the time we know. A city might go with it, as cities have fallen within the last decade from mere earth trembling, but the event remains local. The diamonds are a sort of rain-bow residue of the disaster.

Of course, even larger changes are to be expected, and even read from the record. They are generally slower, perhaps taking millennia. The most evident is the worldwide climate change which brings on polar glaciation. Our species is a creature of the glacial age: we hunted woolly elephants across the tundra of France not so long ago. That was skillful indeed for a bunch of cunning primates who went bipedal in the hot African savanna not so long before that, as the earth counts years.

In spite of their many claims, I hold that the climatologists do not yet know what is the real cause of such big changes in climate. In any case, even if London and Moscow and Peking lie as ruins under a mile-thick layer of ice in a thousand years or so, that in itself can hardly end the species. The coasts will widen as the water leaves the seas; our posterity might raft freely down the Baltimore Canyon across the plateau of the old continental shelf. Even if the change is lightning-swift (some hold that the ice cap might form in a century, though most expect a slower change) we would surely survive it in part. The population might decline, but hardly to zero. There are hopeful engineers who imagine we could defer or modify the climate change, by damming the Bering Straits to confine the coldest waters, or by dusting over the new ice fields with soot to melt them in the summer sun, or in some other way. These are possible delaying tactics; it is not so likely that we can always manipulate clever triggers against such big events, and real macroengineering has shown no signs of viability. We humans still build small perforce; any single well-known mountain dwarfs the whole history of human rock and earth piling, any big crater our hole digging. We are still geologically small, and so are all our works. Rather it is our diversity which seems to mean safety here. Biology itself works in no other way, and we humans share it. Our spread from pole to pole, from alp to atoll, seems to assure the future at least for a good share of our whole genetic and cultural treasury.

One can imagine even chemical changes of worldwide moment. Volcanoes might exude carbon monoxide or some other poison. But the air would quench it pretty well. More subtle changes, like some new substance in small quantities, which would cause the ozone layer to dwin-dle—as it is feared too much freon might do—could affect earth habitability in the large. Against this sort of mysterious effect it is clear that the long geological record of continuous life is our best argument. It has never happened, or at least not beyond the resources of the fabric of life to maintain itself.

Ozone is one small-quantity feature of the world which seems all but necessary. We depend—our crops as well—upon that thin stratospheric layer of ozone to screen out the damaging harder photons of solar ultraviolet. Less ozone would indeed modify life below, though again probably not so far as extinction. After all, we spend only a small fraction of our hours of life outdoors. And farmers could learn to do most of their work in twilight, or even by night. No, not even ozone loss would do us in. The limit would be set by the domestic plants; but they surely vary in response. Some new crops would grow. Just the same, ozone is perhaps the rarest of the known substances on which we heavily depend. The whole earth possesses about one billion tons of this active substance.

I have largely avoided the quantitative till now. But the figure of a billion tons of ozone provides an exemplary case. Human effort produces cereal grains, wood, petroleum, coal, iron ores, stone, sand, gravel, and cement, all major bulk products, in the rough amount of a billion tons each per year, some rather more, some rather less. That—with their waste products—measures perhaps what we can add to the environment, bar some important unusual trigger, like radioactive emissions, which are potent against life in small quantities. But this threshold for human effect on gross features of the environment seems a good guide. There is besides ozone no other rare atmospheric ingredient of known importance present only at the billion-ton level. (The oxides of nitrogen might be included, though their effects are unclear.)

The next rarest substance of world geochemical importance is perhaps carbon dioxide. We exhale it, as do all our fires and furnaces. Plant life depends upon it. But the natural air contains it at a level a few hundred times higher than ozone. We only now begin to modify the carbon dioxide by amounts which compare the natural variations of the span of earth history; that may become climatologically important, but it also does not seem to spell an end. The system can adjust to likely changes over a modest time. It presages only a transient crisis. The oceans provide a reservoir of the gas in solution, and a big if slow source were the atmosphere deficient. Climate change might mean worldwide economic change, but not the end. Human actions begin to approach the scale of volcanic output in some substances, and especially in the heat we release through fire. Perhaps that is the clearest sign of approaching limits on human population. Surely they are not sharply defined by so vague a match; no one has put up a model of catastrophe from such a cause. It can well be argued that we are approaching a limit: ten or so billions of industrious (and industrial) people may mark the prudent end of our growth, whose many signs we now read.

INTRUSIONS FROM WITHOUT

The vacuum of space isolates us on our big planetary spaceship— obviously not completely. We remain creatures of a majestic potentate out there a hundred million miles in space: the great nuclear reactor of the sun. We control it not; yet it controls our life. An irregular cycle of poorly known nature and origin modifies its output in details; we call it the sunspot cycle. There is good evidence that those spots are correlated at least weakly with broad changes in earthly weather. The most success- ful—but still uncertain—theory of the ice ages sees the glaciers as trig- gered by perpetual small changes in the earth's orbit and inclination caused by the big planets. These might enhance winters or summers. Some have found causes in even more remote features of the cosmos, in the great cosmic dust clouds among the stars, into which our sun might drift as over two or three hundred million years it orbits the Milky Way. All these proposals are plausible to a degree; none is proved. What is clear is that humanity was a creature of an epoch of glaciation; whether we arose because of the ice or in spite of it is not clear. But it seems pretty sure that neither the sun's inconstancy—if it exists except in detail—nor the tiny orbital dance has ever threatened to rip the fabric of life, what- ever they might have meant for this or that species. In short, we cannot well change these phenomena; but perhaps we can adapt to them, grow- ing our crops in the tropics instead of Montana, on the plateaus instead of the coast, blackening the snow fields, or whatever the realities demand. No ultimatum there.

Nor is there much sign that the slow orbit of the sun among the stars of the galaxy—over the galactic year of some 300 million solar years—sees much outside influence. True, we may have come from time to time within the sphere of influence of a great star explosion, a supernova event. There is suggestive evidence that the very origin of the sun was in part mediated by a nearby supernova, whose nuclear debris found en- trance into the more normal gas mixture which became the early sun. Since then, the event has not been repeated, or at least not with any strong sign. The most sensitive systems on earth to such distant radiative events are probably life and the chemistry of the atmosphere, especially the trace chemistry, like that of ozone. The handful of supernova neigh- bors implied by statistics during all earth history might have had some effect traceable in life. The proposal has been made many times, but no direct support has ever been offered for such scenarios, to my knowledge.

In the same way, galactic dust clouds may fog up the solar system from time to time. Here again the proposal is plausible, the details not very persuasive, and the evidence lacking. It does not seem that outer space has so far meant anything central to our life, apart from the indispensable endowment of atoms at the sun's birth.

Within the solar system, space is not so dominant over matter. It is rather crowded around here. Worlds in collision are real enough, though that is not to offer the slightest support to wild notions of recent planetary encounters. Every moon crater was made by an intruder. Some of them are big indeed. Meteors strike earth, and in the past there were certainly truly big ones, leaving craters of subcontinental size. But that was in the earth's childhood, before ever life began. Just the same, the errant chunks of the solar system—the most important and erratic are comets— can and do hit earth. A body of mountainous size will produce local catastrophe, and some effects worldwide, from tidal waves to persistent dust in the atmosphere, like Krakatoa, or a super-K. By now we have all heard that such a comet might have ended the rule of the dinosaurs. Certainly there is evidence that the marine life changed everywhere suddenly, so that silt came down instead of chalk on the sea bottom at the end of the Cretaceous era. How ingeniously this has been connected to the great dying of that period is not our story; the case is good, if not yet certain. But it seems to leave the story more or less unchanged. Even a worldwide darkening by dust which lasted for years, so that green plants were mostly killed, would not end human life, it would appear, provided the overall continuity of life was maintained. We would find ways—at least some of us—to live on what was left, the stored seeds and stems, the plants and creatures which could survive the dimming. The actuary also sees that orbital wanderers are no longer so many nor so big; the big erratics in orbit were long ago swept up. All the comets and asteroids which remain do not add up to the mass of a small planet like the earth. Of course, only a tiny fraction can ever collide with us, or even pass nearby. It looks as though there is no major planet wreck to be foreseen, though the effects of past collisions with minor bodies may have been decisive for some forms of past life. Thus the sustaining sun, through its radiation, and some members of its retinue, by direct collision, can affect life; more distant objects probably cannot, and no intruder can annihilate.

BY OUR OWN HAND

Today's forebodings of catastrophic nuclear war are not to be ignored. Indeed, unless international relations take a substantial turn from past patterns, it is hard to avoid the prediction of a large-scale nuclear war some day, whether in decades or in centuries. The coolest argument for this is based on the observation that the energy yield of the weapons grows year by year, without ever declining. But the area of the earth and the volume of our atmosphere do not increase at all. That most typical of all growth industries, the world manufacture of weapons, must saturate if there is to be a long-range future; so much seems tightly entailed by the events. That arms reduction could take so many forms, but it must arrive somehow. The most pessimistic would say the stockpile will go down because the warheads are consumed in use, the population going down along with the weapons stock. The most optimistic see a simple desuetude, or even a final rolling-back of unused and unwanted arsenals. History will decide. Of course, there might be a whole series of calamities, recoveries, escapes. Here the question is simply the chance of survival.

In the last years, grim new attention has been drawn to this possibility of the coroner's verdict of species suicide. In summer 1982 an informal study was published (in the authoritative Swedish environmental journal *Ambio*) by two climatologists, P. J. Crutzen and J. W. Birks. They realized that it is not only some rare constituent of the global atmosphere that can change, but that a trace of some novel but potent stuff might be added. The substance of their concern was familiar enough, merely soot and black smoke from fires burning the organic matter of the forests, fields, cities, and stores of petroleum. A small portion of dark soot spread throughout the upper air can dim the sunlight of life until the soot has been diluted and fallen or washed out of the air. That may take months. In the meantime, the land masses will suffer an unexpected winter. Should the dark clouds arrive in summer, crops will die; so may the animals and plants quite generally. If the smoke-induced winter is protracted enough, even the tropics would freeze, and the effect could spread between hemispheres. Only one cause of fires so widespread is thinkable: general nuclear war. Since the first, several studies have tentatively borne out the early conjecture; nuclear winter is indeed a terrible possibility, even after use of only a modest fraction of the present nuclear weapons stocks. A thousand big explosions over Northern cities could ignite fires that would in days burn an area greater than that which burns in the world's forests during a whole year. The natural processes of dilution and recovery could be overwhelmed. The uncertainties are large; our ability to forecast the weather long-range is not yet a firm one. But a prima facie case has been made that nuclear war puts at real risk not only the targeted peoples, but everyone. Perhaps the most important point is that this hazard, surely not in itself so strange, had not been addressed by the experts during decades of attention. What else has been overlooked? We might learn only too late what our model had neglected.

Yet nuclear weapons, the most present of all dangers, I believe, do not seem likely literally to end our species. Should the worst happen, I would expect a severalfold decimation of the two or three big warring nations. They would sink, their cultural properties as well. All that would remain in the United States, say, would be a few portions of certain less-populated regions, amidst vast unvisitable wastelands. Barren, dying fields and forests might be found worldwide, amidst general hunger. But it still seems to me that some of our far-flung species would survive, its population, wealth, and hope sadly dwindled, but not finally ended. The Southern Hemisphere is actuarially the better off—airborne radioactivity and the dark clouds cross the equator slowly—though it would not remain unthreatened. The best guesses are still that a factor of ten, though not much more, stands against the death of the whole species by nuclear war. Certainly the average danger does not strike every individual; and distances and environmental differences are great. Once again, diversity is the key to survival. The false winter or two have come and gone; the ozone layer is at risk; epidemics of tumors and birth defects persist for centuries; the best croplands are unusable for a long time. The very air holds chemical toxins. The tale is genuinely tragic. Yet there will be people left, plenty of them miserably surviving here and there by their wits on the unused storehouses and the residual life.

Other weapons can be imagined. Plagues and contagions do not appear general enough, though one cannot be sure. There are powerful natural immune mechanisms which have been a long time evolving. Here the nations have been more sensible; biological warfare has not been well developed, and is now proscribed. We can hope that example of good sense is permanent. We could poison some important living forms within the world ecological cycle; the death of the marine plankton by new toxins added to the sea was one scientist's cautionary invention. But the seas are big and poorly mixed; I do not think we could empty them even if we tried; it cannot happen by accident. Our industrial and weapons systems are not big enough for such effects. Once again, we are looking for trigger mechanisms: radioactivity, ozone reactants, and the like.

What of the will to survive? Physical attack by weaponry is only one means of self-destruction. It is not necessary to invoke the macabre vision of a universal Jonestown to imagine an end to the species by quiet consensus. All that is required, of course, is a gradual end to new births. That seems to have happened in one or another small culture once placed into an intolerable bondage by a powerful invader or colonizer. Now that the imperative instinctual arrangements of biology have been cut away from procreation by consciousness and culture, this possibility is opened more widely. Surely a physicist is here on poorly understood ground. Once more the diversity of the psyche can be counted upon to avoid the danger, all the more since the feedback loop, awareness of the predicament, seems easy to activate: local information is enough for alarm. It is true that the growth of the unity of mankind, plainly evident over the last millennia, suggests the possibility of a psychological unity, mediated by travel and communication, which was not at hand when the races of mankind differentiated under strict geographical isolation. The slow return of one world—we had it in the Rift Valley when the genus was young—holds the sort of risk under discussion. But the turmoil of the present world of resurgent nationalism and regionalism seems to presage just what sort of limits arise to the dreams of a universal brotherhood and sisterhood. Given genetic diversity and experiential variety, we will not become all of a mind. If some become sheeplike, others will become more solitary or even enterprising. Fluctuation is not merely a thermodynamic notion; it has mechanisms deep in culture.

We are predators worse than wolves, man to man, but predation does not often end species, except for the power of human culture, and the old human rivalry for a niche. Even the latter is perhaps more an end by incorporation than by hostility, with one example perhaps in the relationships of Neanderthal and early *sapiens* in Europe.

We risk terrible damage to ourselves; it is in every tax return and news story. But self-destruction, down to the very end, does not seem indicated by our powers or by our nature.

WHEN THE SUN DIES

Two paths of endurance are plain. The one is that which has saved the horseshoe crab and the works of Aristotle: multiple copies widely dispersed. The other is the path of the sun, or of the Blue Ridge Mountains: construction of such durable material on such a scale that the tooth of time must gnaw for a long while. But of course in the end the mountains will erode to basins of silt, and the sun will die. The death of the sun is likely to be a fiery one, we believe, not a mere cooling, but an expansion and a feverish glow. The earth will be ended by that, let alone the life upon it. Even the outer orbits where spaceships might dwell will have a hard time adjusting to the erratic and gusty course of sunlight and solar wind.

Will we emigrate from this home system out among the other stars? Science fiction, of course, sees that as a commonplace. After all, the sky is filled with stars in our galaxy, among them a couple of hundred million old enough, stable enough, single stars, with temperatures like our modest sun. They lie far away, indeed, but not beyond any hope of reaching them by human transport over generations. So one admits the possibility that our species will become wanderers in space seeking homesteading rights. But that will almost surely be a sporelike venture: the whole of our number will not go, but only a few representatives, able perhaps to maintain the memory of earth.

Even more plausible than this plot, which implies forecast over billions of years until the sun does undergo serious change, is quite another. Are we alone as self-conscious appraisers of our future? Or among the suns are there many like us in insight, however different in biology? It seems probable that we will know that within a modest time, perhaps by catching radio signals from Others far away. Perhaps we are The People, solitary on our planet-island, someday soon to be surprised by other beings from far away, with radio beams if not white sails, easily our masters in many domains of life. It has happened before: it may happen again. We do not know, but perhaps we will find out by an active if vicarious radio or laser search. To be sure, those Others will not be of our species, but they will by hypothesis share the niche we hold: conscious beings, surviving and spreading by a new form of evolution, changing more by hand and eye than by the gamble of inheritance.

We have never seen anything like that before: a new species which shares our functions though not at all our image, our descent, even our biochemistry. If our culture and our history pass into the keeping of a wider society than earth's, the issue of species survival becomes somewhat moot. Here we touch questions of philosophy, of the very definition of the end. What does it mean? Would we be held to survive if our new partnership with natural selection led to a filiation into something rich and strange? The older speculators, say George Bernard Shaw, saw the deep future as the rise of an etiolated but powerful race of philosophers, perhaps even of pure thought: the more silicon-bound speculators of our day foresee the inheritance of our culture by subtle machines we set on a path of machine evolution.

I shall not worry this point unduly; here imagination is hardly constrained by experience. It would appear that such changes will not in fact preserve us; that they might keep our echo, the kind of echo we hear faintly of the Olmecs or the Etruscans, without any lineal descendants, is plain. We will have been transformed away, reborn if you like, through a channel as compact as a seed. The likelihood seems high that we will share a wider interstellar culture one day, unless indeed ours is first of all the hundred million suns to engender the carriers of thought. That case is logically possible; but it seems a poor bet.

All that I have argued has been built on the science of our times. Surely the past teaches us that much of what we hold true is in error, and more incomplete. How can this be a guide to actuarial forecast? Here is the most troubling of all the estimates I have made. In spite of the clear precedents, it is hard to see where new knowledge will change these remarks to a serious degree. What will we learn before science itself comes to an end? A closer approach to the ultimate structure of matter, to the ends of space and time—if they exist? The inwardness of the development of living forms? The architecture of the mind? Surely all these and more that I cannot foresee, with a plentiful triggering out from every present scientific branch. We will find cause in the domain of chaos, and no doubt chaos behind the apparently causal, as we have often done.

Yet in a curious way science has told us what we need already. It has defined the space-time volume of our life, the nature of stars and galaxy, the age of earth and sun, the epoch of organic evolution. Just as we can be sure that there is no mountain on earth a kilometer higher above sea level than Everest, I believe we can be sure of the minimal extent of our space-time history, even if we cannot yet see its farthest boundaries, or understand its initial phases or final fate; its infinities are beyond us. But can they matter? I do not believe we will find how to work magic. We fly now with thrust and wing, not on carpets or by wands. We travel through space freely, but at the cost of time, and never through time against its current. Mind indeed masters matter, but not by telepathy or by spell, only by the cunning disposition of structures, circuits, and energy sources. Unless the writers of fiction prove correct—time travel, starlike intelligences, instant mind contacts over arbitrary space, and other timeworn marvels of wishfulness—I do not see new science confounding what I have somewhat cautiously outlined. If we cure all disease, make life freely, travel at near light-speed, all those things will not free us from the constraints and the supports of time and space, from sun energy or a surrogate fuel. We will remain finite beings, with finite powers, bound like the cosmos itself by the laws of thermodynamics. I doubt much that we will turn the galaxy into a park, or visit the ends of the cosmos. It costs too much, in energy, time, and plan.

The best glimpse into the dim future we can hope would come, if it comes at all, from the signals of our peers and superiors out there among the suns. If that happens, the actuary will have some statistics. Until it happens, the best guess seems to be that we will survive, surely for longer than our written history so far, surely beyond the return of the ice, probably long beyond that to a time as long as our evolutionary span so far, the couple of hundred thousand years since *sapiens* came on earth. If we allow for changes, our modified cultural posterity might with good fortune go on for geological epochs, as far as I can see. Maybe our new evolution can persist as long as has the cockroach or the cycad. The odds go down with time, but slowly. One day, the sun dead, the universe itself perhaps collapsing to a fiery rebirth, it will all be over, long before matter itself decays away as likely it will do. But we are now a long-lived, widespread, and marvelous species, all the same, marked by a symbiosis unique on earth, living intimately with a creature of wonderful talent and sinister cunning, our Monkey of the Mind.

INDEX

ABOUT THE AUTHORS

EDITORS

DR. SAUL FRIEDLÄNDER is Professor of European History at Tel Aviv University and the Graduate Institute of International Studies in Geneva, the author of many publications on Nazism, the Second World War, and the psychological dimensions of history. His most recent book is *Reflections of Nazism*.

PROFESSOR GERALD HOLTON is Mallinckrodt Professor of Physics, and Professor of History of Science at Harvard University. Among his recent books are *Thematic Origins of Scientific Thought: Kepler to Einstein* and *The Scientific Imagination: Case Studies*.

PROFESSOR LEO MARX is William R. Kennan Jr. Professor of American Cultural History in the Program in Science, Technology, and Society at the Massachusetts Institute of Technology. He is the author of many essays in American studies and of *The Machine in the Garden: Technology and the Pastoral Ideal in America*.

PROFESSOR EUGENE B. SKOLNIKOFF is Professor of Political Science and Director of the Center for International Studies at the Massachusetts Institute of Technology. He has written extensively on science policy and has held positions in government, including service in the science office at the White House. He is the author of *Science, Technology and American Foreign Policy* among other works.

CONTRIBUTORS

PROFESSOR HARVEY BROOKS is Benjamin Peirce Professor of Technology and Public Policy in the Division of Applied Sciences and in the Kennedy School of Government at Harvard University. He chairs the Program on Science, Technology, and Public Policy at Harvard. He is the author of many articles on science policy and of *The Government of Science*.

PROFESSOR MATEI CALINESCU is Professor of Comparative Literature and West European Studies at Indiana University, Bloomington. He is the author of numerous essays on contemporary Western culture and of *Faces of Modernity: Avant-Garde, Decadence, Kitsch*.

PROFESSOR AMOS FUNKENSTEIN is Maser Professor of Philosophy and History in Tel Aviv University, and Professor of History, Department of History, University of California, Los Angeles. He is the author of various publications on the medieval philosophy of history, Christian and Jewish exegesis, the history of Jewish thought, and the history of science. Forthcoming is his book *Theology and the Scientific Imagination from the Middle Ages to the Seventeenth Century.*

PROFESSOR FRANK KERMODE teaches at Columbia University. Of his many books the most recent are *The Genesis of Secrecy, The Art of Telling,* and *Forms of Attention.*

DR. ROBERT JAY LIFTON is Distinguished Professor of Psychiatry at the City University of New York. His most recent books are *In a Dark Time: Images for Survival,* edited with Nicholas Humphrey, and *Indefensible Weapons: The Political and Psychological Case Against Nuclearism,* coauthored with Richard Falk. He is now completing a study of Nazi doctors.

DR. ROBERT MORISON is Professor of Biology Emeritus, Cornell·University, and Visiting Professor of Science and Society at the Massachusetts Institute of Technology. He is the author of papers on the physiology of the nervous system, and, more recently, on the ethical and policy implications of advances in biomedical technologies.

PROFESSOR PHILIP MORRISON is Institute Professor of Physics at the Massachusetts Institute of Technology. His research interests are in astrophysics. For twenty years he has been the book reviewer for *Scientific American.*

PROFESSOR RICHARD POIRIER is Marius Bewley Professor of English at Rutgers University, the editor of *Raritan Quarterly,* and vice president of the Library of America. He is the author of *The Comic Sense of Henry James: A Study of the Early Novels, A World Elsewhere: The Place of Style in American Literature, The Performing Self: Compositions and Decompositions in the Language of Contemporary Life, Robert Frost: The Work of Knowing,* and of many essays and reviews.

PROFESSOR HARALD A. T. REICHE is a classicist on the History Faculty of the School of Humanities and Social Science at the Massachusetts Institute of Technology. He is the author of many publications on the interface of ancient science, philosophy, and religion.

PROFESSOR ANDRÉ RESZLER is Professor of European History at the Graduate Institute of European Studies, Geneva. Among his recent publications are *L'Intellectuel contre Europe* and *Mythes politiques modernes.*